# A DISTANCE
# TOO GRAND

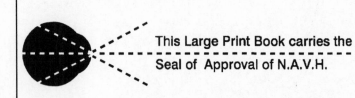

This Large Print Book carries the
Seal of Approval of N.A.V.H.

# AMERICAN WONDERS COLLECTION, BOOK 1

# A DISTANCE TOO GRAND

# REGINA SCOTT

**THORNDIKE PRESS**
A part of Gale, a Cengage Company

**LIBRARY OF CONGRESS CIP DATA ON FILE.
CATALOGUING IN PUBLICATION FOR THIS BOOK
IS AVAILABLE FROM THE LIBRARY OF CONGRESS**

ISBN-13: 978-1-4328-7193-2 (hardcover alk. paper)

Published in 2019 by arrangement with Revell Books, a division of Baker Publishing Group

Printed in Mexico
1 2 3 4 5 6 7 23 22 21 20 19

To Edward and William,
for understanding Mama's
need to create,
and to the Creator, for all the wondrous
places he made for us to find.

# 1

*Fort Wilverton, Arizona Territory, August 1871*

"You can't be the photographer."

Meg Pero blew a stray blonde hair out of her vision, aimed her sunniest smile at the Army clerk, and laid a gloved hand on the contract sitting between them on the scarred wood counter. "This is a legally binding document, and that is a senior officer's signature, is it not?"

The clerk squinted down at the scrawl. "Yes, ma'am. But I was told the contract was with Matthew Pero. You're not Matthew Pero."

Indeed she wasn't. She'd worked most of her life to be as good a photographer as her father. Few knew that she had taken many of the pictures attributed to him the last three years.

"If you look closely," Meg said, bending over the contract, the sunlight from the door behind blazing across the crowded quarter-

7

master's office, "you'll see the name is M. Pero. M for Margaret."

Corporal Dent bent lower as well, dark wool cap slipping on his short brown hair, then raised his eyes to meet her gaze. "But you can't be the photographer."

She sighed despite herself. She'd been expecting the argument ever since she'd discovered the contract among her father's effects. He had to have negotiated it more than five months ago, before he'd fallen ill. Papa had always been the one to negotiate their services.

"Men don't like haggling with women, Meg," he'd explained more than once. "Just smile and look pretty, then show them you can do the job better than any of them."

She'd never liked that advice, but she certainly couldn't follow it now if the clerk wouldn't even give her a chance!

It had been like that most of her trip — arguments, protests. Women couldn't be seen here, sit alone there. She was too short and slight to look imposing, more likely to smile than scowl. Normally men hurried to help when she glanced their way. But sweet words of persuasion and eager looks had not availed her much this time.

Things had been so much easier when Papa was alive. He could charm his way into any situation, make her presence seem perfectly reasonable. He'd probably have found a way to explain why she'd come riding up with the supply train to the dry redrock plateau that held the adobe buildings of the fort, pulling ten mules loaded with photographic equipment that the clerk of the fort was attempting to turn away.

"It's a perfectly good contract," she said. "There were probably lawyers involved."

He scratched at his navy wool jacket, and she envied him the uniform's warmth. Though the last few days of travel from Utah had seen warm temperatures, the nights were cool. As it was, she wore her navy wool cloak over her sky-blue cotton blouse and tan twill skirt.

"I don't doubt it's legal, ma'am," he said. "I also don't doubt Captain Coleridge would put me in irons if I added you to the payroll."

Captain Coleridge? Funny. She was certain Fort Wilverton's commanding officer, who had signed the contract, had been a Colonel Coleridge. Not that she had any interest in making his acquaintance. That was one of the reasons she'd headed straight for the quartermaster's office instead of fort headquarters. Someone would eventually inform the colonel of her presence, but perhaps she would be able to make her escape with the survey team without meeting him again. How could she reintroduce herself to the famous Army colonel when she'd broken his son's heart five years ago?

"Captain Coleridge," she said, "will be as bound by that contract as you are."

He pushed the paper at her as if afraid it might bite. "But you're a woman. Women aren't photographers."

Meg kept her smile in place. "On the contrary. There are ladies right now who run photography studios in England, Germany, and New York."

"All well and good, ma'am," he said. "But we can't have women on a survey expedition."

Now, that point she'd come prepared to argue. "Your commanding officer told my father in a letter that the cartographer's wife will be joining the survey."

"Yes, but Mrs. Newcomb can cook," he protested, backing up until his shoulders bumped the rough-wood shelves behind him, setting the canteens stocked there to rattling.

"And I can take pictures," Meg informed him. "I see no difference."

"You would if you knew Mrs. Newcomb," he muttered.

Meg refused to dignify the comment with a response. She'd traveled more than two thousand miles — by rail, wagon, and finally mule — to reach the fort. Corporal Dent couldn't know the danger she'd left behind, a threat to everything she'd ever known. She could still see the glitter in her aunt's green eyes as the family had returned from Papa's funeral.

"You've been terribly cozened, Margaret," she'd said, leading Meg into her dingy little house in Norfolk. "As far as I can see, your father filled your head with nonsense about your place in this world. At six and twenty, a young lady should be wed, with children playing at her feet."

"But that would make it terribly hard to get the shot," Meg had replied.

Aunt Abigail had not been amused. But then, Meg had learned, Aunt Abigail was never amused.

Truly, had there ever been two more different siblings? Her father had been joyful, carefree, expansive in gesture, vocabulary, and choice of living. His widowed younger sister seemed grim, weighed down, and tight-laced in body and spirit. Her son, Meg's cousin, had been equally as restricted.

"You can have no further use for that

camera equipment," Cousin Harold had maintained, standing with his arms crossed over his broad chest in the door of the prison cell of a room they'd given her. "By rights, it should be mine. I'm sure I could get a pretty penny for it."

Over her dead body.

Neither of them understood. She loved the trade she'd been baptized into, the way the world opened through the lens of her camera. It was a challenge and an art to choose the exact right angle, the exact right light, to create something extraordinary out of the ordinary, to share a glimpse of the divine. How could they ask her — no, order her — to give it up, as if it were something shameful?

Papa had refused to allow her gender to get in the way of their trade. He'd taken her with him to the edge of the battlefield and the wilds of the frontier. She'd met women who nursed wounded soldiers, taught natives to read and write, forged a home in untamed territory. She knew her life didn't have to be confined to the sitting room and the kitchen.

Aunt Abigail and her son had other ideas. They seemed to view her gender as a limitation, and one that must never be overcome. She'd only met one other woman with such rigid ideals. A shame she'd been the mother of the man Meg had thought she might love.

She'd tried to play the demure miss for a time when her father had had a studio. She'd taken tea in the afternoon, attended balls and soirees. She'd never fit in. Indeed, she sometimes wondered whether she was constitutionally capable of it. Her ideas, her hopes, her skills were as expansive as her father's. She'd escaped her aunt's narrow expectations by working with a friend of her father's to sneak her equipment out of the house and used the money Papa had left her to purchase the transportation she'd need to head West. She'd escape this clerk's expectations as well. Too much depended on it — her freedom, her future.

"Perhaps you should speak with Captain Coleridge," she said, straightening. "He signed the contract. Only he can renegotiate it."

"Colonel Coleridge signed that," the clerk said. "He went missing two months ago. Our interim officer in charge of the fort, Colonel Yearling, will back me up. He likes regulations."

Meg frowned. "So is Mr. Coleridge a colonel or a captain?"

"Both," said a familiar voice behind her.

Summer turned to winter. She must have

been staring at the clerk, for he was reddening. She rather thought she was white.

*God, if you're still there, if you still care, not him. Not now.*

"Is there a problem, Corporal?" the man behind her asked. Oh, but she couldn't mistake that voice, even ringing with command. It seemed God wasn't going to answer this prayer either, just as he hadn't seen fit to allow her father to survive his illness.

Corporal Dent squared his shoulders. "No, sir. This citizen says she's to go on the survey expedition to the North Rim, but it's clearly a mistake. I can deal with the likes of her."

Meg bristled, but the voice behind her was now all commiseration. "No need to be rude, Corporal. I'd be happy to explain the situation to the lady. If you'd tell me your name, miss?"

So well meaning. That was one of the traits that had originally drawn her to him. That and his unrelenting confidence. Easy to turn now, to greet her long-lost love, to let him convince her she should go back home.

But there was no home and never would be if she didn't win this commission.

She raised her chin and turned. Even

14

though she knew who she would find behind her, the sight of Benjamin Coleridge still shook her. That shock of golden-brown hair, so thick and silky; those blue-gray eyes that could look deep inside her. The chiseled chin that could soften with emotion, that strong physique outlined in the navy wool of his uniform jacket, two silver bars on his shoulders. Oh, but she could hear the ladies sighing from here.

Once more she put on her best smile. "Good afternoon, Captain Coleridge. I must insist that I join your expedition. I'm your photographer."

Ben Coleridge stopped, hand extended in greeting. He'd assumed he'd been about to meet someone's sweetheart or sister. But Meg Pero? Here? How? Had the Arizona sun addled his wits?

Just looking at her took him back to West Point, the walks among the trees, the stolen moments at balls. She was as beautiful as he remembered, pale blonde hair wound up under a surprisingly practical broad-brimmed straw hat, figure swathed in a dark wool cloak. The fire in those green eyes dared him to argue with her. He never had been able to argue, even to beg her to stay.

He inclined his head as he pulled back his

15

hand. "Miss Pero. I take it you're here with your father."

She raised her chin a little higher, all bravado, though her cheeks held little color. He remembered them pink with delight, soft to his touch.

"My father passed away," she said.

Sorrow washed over him. Matthew Pero had been a friendly fellow, always ready to talk, to laugh. His daughter had been much like him. The two had been nearly inseparable, unlike him and his father.

"My condolences," he said. "Your father was a good man, and a great photographer."

That determined chin inched higher. "Which is why I intend to carry on his work."

Corporal Dent's sigh was audible. "You see, Captain? She won't listen."

She never had. Meg Pero did what she liked and never mind the consequences. He'd had to accept her decision once. Not this time.

"Corporal Dent is correct," he told her. "You cannot serve as an expedition photographer."

Once more her green eyes flashed, and she gathered her skirts and swept up to him. He'd faced hailstorms that had threatened to flatten him, rising rivers set to sweep him

16

away, and Apaches out for his blood, but this was the first time he'd considered re- treating.

"I have worked as a photographer for eighteen years," she said, head tilting back to meet his gaze, "ever since my father started having me position the equipment at age eight. Though my father was given credit for much of it to assuage the sensibili- ties of editors, my work has appeared in the *Atlantic,* the *New York Times,* and the *Boston Evening Traveller.* I have shot portraits, still lifes, campaigns, and the greatest works of nature. In short, Captain, I have more experience than most photographers the Army hires, and I have a contract."

Corporal Dent helpfully lifted the piece of paper and held it high.

She was all fire, all ice, every inch of her bristling. He couldn't agree.

"I don't care if you have an invitation from the president," Ben told her. "I'm not bring- ing you on this expedition. Take pictures of the fort if you must. Corporal Dent will schedule you on the next pack train north. Good-bye, Miss Pero."

He turned on his heel, but he heard the scuffle of her boots as she followed him out the door.

"Wait! You need me!"

Once he had thought so. He had been certain she was the only one for him. Her response to his proposal had proved him wrong.

Now he turned to eye her as she came out of the quartermaster's office. Her cloak belled around her like wings, betraying a figure as slender and elegant as he remembered. Something nudged at him, told him to apologize.

Not now. Not again. He widened his stance, gave her the glare that made the men under his command rush about their duties. "The answer is no, Miss Pero."

She drew up beside him, hands fisted in her skirts. "Even though you're already late in the season? You won't get another photographer here for months."

She was right. He'd heard that Timothy O'Sullivan was engaged with Wheeler, William Bell at Kanab. There were only so many photographers skilled enough to take their equipment into the wilderness and capture the grandeur of new territory. The Army had been making use of them since the War Between the States. Many had forged a reputation for themselves and no small income selling prints and stereographs from their work. He'd known starting out that a photographer would be key to this expedition.

"Don't worry," his commanding officer had said, clapping him on the back as Ben took his leave to head for Fort Wilverton. "I hear the Army hired Matthew Pero. He's the best. He's been alerted to the delay but should arrive shortly after you do."

Ben could only be thankful. Matthew Pero had photographed many a landmark across the country, Meg at his side. Their stereographic views were famous, enjoyed by thousands. He had no doubt she knew her way around a camera. But she couldn't appreciate the dangers she'd be facing. His mother and sister had hesitated to join his father when he'd been made commander of the fort. Arizona had been its own territory for less than a decade and was known more for its vast vistas and copper than any sort of society. Likely his mother and Diana would never come now that the Colonel had disappeared.

And would he have any chance to discover why his father had gone missing if he delayed much longer?

Something of what he was feeling must have shown on his face, for she took a step closer and laid her hand on his arm. "Please, Ben. I need the work. I won't let you down. Take me with you."

How could he? He could think of a dozen ways she might be harmed by nature alone. The wildly fluctuating temperatures, scant water, predators like mountain lion, vermin like rattlesnake. Flash floods, wildfire, lightning storms. The glory of God's creation was nearly as commanding as his father.

And he couldn't tell her the other dangers he feared.

Yet it was already August. They had at best two months, barely enough time for the survey, before snow began to fall along the North Rim. The Grand Canyon, they called it, and everything he'd read said searching for a way to ford it by wagon would be a great adventure, the kind he'd always imagined. That was why he'd abandoned his father's dreams for him and become an engineer instead of a cavalryman — to explore new lands, chart new territory.

Besides, the Army Corps of Engineers had invested considerable funds equipping a survey team and a photographer, the effort planned months ago and plagued by delays. The work was to augment the efforts of the Wheeler Survey of 1869 to find a wagon road across the West. But Wheeler had his eye on bigger game. He was proposing to document and map the land south of the one hundredth meridian, with the hope to identify locations for Army outposts and opening the area to settlers. Ben heartily agreed with the approach. He'd served on the 1869 survey and knew the potential.

Finding a way to cross the Grand Canyon was critical. Troops, settlers, and the sutlers to supply them had to make long detours east or west to avoid it. Congress wanted to change that. Already John Wesley Powell was making a second attempt to navigate the Colorado River down the canyon with a government-backed team of ten handpicked men and specially built boats. If Ben didn't leave within the week, he'd have to wait until next May.

And he'd lose all opportunity to learn what had happened to his father.

"Do you have any idea how dangerous this could be?" he demanded.

She squeezed his arm. "Yes. My father always said nature would kill him if man didn't do it first. I'm not afraid, Ben. This is a grand adventure. Think of the vistas we could capture."

*Think how easily she could recapture your heart.*

He shoved the thought away. He was immune to Meg Pero's charm. Her sweet smile, the touch of her hand, wasn't why he was about to agree with her outrageous request.

He couldn't leave without a photographer, and she was the only one available.

"Very well," he said and was rewarded with a barely suppressed squeal of joy. "Join me at the enlisted mess at five, and you can meet the rest of the team."

# 2

Corporal Dent showed her to her quarters.

"We don't have lady visitors much," he explained as he opened the door to the stuffy little guardhouse. "Leastwise, not unmarried ones. You can bed down here for a night or two." He dropped her case, which he had insisted on carrying, on the packed red dirt floor.

Meg glanced around at the narrow wood bunk, the barred window high in the wall. "I've had worse than a jail cell." She held out her hand. "I'll be fine, so long as you leave me a key."

The corporal reddened as he handed it over. "And you'll want to bar the door before you go to sleep, ma'am." He scuttled out as if afraid of being locked in with her.

Bar the door. She certainly hoped she needn't take such precautions, but she would just in case. Funny that the colonel in charge of the fort hadn't invited her to stay in the officers' quarters, but if he was so determined to follow regulations, as Corporal Dent had said, perhaps this was the most he'd offer a civilian.

Either that, or Ben was more vengeful and influential than she'd thought.

She went to twitch the wool blanket off the thin tick. Nothing moved, but that didn't mean it wasn't infested with lice or bedbugs or some other sort of creature. She'd bring in her bedroll. It wouldn't be the first time she'd slept on the ground.

Melancholy beckoned, as it had so often since her father had died. How could he have left her alone? He was the only family she remembered, her mother having died in an accident when Meg was four and her aunt and cousin occasional hoteliers between travels. They believed it their duty to see her *civilized*. She was thankful they'd never quite managed it. Whenever Aunt Abigail started prosing on about schooling and settling down, Papa would announce a new scheme and whisk Meg off.

To capture crystal-clear waterfalls in the White Mountains of New Hampshire.

Slender boats gliding through the Erie Canal.

Impossibly tall buildings in New York City.

Massive monuments and churches in the

nation's capital.

Cocky cadets at West Point.

They had been a team, inseparable. So why had he let his illness progress so far without consulting a physician? He must have known he was sick. Why not seek help? He went through money as quickly as he earned it, but surely there'd been enough for his care. All that talk of training her — mixing the collodion on which the picture formed, preparing the plates, having her set up the shot and develop the negatives — all to mask that his health was failing. If only she'd guessed, but she'd been so happy he'd finally fully trusted her with the work that she hadn't questioned his orders.

And now he was gone.

Tears were gathering again. She dashed them away with her fingers. The time for grief was over. She had one opportunity, this opportunity, to make herself a future, and she wasn't going to waste it being maudlin. If she distinguished herself on this expedition, the Army might be persuaded to hire her for others, so long as another lady was in the group. And if she could take the stereographic views she hoped, she could sell them and live off the income for some time.

She located the enlisted mess by a quarter

25

to five. It was a room set off the back of the barracks. Like the other buildings at Fort Wilverton, the square structure was constructed of adobe brick, made from the soil of the plateau. The Army could have had little choice in its building material. The few trees in the area were stunted things of no use in making lumber, and it would have taken years to transport enough planks for the dozen or so facilities. As it was, they must have brought most of their furnishings with them, for the two long tables and flanking benches in the shadowy mess looked worn beyond the years they could have been in use here.

Four men were gathered at the closest table, and they were all staring at her. The lone woman among them rose from the bench and strode toward Meg. She was perhaps forty years of age, with dull brown hair tightly wrapped to her head, her figure bulky in the loose calico shirt and denim riding skirt. Her boots thumped with each step across the hard-packed floor.

She stuck out her hand, back spotted and nails chipped. "Dot Newcomb. You must be Miss Pero."

"That's me," she said, shaking Dot's hand. "I understand I have you to thank for the opportunity to join this expedition."

Dot cracked a smile. "First time I've been called upon to play chaperone. And we may need one. No one told me you were a beauty."

Meg felt warm. "I'm here as a photographer, nothing more."

Dot cocked her head. "You sure? Some of the boys at the fort have fancy careers ahead of them, if they don't fall prey to sunstroke or rattlesnake."

"I'm sure," Meg promised. "I just want to take pictures."

"Like your father." Dot nodded. "I heard of him. He took the picture of Niagara Falls that was in the paper. It was like you were about to go over."

Meg smiled. "Because he went out to the farthest point, beyond where anyone would have considered it safe. Nothing was more important to my father than getting the shot."

Dot linked arms with her. "I feel the same way about my rifle and whatever's heading for the cook pot that night. Come on, then. I'll introduce you to the others."

She drew Meg over to the group of men. The two youngest popped to their feet.

"Oh, sit down," Dot said with a wave of her free hand. "This is an expedition, not a fancy tea. Meet Miss Meg Pero. She's our photographer."

The privates, judging by the lack of insignia, elbowed each other and grinned as they returned to their seats. One blond, the other a brunet, both tall and wiry, they reminded her of the cadets she'd met at West Point: bright, eager, ready for anything even if they had no idea what they might face.

The large-boned bearded man near the head of the table looked her up and down. "Where'd you learn to take a picture?"

She'd heard the question too many times to not have an answer. "My father was a photographer. I've been helping him since I was eight. I'd be happy to show you my portfolio."

He frowned as if he wasn't sure of the word, but Dot aimed a scowl around at them all. "No need to question the lady, now. Captain Coleridge approved her, and I approve her. That should be good enough for you."

They all dropped their gazes, but Meg thought she heard a grumble. Dot tugged her toward the foot of the table.

"They'll be fine," she assured Meg as she slid onto a bench. "And if they aren't, the Captain and I will deal with it."

"Let me deal with it," Meg insisted, seating herself opposite the woman. "I need to prove to them I can stand on my own."

Dot leaned forward to gaze down the table. "Shouldn't be too hard. Most of them are used to me, so another lady in the group shouldn't seem so odd. But I'd watch out for that big fellow on the end who questioned you. That's Rudy Pike. He's traveled all up and down these lands and likes to brag about it. He's our guide."

Big as a bear, with dark hair and a full beard to match, Mr. Pike hunched over the table in his homespun, gnarly hands working at peeling a wizened apple with a knife large enough to carve a tree.

"The fellow across from him is Corporal Christopher Adams," Dot went on. "Educated fellow. You can tell by the way he talks. Fussy, though. He keeps all the notes and specimens."

The corporal was as thin as the guide was broad. His hair was already beginning to recede from his high forehead, and, by the red of his skin, he'd forgotten to wear a hat a time or two.

"The two youngsters are Frank Larson and Josiah Meadows. They're greenhorns — showed up at the fort four months ago with the former commander."

"Colonel Coleridge?" Meg asked.

Dot nodded. "Sad doings there. He rode

off with a guide and never returned. I didn't hold with the decision to stop searching. Neither did my Hank, our cartographer. That's him coming in with the Captain."

Meg could see why the imposing, red-headed Hank Newcomb would have won Dot's heart. He walked across the dirt floor as if he owned it and the fort around them, beard neat and head high. But one look at Ben Coleridge and all at once she was back at West Point.

Papa had decided to become respectable, as he called it. He'd just finished months of photographing the war, leaving her for a time with Aunt Abigail's endless lectures, and she'd wondered whether what he'd witnessed on the fields of death had motivated his change of heart. Regardless, he'd promised to give up traveling for a time to take photographs at the portrait studio in West Point, New York. After all, every cadet, faculty member, and their families wanted a photograph to commemorate their time at the prestigious academy. It had been a comfortable position, while Papa had been enamored of it. They'd had a house with a parlor, kitchen, and two bedrooms. And he'd been very understanding when she burned half his meals and forgot to make the beds because she was busy taking her own pictures of the area.

And attempting to enter society.

It had been a lark, an opportunity to see whether she really was missing anything by following her father. Reining in her usual enthusiasm and pretending to be a typical young lady had been a challenge, but she'd consoled herself with the thought that it was only temporary. If she made some gaffe, didn't behave as expected, they would eventually forget after she and Papa moved on.

Then one day, at a ball sponsored by an old Army friend of her father's, the crowds had parted and there he'd stood.

Tall, muscular, chin forward, arms akimbo, grin as bright as the brass buttons on his uniform. Like the privates here, his friends were elbowing him, patting him on the back as if to encourage him. He'd squared his shoulders and marched across the room.

"Pardon me, ma'am," he'd said to Meg, "but I'm on a mission for the Academy, and I need your assistance."

"A mission?" she'd asked, amused. "How could I possibly help?"

"I assure you, you are critical to the mission's success." His words were serious, but his blue-gray eyes held a twinkle of silver.

31

"You see, I promised myself I'd dance with the prettiest girl in attendance. It's a matter of honor, for me and the Academy." He offered her his arm. "Would you join me on the floor?"

She sighed, swinging her fan by its silken cord. "What a shame. If you'd said the most intelligent or the most talented lady in attendance, I might have been tempted to accept. I fear you'll have to make do with another lovely lady."

She turned and strolled away. Across the room, his friends were making shooing motions with their gloved hands. She wasn't surprised when he appeared at her side again.

"You must forgive me," he said, sweeping her a bow. "We haven't been introduced. I don't even know your name. I couldn't know how intelligent or talented you are, or you can be sure I would have praised those qualities."

Perhaps. But perhaps she'd just been a pretty girl across the room. While there was nothing wrong with that, she supposed, she wanted to be considered more than a beauty.

She eyed the blue of his dress uniform. "You are studying military endeavors, are you not? Gather intelligence before approaching your target, sir." She turned once more.

This time he didn't follow her, but she saw him moving from group to group, noticed the looks being directed her way. Her pulse started beating faster as he came closer for the third time.

"Miss Pero," he said with another bow, this one more respectful than bold. "I'm Ben Coleridge. I'm told you're a photographer. I wonder if you'd be willing to share how you compose your shots."

She smiled at him. "I'd be delighted, Cadet Coleridge. Perhaps we could talk after we dance?"

His grin had appeared as he'd offered her his arm once more.

The memory faded as he approached the head of the table now. She'd sent him away one time too many, at the end. It was for his benefit, even if he hadn't realized it then. She had tried, but whatever her talents, her pretentions to beauty, she would never be the kind of wife men seemed to expect. Certainly she was a poor choice for a rising officer. She was too outspoken, too determined to follow her own path. And nothing Ben Coleridge could say would change that.

Looking down the table at the men and

women he was about to command, Ben found his gaze stuck on Meg. She was leaning forward, eyes narrowed. He couldn't tell what she was thinking, but that was nothing new. Her dismissal of him had proven that he'd never known her at all.

As Newcomb went to sit next to his wife, the three cavalrymen who had been assigned to the survey — Adams, Larson, and Meadows — came to attention. Ben nodded them back into their seats. "Gentlemen, ladies, have you all been introduced?"

"Good enough," Pike grumbled. He twisted his knife idly in his thick fingers. "You sure about bringing a woman on this trip?"

"Hey!" Dot's voice echoed against the rafters. "It's two women, ya big galoot. And I'd like to see you cook a meal or take a picture anyone would recognize."

Something tugged at Meg's mouth. A smile? Ben kept his face stern. "Every member of this expedition is critical to its success. You were each chosen for a specific skill. We have a job to do. I expect you to work together and do it."

The others nodded. Pike stuck the tip of his knife into the wood. "So, when do we leave?"

"The day after tomorrow," Ben told him.

"Corporal Adams, double-check our supplies and equipment. We won't have time to send for more. Private Larson, Private Meadows, make sure the mules are ready and loaded. Miss Pero can show you how to deal with the photographic equipment."

They both looked to Meg, who inclined her head as regally as a queen.

"I trust you have a closed wagon or van for me?" she asked.

"Yes, ma'am," Larson promised, and Meadows nodded so eagerly he looked as if his clean-shaven chin was bouncing off his uniform.

He'd have to watch those two. He could easily see them falling over themselves to please her. He'd done the same when he'd been about their age.

Adams seemed less inclined to make a fool of himself, though he too directed his look toward Meg. "And I have the honor of driving it, miss."

Did he know how much of an honor? Meg was easily the most famous person on the team, even if some didn't realize it.

"And the route?" Pike asked, pulling his knife from the wood.

"We'll head due south," Ben said, "work our way east onto the plateau, then south again until we hit rim territory. We should

35

start to see portions of the canyon by late in the third day."

Now Pike narrowed his eyes. "You'll be moving fast, then."

Faster than usual, but he couldn't tell them what drove him. That part of his mission had been disclosed to him alone.

"We have a lot to do before the snow flies, Mr. Pike," he said. "We'll be following the line of the side canyons, dipping down where we can. Our goal is to find a way for wagons, while Powell's survey team follows the river looking for a way across and up the other side. We'll keep going until we run out of canyon or we spot the first sign of snow. Any more questions?"

They looked at each other, then him, many shaking their heads. Once again his gaze was drawn to Meg, who nodded, smile widening. He had a feeling she was the last one he had to worry about being ready. She'd always been ready, for everything but commitment.

She'd been the most beautiful girl he'd ever seen, and it hadn't taken much encouragement from his friends to seek her out. She'd made him work for that first dance, but the other dances, the picnics, helping her as she captured photos of the area, those had been some of the best moments of his life. There'd been a sense of adventure about the Academy, the idea that when graduated they would be building the future, that made him dream of building a future with Meg. That was when he'd introduced her to his family.

The Colonel, who had been visiting West Point between assignments, had approved, as Ben had hoped. "Smart, beautiful, engaging. She'd make an excellent officer's wife."

Mother had been less complimentary.

"Who is she?" she'd complained, hitching her silk-tasseled shawl closer. "I've never heard of her family. Not a single military man that I can tell. If you ask me, she's trying to further herself through you."

He hadn't believed it for a moment. Meg was everything his father had said besides being a genius behind the lens. He was the fortunate one.

He'd convinced himself she cared as much. Certainly her father had liked him. But the night he had attempted to propose, she'd cut him off.

"Oh, Ben, I'm sorry. We're simply too different to make a marriage. Forgive me for not realizing it sooner. Father's already planning to travel West. Of course I'll accompany him."

Too different? In what way? They conversed easily, about anything, everything. They were both eager to see what lay behind the horizon. He'd blindly thought the camaraderie, their closeness, would go on forever. How could she cut him off like this? Stunned, he could only watch, immobile, while she stood on tiptoe and pressed a kiss against his cheek. He hadn't said a word as she'd turned and walked away.

How could he have so mistaken her? Was he so arrogant? Was his focus narrower than that of her camera? Had he made rash decisions, thinking only to benefit himself?

Time for that to end. He wanted to lead men, open new lands, not push himself forward to glory out of a mistaken sense of pride. He'd tucked away his feelings, focused on his studies, each decision made with careful forethought, detailed planning. No more did he listen to his heart first. Funny how just seeing her brought all those memories rushing back.

But he wasn't that boy anymore. He'd led details on his own, helped build ramparts, mapped stretches of land untrammeled by booted feet, faced the worst nature and man could throw at him. He had a job to do now. Meg Pero was no different than any other expedition member.

Perhaps if he kept repeating that, he might come to believe it.

# 3

They left on schedule two days later. The first leg would be on an established trail south toward Camp Mohave. Dot drove a short-bed wagon and team with most of the supplies, a canvas top stretched over for protection. Corporal Adams drove the photography van. The rest rode on horses. Meg caught the cook eyeing her riding habit as she prepared to climb into her sidesaddle.

"Mighty fancy, Miss Pero."

Meg swished the dun twill skirt aside to show Dot the denim breeches and leather boots underneath. "Mighty practical, Mrs. Newcomb. And it has pockets."

Dot's brows went up. "Might need to order one of those myself."

Meg looked past her to where the two privates were checking the closed van that held her photographic equipment. It was square and narrow, perhaps six feet deep and high and four feet wide. Railed shelves inside held the bottles of her chemicals securely, while drawers fitted into one side sheltered pans and utensils. Corporal Adams was already at his place on the bench, four mules in harness in front.

Dot must have interpreted her look. "Don't you worry about your plates, now. You packed them well."

"Just like my father taught me." It had taken her a while to prepare the glass, secure it in wooden frames, and slip them upright into boxes cushioned with lambs wool. Longer expeditions had been known to use one hundred plates on mammoth cameras up to twenty-four inches in width, besides fifty or so of the narrower stereographic views. She could only hope the fifty plates and twenty stereographs she'd brought for her smaller cameras would be enough.

She had been so concerned about the van that she hadn't considered her own transportation until Private Larson brought her a chestnut mare. The lanky cavalryman had proven the more talkative of the two younger men. The most she'd gotten from Private Meadows so far was a shy smile.

"With nigh unto a thousand horses and mules at the fort, they don't generally name the spare mounts or pack animals," Private Larson had confided as he'd handed her

41

the reins. "But I call her Stripe for the white down her nose."

Papa had generally purchased their horses, and he'd tended to buy whatever was convenient rather than looking for a horse likely to give them a comfortable or easy ride. She'd ridden her share of swaybacked nags, including one that had attempted to take a bite out of her every time she mounted.

Stripe, however, appeared to be a gentle beast, with warm brown eyes and a luxurious mane. Her chestnut coat and hooves seemed in good shape, but Meg would have expected no less from a cavalry horse, spare or no. She'd stood patiently while Meg cinched the sidesaddle in place and didn't flinch when Private Larson slung on saddlebags with Meg's personal gear. Meg had just mounted when Ben rode past on a sable-coated beast, broad-brimmed black felt hat pulled low, gloved hands gripping the reins in an easy fist.

"Ready?" he called.

"Of course," she answered.

She thought she caught sight of his grin before he turned the horse for the front of the column. "Move out!"

Something hitched inside her. Excitement? Anxiety? Perhaps a little of both. Determined, she clucked to Stripe, and they headed south.

Ben led the short column, with Mr. Newcomb right behind. Corporal Adams came next with the photography van, followed by Dot with Meg at her side. The two privates brought up the rear, each towing a train of eight mules. Mr. Pike ranged ahead, dark horse soon dotted with red from the dust of the trail.

The guide had intimated he thought the pace of the trek Ben had planned might be too fast. He appeared to be correct, for Ben broke into a canter that forced the others to follow at the same jarring gait. Ben had said they must be back to the fort before snowfall, but as she glanced around at the rocky ground, the sharp emerald spikes of grass and the minty clumps of sage, she found it hard to imagine the area covered in white.

"Are we expecting trouble?" Meg asked Dot.

"Not that I heard," Dot said over the rattle of the wagon. "Maybe he wants to make the spire by noon, rest the mules."

Meg shook her head. Had he learned nothing of planning since his days at West Point? "He might not need to rest them if he slowed down."

The trail lay straight across the plain, past odd little knobs of red rock and through the occasional dry draw she assumed carried runoff during the rainy season. As the sun climbed, the temperature rose. Meg unbuttoned the top flap of her habit, let the dry breeze cool her neck.

Dot wiped sweat off her brow with her sleeve. "Ever been on one of these before?"

"Columbia Gorge, with my father," Meg told her, guiding Stripe around a particularly large clump of sage. "It was a private expedition, and the wife of the guide was along, so one more woman wasn't any trouble."

"Speaking of trouble." Dot nodded at Ben as he rode back toward them. "Here it comes." She raised her voice. "Indians on our trail, Captain?"

"Nary a sign," Ben assured her. "How's the wagon holding up?"

"Fine," Dot said. "Though I may have to repack the pots and pans the way they're jangling. I didn't expect quite this pace."

"We're late," he said. "Until we aren't, we move." With no more than a nod to Meg, he rode around the wagon and headed back toward the front of the cavalcade. She supposed she should be glad he hadn't questioned her about her ability to keep up.

He must have taken Dot at her word, though, for he called a halt as the sun

44

reached its zenith. Meg was glad to dismount and sit in the small patches of shade afforded by a copse of pine while Dot passed around water. Corporal Adams and Dot's husband followed her back to the wagon to help with the repacking.

"How much farther to camp?" Private Larson asked, leaning his back against a tree.

"Good five hours," Mr. Pike said before taking a long draw of the water.

The two privates sighed in unison. Meg was more interested in Ben's behavior. Instead of sitting, he paced across the area, gaze on the ground. What was he looking for? This was an established path. Surely it had been surveyed before.

Mr. Pike rose, adjusting his battered hat as if to better shade his eyes. "Come rest, Captain," he called. "It's a harder ride from here. We'll leave the trail in about an hour and head across country, right past Deadman's Tower."

Meg perked up. "Deadman's Tower?"

The guide chuckled. "Scared of ghosts, are you, Miss Pero?"

"No," Meg told him. "I don't believe in them. The place just sounded picturesque. What is it?"

"It's a sandstone spire," Ben said, joining

45

them at last and propping a booted foot up on a rock. "Legend has it the first explorer who tried to climb it fell to his death."

"How horrid," Meg said with a delighted shiver. "I'll want a picture."

He straightened. "No time."

What? Was he trying to beggar her? Meg scrambled to her feet. "But this is an expedition. You're supposed to take pictures, collect samples."

"Which we will do when we reach the rim," Ben promised her. He glanced about at the others. "Rest's over. Mount up and move in five." He stalked off.

"Who put a burr under his saddle?" Mr. Pike muttered, but he went to get his horse.

Meg climbed a rock to slide herself back into the sidesaddle. She'd used their late start to convince Ben to bring her along, but what difference did an hour here or there make? She had every intention of documenting the expedition in photographs, but the stereographs would make her the money to be self-sufficient. Pictures of western landscapes could reach one hundred thousand printings. Papa had been living off the proceeds of his pictures for years, but on his death the rights to his photographs had gone to the distribution company. If she wanted income of her own, she had to create her own pieces.

As the next hour passed, Meg grew more restless. She'd spotted a butte rising on the east that would have made an excellent stereograph, a sweeping view across the plain that begged to be captured. But Ben continued resolutely on, seemingly oblivious to the growing grandeur around them.

"Why did he want a photographer if he refuses to stop long enough to take pictures?" she complained to Dot as they neared Deadman's Tower. The ragged red rock jutted out of the ground, boulders tumbled around the base, like a finger pointing accusingly at the sky. "Look at that thing. Have you ever seen anything more striking?"

"It would make a pretty picture," Dot said. "A shame the wagon's about to break down so I won't see you set up your equipment."

"What?" Meg asked, but Dot reined in the team and Meg slowed as well.

"Hey!" Dot shouted, and Private Larson brought his mount closer, tugging the mules along behind him.

"Got a problem," Dot told him. "Need to stop, and I'll want Corporal Adams's help. Pass it up to the Captain."

"Right!" He drew back, handed the lead

of his train to his buddy, then urged his horse into a gallop to catch up to the front of the line. Corporal Adams reined in as well and glanced back around the side of the van.

Dot set the brake of the wagon and climbed down. "Well, what are you waiting for? I can only fuss about so long. Go get your picture." She waved the corporal over.

With a grin, Meg slipped out of the sidesaddle and hurried to fetch her equipment.

"Captain!"

Ben reined in as Larson rode up to him and Pike.

"Problem with the wagon," he explained. "Corporal Adams's gone to see how he can help. I'll stay with the mules." Wheeling his mount, he headed back.

"I'll scout ahead," Pike offered.

Ben nodded, turning in the saddle to glance behind. Meadows had stopped just short of the wagon, mules milling about uncertainly. Hank must have decided to help as well, for he and his wife were examining a hoof on one of the horses while Adams lay on his back under the wagon as if inspecting the undercarriage.

Ben scanned the way ahead, seeing nothing but more red earth dotted by shrubs and grasses growing brittle with the summer sun. His father had traveled this way two months ago with only a guide. He'd claimed the need to personally check the route for the upcoming survey. Why? There hadn't been trouble for months. The Colonel had even joked with Mother and Diana about how safe it was, encouraging them to join him during his expectedly short tenure. One of his duties in taking command had been to assess the continued need for the fort.

His father was in excellent health, a crack shot, and a brilliant strategist. The guide, by all accounts, had been experienced and reliable. The weather had been good, and there'd been no reports of unrest. What had prevented them from coming back?

The Army hoped to find a way across the canyon to encourage settlement. He'd become an engineer rather than a cavalryman like his father for that very reason — opening areas, giving people more opportunities. He'd become painfully aware that many of his opportunities had been gained because of his father's influence. Other men deserved the right to try.

A movement caught his eye. Meg had dismounted and carried a camera and tripod toward the spire. Frustration warred with admiration. He urged his mount forward.

She had her head under a cloth draped over her camera when he reined in, but she must have heard him for she called out, "Almost finished. Just a few more minutes, and I'll have a fine stereograph."

He shook his head. "Stereographs must be taken at precise angles. You taught me that. We could be here another hour."

"Not at all." She emerged from the cloth, hair spiking with the static of the dry air, like a dandelion turned to the sun. "I have a stereographic camera now. Two lenses, one shot, and just a few moments for the exposure."

"That easy?" he mused.

She grinned at him. "Well, I did have to coat the plates first. But at least I don't have to bribe the spire with a lollipop to get it to stand still."

"Lollipops would be safer," he said, fighting not to share that grin.

She wrinkled her nose. "But so much more boring. Give me the sky, the sweeping vistas, any day." She dove back under her cloth.

She might be busy with her camera, but did she have any idea of the picture she presented? Trim figure bent at the waist, riding habit twitching as she shifted. Ben shot his gaze skyward, counted the few wispy clouds. Behind him he heard Larson call to Meadows to let the mules graze while they waited.

"There," she proclaimed, reappearing once more. "All done."

"Impressive." He swung down from the saddle to help her with the tripod. "But what about developing the plate?"

She made a face as she cranked the bellows on the camera closed. "That *will* take a few minutes. I have everything set up in the van. We can look at the negative tonight if you'd like."

She had thought it all out. He carried the tripod in one hand and led the horse with the other. "Is there really something wrong with the wagon?"

She cast him a quick glance, then fiddled with the camera. "You'll have to ask Dot."

He sighed. Just as he'd suspected. Either Meg had convinced the cook to pretend they had a problem or Dot had thought of it and Meg had gone happily along because it furthered her plans.

"This isn't a private expedition, Meg," he warned her as they headed for the van. "It's a military operation. You and Dot and the

51

others are under my command. I'm responsible for your safety."

"I understand that." She offered him one of her sweet smiles. "But there's nothing dangerous at the moment."

He wished he could be so sure. Something had stopped two grown men, both fully capable of defending themselves, from returning to the fort. A band of Navajo warriors intent on revenge? A rockslide or flash flood? Or something worse?

"This is the wilderness," he informed her. "Unless you know otherwise, it's best to assume everything's out to kill you."

She raised her brows. "The Ben Coleridge I knew was ready for anything."

"I'm not the man you knew."

She shivered, as if she'd felt the frost in his tone. "Pardon me, Captain. I never intended to countermand your orders. But the Army hired a photographer to document the survey, and you won't have much documentation unless you allow me to take pictures."

They had reached the van, and she picked up her skirts to clamber inside. He caught a quick glimpse of shelves, one of which was wider so that it could be used as a table, before she shut the door. He turned to find

Dot back at her place on the bench of the wagon.

"Thought one of the horses might have picked up a stone," she said. "My mistake. Corporal Adams is looking over the wagon just in case. You ready to move on when he's done?"

She made it sound as if he'd been the delay. "Sure," Ben drawled. "Sorry to have kept you waiting."

"No problem," Dot said. "Just don't wander off again. We need to make water by sundown."

With a shake of his head, Ben went to check on the corporal.

Adams was running his hand over the iron rim of one of the rear wheels. Ben had only met the fellow on arriving at the fort, but the clerk had struck him as meticulous and cautious. He also tended to speak in a slow, considering manner that said he had an education beyond many of the Colonel's men.

He glanced up at Ben's approach.

"Any trouble?" Ben asked.

"Everything appears to be in order," he replied. "I can find no indication of a flaw. Perhaps the rocky terrain misled Mrs. Newcomb."

"Perhaps," Ben agreed, though he still

53

wondered how much Meg had had to do with the stoppage.

"Corporal," Dot shouted from the front of the wagon. "Stop dawdling and help Miss Pero remount."

Meg had come out of the van and taken her horse's reins in hand. Now she glanced around, likely looking for a rock, so she could push herself up into the sidesaddle. Ben handed his reins to Adams, who pulled up short. Ben went to join her.

"Allow me." Setting a hand on either side of her narrow waist, he boosted her up. Once more memories threatened — twirling her in a dance, lifting her onto a rock so she'd have a better vantage point to shoot her picture, holding her close for a kiss.

As if she'd been privy to his thoughts, her face turned pink. She draped her skirt about her, avoiding his gaze. "Thank you."

He sighed. "I'm not your enemy, Meg."

She turned to gaze at the spire. "I know that. And I'm not your enemy either. I want this expedition to be a success."

"Then it seems we share the same goal."

Her light dimmed, as if she expected him to refuse her next request for a photograph. His resolve dipped as well. "Let me know if you notice something else that must be documented, and I'll see what I can do."

She smiled and met his gaze at last, and the whole world brightened. "Thank you."

He could have stood there for an hour, basking in the glow. He made himself turn and retrieve his reins from Adams, who was staring at him. Ignoring the corporal, he mounted and rode back to the front of the line.

He expected to hear a request to stop at least twice more before they reached their evening camp at Mesa Springs. He even glanced back when they hit the edge of the escarpment late in the day. The plain dropped off through a steep set of stairs to the plateau below. Surely this deserved a picture.

But Meg must have taken his warnings to heart, for she merely waved him on. No dulcet voice ever called out as they zig-zagged down to the plateau, and the wagon and van never stopped again. They reached camp well before sundown, set up the tents around the little springs, and gathered downed wood from the trees for a fire.

"Enjoy your dinner," Dot said as she carved off the beef she'd seared over the flames. "This is the only fresh meat we brought. You want more than salt pork tomorrow, you better shoot it."

The others dug in, but Meg was sitting by

the tent she would share with Dot, deep in study. Ben moved closer.

"I know the first day on the trail can be hard," he told her, "but you should eat something."

She glanced up, face puckered. "It's not the ride that's troubling me. I was checking the negative to make sure it turned out."

"I take it the picture was flawed," he said, bending closer.

"Not exactly." She pointed toward the spire. "Look there."

Her cheek was an inch away. He caught the scent of honeysuckle over the smoke from the campfire. If he turned his head, their lips might meet.

He glued his gaze to the plate of glass. Even though the light and shadow were reversed from what the picture would show, he made out the imposing finger of the rock, the tumble of boulders about its base. "It looks fine to me."

She shook her head. "Right there, near the largest boulder on the right, that small patch of white. It's a shadow."

"Aren't shadows good?" he asked, straightening. "They make the picture look more real. Everything casts a shadow."

Her frown didn't ease. "Indeed. You can see the length of the spire's shadow along

56

that line. This shadow was cast by something else, or rather, I suspect, someone else."

Ben reared back. "You can't know that. It could be a smudge."

Her eyes narrowed. "I know my photographs, Captain Coleridge. I know what I saw and what I took. There was another person at Deadman's Tower, watching everything we did, and taking some trouble to make sure we didn't know it."

# 4

He didn't believe her. Those blue-gray eyes were entirely too sharp, narrowed now as he gazed down at her. Oh, to have a commanding voice, the presence of an Amazon! Why did so many people think she could not know her craft because she was female?

"Fine," she said, wrapping the negative and slipping it back into her case for safekeeping. "You are the leader of this expedition. You've made that perfectly clear. Do as you please."

"Meg." The word was half appeal, half apology. "Be reasonable."

"Hey!" Dot's voice cut through the twilight. "You can't expect your photographer to work all night, Captain. That lady needs to eat."

Ben rose, tipping his hat in Dot's direction. "I know the folly of standing between a soldier and his — or her — mess."

Still smarting, Meg stood and approached

the fire. Dot and Hank had gathered stones to circle the blaze. A big cast-iron pot was wedged into the heat, with a kettle suspended over the fire on a cast-iron tripod. She accepted a tin plate and wide-handled knife, fork, and spoon from Dot and perched on a larger rock to eat the beef and beans the cook had prepared. The smoky flavor rolled over her tongue. She washed everything down with the clear, cool water.

"This is very good, Dot," she said.

The cook grinned at her. "Thank you kindly. The Army's got its own ideas about what supplies we need — flour, bacon, saleratus, beans, cornmeal, salt pork. But I find a little rub off a cinnamon stick improves everything."

Mr. Pike must have finished earlier, for he was sketching in the red dirt with a stick, while Mr. Newcomb and the three cavalrymen looked on. The firelight flickered over his constructed hills and valleys.

"Tomorrow, we cross the plateau," he said in his gruff voice. "It will be dry going, so make sure the canteens and water barrel are full before we leave. There's another spring here." He stabbed the stick into the dirt. "That will be our next camp."

The hairs lifted on the back of her neck as

Ben joined them to gaze down at the crude map.

"Why head for the western end of the canyon?" he asked. "We'll only end up backtracking."

Hank nodded. "Better to start at the eastern end and work our way west. Easier to map."

The guide pulled out the stick. "The eastern end is too rough for present company."

Dot glanced up from carving another slice of beef for Private Meadows. "You better not be talking about me, Rudy Pike. I was driving a wagon across the prairie when you were knee-high to a grasshopper."

"Prairie," he grumbled. "I'm not talking about a flat stretch of wavy grass. It's rutted and seamed and rocky. We'd be smarter to avoid the area."

"Which is precisely why we must map it," Ben said. "Families moving out this way need to know what they're facing. The Army needs to know where it can move supplies and troops, position new outposts. On his first expedition, Powell indicated several possible side canyons in the area that might prove useful for crossing. We'll head toward the eastern edge of the plateau tomorrow."

He didn't wait for the guide to argue

further but turned to Adams. "Corporal, I want someone on watch through the night."

"Yes, sir," he said with a look to the two privates.

Mr. Pike climbed to his feet, tossing his stick into the fire. "Is that necessary? We haven't seen hide nor hair of another soul."

"Standard procedure," Ben answered. "I'll take the first shift."

Corporal Adams nodded. "If you'd be so good as to wake me at moonrise, sir, I'll wake Larson at midnight and have Meadows step in toward morning."

"Everyone else up at sunrise," Ben agreed. With a look to Meg, he strode toward his tent.

Was all that really standard procedure? Or was he mounting a guard because he believed her after all?

As the others moved away from the fire, Dot waved a knife at them. "Coffee and hardtack in the morning. And you may have to wash it down in the saddle by the sound of it."

Meg finished her dinner and took her things to where Dot was pouring some of the hot water from the kettle into another of her big pots. She dropped a cake of soap into the water and followed it with some cold water from the spring. Bubbles speckled the surface.

"May I help?" Meg asked.

"Sure." Dot nodded toward another pot nearby. "I'll wash, and you rinse. We have plenty of water tonight. Can't say the same about the next few days. Might as well keep things tidy as long as we can."

Dot was more fastidious than some cooks with whom Meg and her father had served. She used soap on the plates, cups, utensils, and cookware, scrubbing at them with a rag, then handed each item to Meg to rinse off in hot water before laying out to dry on the rocks around the fire. As they worked, Meg kept glancing to where Ben sat in front of his tent. He'd taken his rifle apart as the others prepared for bed and was cleaning it more thoroughly than Dot cleaned her dishes.

"Have you known Captain Coleridge long?" she asked the cook.

Dot smiled fondly. "Since he was a boy. Hank and I served with his father out at the Presidio in San Francisco. That's a fancy name for a fort. After he graduated from the military academy, he worked with us on the Wheeler survey. He came out to Fort Wilverton to replace Captain Reynolds." She eyed the stain on the plate she was washing and gave it an extra rub with her rag.

"Captain Reynolds?" Meg asked.

"He was supposed to lead this survey. We were all set to start out in June, but he was thrown from his horse. Broke his leg. Army sent him north to recover, but he wasn't expected to return in time for us to set out."

So how much experience did Ben have with this sort of thing? "Did Captain Coleridge conduct the survey with Mr. Wheeler or merely serve as an escort?" she asked, laying out the last rinsed plate as if the answer made no difference to her.

Dot shook soap off her hands. "Far as I recall, he worked with the scientific folk, but Hank would know for sure."

So would Ben. She could ask him directly. They used to be able to talk about almost anything. She'd loved listening to his plans.

"This country's going someplace," he had said, a gleam in his eyes as if he could see what lay ahead. "I'm going to help."

Would he confide in her so readily now? She could find out.

Or she could get some sleep. Already Mr. Pike was rolled up in his blankets, feet to the fire and head away.

"That's why they say you need to keep a cool head," her father had once told her.

Her own bedroll called from the canvas tent she'd be sharing with Dot.

Yet she wanted to talk to Ben. She wanted to know his plans, his ideas about this survey. What drove him so hard and fast toward the canyon? Her safety and the safety of everyone else on the expedition depended on his judgement. Surely she should try to understand him better.

She and Dot finished the dishes, then she picked up the skirts of her riding habit and went to join him in the growing dark.

He glanced up as she approached. "Something wrong, Miss Pero?"

She'd been demoted. A while ago she'd been Meg. She chose not to think about when she'd gone by other names.

Darling.

Dearest.

Sweetheart.

"Nothing wrong," she answered. "But I'm not ready to sleep just yet. I'm more interested in your thoughts."

He cocked his head, and she took that as an invitation. She sat across from him on the hard ground.

"It's clear you're concerned about the pace," she said. "But everyone seems determined to make good time. Why push so hard?"

64

He eyed the wooden stock instead of her. "We have work to do. That's all."

She didn't believe him. "It's more than that, like something's chasing you."

He raised his brows high enough that they disappeared under the shadow of his hat. "I don't chase easily."

Very likely not. Yet something was riding him. Had the Army given him orders he wasn't at liberty to share? Was there some other reason they had to rush to the canyon?

What was waiting for them on the north rim?

Ben finished the last of the cleaning as Hank and Dot headed for their tents. The Colonel had shown him how to clean his rifle at an early age.

"Sometimes all that's standing between a man and death is a fast horse and a well-maintained gun," his father had stressed. Ben had done the drill so many times now it was second nature.

But not even the Colonel's eagle eye had made him linger so long at the task. Some part of him seemed to think the longer he polished, the longer Meg would stay by his side.

The light was nearly gone now, her hair the bright spot beyond the fire. On other moonlit nights, her eyes had mirrored the stars. He gave the stock an extra rub and began reassembling the rifle. "You should get some sleep."

As if to prove as much, she yawned. His mother or sister would have covered their mouths with a gloved hand, if they had deigned to yawn in public at all. Meg was natural, unaffected, like the land around them. He'd always admired that about her.

Her hair flashed as she glanced up into the night. "How can I be tired? Look at that sky. I almost forgot how you can see forever."

He glanced up as well. Thousands of pricks of light pierced the black of the canopy, the center denser, opaque, like a lace veil on velvet. Cool air brushed past them, and an owl hooted from the wood. Though they were surrounded by companions, they might have been the last two people on Earth.

"Papa wanted to take that shot," she murmured as if awed by what she saw above them. "But no camera was up to the task."

"What happened to him?" Ben asked, dropping his gaze and laying the rifle across his knees.

"I'm not really sure." Her voice was as mournful as the call of the owl. "His hands

66

started shaking. Then his eyes began to fail. I didn't realize how sick he was until he'd gone."

Her sorrow clung to him like wet wool, leaving him heavy. "I'm sorry."

"Me too." She was quickly becoming another shadow in the night, but he thought she lowered her chin to gaze at him. "And I was sorry to hear about your father. I know how much you admired him."

He had. He did, he hastily amended. There was still the possibility that the Colonel was alive — held hostage by natives, perhaps, or holed up with a broken leg. Still, more than two months had passed since anyone had heard from him. Every day the chances of finding him alive grew slimmer.

"The Colonel was a force to be reckoned with," he agreed. "I know what he'd say now. You need your sleep. Dismissed, Miss Pero."

She climbed to her feet, and he rose with her.

"I'll go," she said, voice once more precise and controlled. "But not because of any order. I'm a civilian, Captain Coleridge. You have only so much authority over me."

"You're here in the service of the Army," he countered. "My orders apply to each member of this expedition."

She saluted, head high. "Yes, sir." He caught a flash of teeth as she lowered her hand. "But see that you keep your orders civil and sensible, or you might have a mutiny on your hands."

She headed for her tent before he could tell her that mutinies were for sailors. Soldiers just turned tail, and that he would never do.

He kept watch until moonrise, but aside from the howl of a coyote and the occasional hoot from their friend the owl, he never sensed the presence of another living being. Adams came out promptly when Ben rattled the canteen hanging from the pole at the front of the tent.

"All clear," Ben told him. "Call if there's any change."

"Yes, sir," Adams promised.

Despite the narrow, Army-issued cot and stuffy canvas tent, Ben generally slept well on a survey. A sign of a clear conscience, the Colonel would have said. Tonight, his mind drifted to concerns — his father's safety, his mother's fears, the unknown shadow on the negative. Perhaps because he could not solve the first two issues at the moment, he focused on the third.

Meg knew her work. If she said that shadow shouldn't have been there, he believed her. Did it follow, however, that whoever or whatever had made that shadow harbored ill intent? His team consisted of a company of eight well-armed and mostly experienced members. A single entity could do little against them.

Still, wasn't it better not to take chances, given his hopes for this expedition? Something or someone had prevented the Colonel from returning home.

He must have fallen asleep, because the urgent hiss of a whispered conversation woke him. His tent was dimly lit; it couldn't have been dawn yet. The moon must be out, for the darker shadows of two people loomed outside the flap. Drawing his gun from the holster on the ground beside his cot, he slid out from under the covers, stood, and aimed.

"Who's there?" he demanded.

The voices hushed. Then came Larson's voice, creaky and contrite. "Sorry to wake you, sir. I thought I saw something."

Pulling the suspenders up over his shoulders, Ben moved to the opening of his tent and ducked under the flap.

The fire was a dull orange where Dot had banked it against the cool night air. Silvery clouds drifted past a moon that was just narrowing from full. His two privates stood at attention in front of his tent, their faces in shadow.

"Report," Ben said.

"I was patrolling the campsite, sir," Larson said, "when I thought I saw something move under the trees." He pointed toward a gap between the pines. "When I got closer, I heard something."

"Something?" Ben pressed.

"Yes, sir." The next sound was suspiciously like a gulp. "Real heavy breathing."

Ben could only hope the moonlight wouldn't give away his quickly suppressed smile. "Is this heavy breathing still evident?"

Larson shook his head. "No, sir. I went to fetch Josiah, that is Private Meadows, to confirm it, but he didn't see or hear anything."

Meadows nodded.

"Show me," Ben said.

The two scurried across the camp. The ground was littered with pine needles — he could feel the slippery prickles and occasional poke under his stockinged feet. If Meg's shadowy watcher had come close to camp, he would have left no tracks.

"Is Fort Wilverton your first trek out West?" Ben asked, listening to the melancholy sigh of the breeze through the pines.

"Yes, sir," Larson admitted. "For both of us."

Ben thought he understood. An edgy private on the frontier for the first time might easily mistake the wind for the breath of an unseen enemy.

"Well, you were right to investigate the noise," Ben said. "Can't be too careful. If you hear it again, come get me and we'll trace it to the source."

"Yes, sir. Thank you, sir." Larson saluted, and Meadows copied him.

But the two must have settled down after that, for Ben returned to his tent and didn't wake again until someone rattled the tent flap. Pearly light trickled through the crack in the canvas. Dawn. He tossed back the blanket and rose.

As he pushed open the flap and came out, he was pleased to see everyone else up and moving. Meg was striking her tent while Dot offered coffee and hardtack to a yawning Adams and a tousle-headed Hank. Larson and Meadows were checking horses and mules. They'd be loading the wagon and packs next. He intercepted them.

"The rest of the watch uneventful?" he asked, glancing from one to the other.

Larson scratched his ear, pushing his

brown hair back. "Never heard anything else."

"Owl," Meadows reminded him.

"Oh, right," Larson said, dropping his hand. "An owl. Two of them, actually. One on one side of the camp, one on the other, like they were having a chat."

"But no more breathing?" Ben asked.

They shook their heads.

"Listen while you're riding today," he advised them. "See if you hear anything like it."

Hoping they'd accustom themselves to the sounds of the West, he went in search of Pike.

The big guide was checking his saddle. He looked up as Ben approached.

"There's a possibility we're being followed," Ben said.

Pike's heavy black brows drew down. "What makes you think that?"

Ben didn't want to mention Meg or Larson and have either face the guide's disdain. "Just a feeling. Swing back a little, and see if you spot any evidence, then rejoin us. I'll follow the route we discussed."

Pike scratched his chest with a broken nail. "Will do, but I doubt I'll find anyone. Mesa Springs is the only water for miles. If someone else is out there, he's mighty

72

thirsty by now."

Ben could believe that as they set out a short time later. Their path led through stands of pine that scraped at the low-hanging clouds. Downed limbs and fallen trees spanned the forest floor, making a difficult crossing for the wagon and van. Any grass had turned yellow with the summer heat, and red soil showed through. Even the air felt dry.

"Not quite as rough as Pike predicted," Hank ventured, riding beside Ben at the head of the column. "The land's fairly flat. Still, I can't see too many homesteaders coming this way."

Neither could Ben. "But any Army road from the south or north would have to cross through here. We just need to find the easiest route."

That this wasn't the easiest route was apparent by mid-morning, when a shout came from behind him. Ben reined in, then turned in the saddle to find the wagon at a precarious angle. Clucking to the horse, he rode back, Hank beside him.

Meg was on the ground next to Dot, and both were examining the underside of the big wagon. Meadows and Larson were controlling the milling animals behind. From where he sat, Ben couldn't spot

73

anything wrong. Frustration made him shake his head.

"So, like your father, you'll go to extremes to get the shot," he said.

Meg glanced up with a frown, hat failing to hide the red dust speckling her cheeks like freckles. "I had nothing to do with this."

"It's no trick, Captain," Dot assured him. "Wagon's been rolling strange since we started this morning. I think all this jolting set the rear hound out of balance." She pointed to a long strip of wood that connected the back axle to the longer strip of wood that reached from axle to axle. "Wouldn't have thought one would crack so soon into the trek, but I'm guessing this isn't the first time this wagon's left the fort."

"How long to fix it?" Ben asked, trying to ignore the call of the canyon ahead.

"Couple of hours, if I can have Hank and the corporal to help."

"They're yours. And once it's fixed, double time to camp."

Hank grimaced, then quickly dismounted to help his wife. Ben felt Meg's disapproval more surely.

He couldn't tell her what drove him, last night or now. He was under orders. Besides, if Meg and Larson were right, and an enemy stalked them, the last thing he wanted was to be caught in open country after dark.

## 5

He made it sound as if this was all her fault. As if she would damage government property and risk their food supply, much less Dot's safety. She'd never been that desperate to get the shot.

Though the pine forest did have a rustic charm.

The trees were tall, their resin scenting the air. She'd spotted a jackrabbit bounding away from their approach and felt a little selfish for hoping the fellow escaped anyone's sharp eye and fast bullet. A few wildflowers clustered here and there. She could imagine framing that cluster of blue asters between the pine and spruce, and catching a cloud at the peak, white against the sky. The scene would be uplifting, hopeful.

Rather like her feelings at the moment.

By tomorrow they should reach the rim, and her work would start in earnest. Plodding along in the saddle, warm air drying the perspiration from her forehead, was only a prelude to something finer.

If only she could convince herself she wasn't being watched.

It was an odd feeling, creeping up on her from time to time as they moved through the forest. She'd peered around but sighted nothing she wouldn't have expected. Still the plentiful trees, the occasional gulley, provided sufficient cover. And she hadn't missed the fact that Rudy Pike had ridden north this morning instead of southeast. Combined with the posted guard last night, she could only conclude that Ben was concerned too. Was that what fueled his determination to continue at a faster pace?

Corporal Adams had crawled under the wagon to examine the hounds, mallet in one hand, with Hank calling instructions and Dot issuing contrary ones. Private Larson had gone to hold the mules on the photography van. Meg went to the back of it and lowered the steps to climb inside.

Shut off from air, the interior was close and stuffy, and it took a moment for her eyes to adjust to the dim light. Corporal Adams had helped her outfit the van, which had previously been used as an ambulance to carry wounded soldiers.

"Though I'm thankful we haven't had many," he'd explained as he'd tucked her chemicals onto the shelves behind the rail that kept them from falling in transit.

Now her hands moved from long practice — mixing the light lemon-colored liquid of gun cotton dissolved in alcohol and ether into a brick-colored solution of iodine potassium bromide in her tray until the color turned rosy, then submerging her glass plate. She no longer sneezed at the sharp scent of the chemicals as she set the plate in its frame to dry, though she still felt as if something was burning the inside of her nose. After returning the chemicals to their places, she pulled down the nitrate of silver, waiting only until the plate was dry before immersing it in the shimmering bath.

"Amazing grace, how sweet the sound," she sang to herself as she gathered the camera and popped open the hinged top panel, so she could insert the plate when it was ready. "That saved a wretch like me. I once was lost, but now am found. Was blind, but now I see."

The words were as routine as her movements. The plate had to soak for several minutes, about the length of time it took her to finish all four verses.

Up came the plate, all wet and silvery. She

slid it into place, then picked up her camera and opened the door to the van.

Sunlight set her to blinking. Ben was standing near the base of the steps, looking for all the world as if he'd been waiting for her. He'd never worn such a frown at West Point.

"So you did want a picture," he said.

"I always want a picture," Meg replied, descending. She nodded to the tripod hanging on the inside of the door. "You could help."

She thought he might argue, but he took down the three-legged contraption and followed her to a spot well away from any dust the mules might kick up.

The vista through the trees wasn't quite what she'd hoped. The cloud had moved on, but she could still capture something pretty. Ben leveled the tripod, and she positioned the camera, screwing it into place on the broad top rail.

"What do you think?" she asked him. "More trees and ground or sky?"

He didn't answer, and she glanced up to find that his gaze had gone past her. Following it, she saw their guide approaching. He didn't appear to be coming at a particularly fast clip, one arm loose at his side while he held the reins in the other, so he didn't seem to think they were in any danger. Still, she went no further in setting up her shot. For one thing, his movement would quite spoil the frame. For another, she wanted to hear what he had to say.

He reined in beside them. He'd removed his coat, which was rolled up in front of him, and perspiration circled his arms and neck. Even his black beard glistened.

"Captain," he acknowledged with a nod of his head that somehow took in Meg as well. "All clear."

So the guide had been looking for trouble. She wasn't sure whether to be glad or disappointed he hadn't found any.

"Good," Ben said. "We've had some difficulty here. See if you can help Corporal Adams."

Mr. Pike headed for the wagon.

"Thank you," Meg said.

Ben swung a gauntleted hand to brush flies away. "Just doing my duty, ma'am."

Maybe. But she preferred to think that he'd taken her concerns seriously. She bent to her work.

The view was quaint. It might make a popular stereograph, particularly if she titled it something romantic. "Glen in Far-Off Arizona Territory," perhaps, or "Forgotten Wilderness." People slid her pictures into their stereoscopes and peered through the dual lenses to view exotic places and foreign cultures they'd never visit in person, after all. The best pictures told a story.

She had barely finished washing and varnishing the negative and packing it and her camera away when Corporal Adams reported the wagon repaired and Ben called the order to saddle up and move out.

"I'm going to be sore tonight," Dot's husband predicted, pausing to pat his wife on the shoulder.

"I've got liniment," Dot promised. She glanced to the head of the column, where Ben sat, finger drumming on the cantle as he gazed back at them with a frown. "But I may not share it with everyone."

If the pace Ben set that morning had been bad, the one they attempted the next two hours was worse. Even after the repair, the wagon continued to list to one side, bumping and swaying. The van was nearly as bad, though Corporal Adams seemed to be trying to avoid the worst of the dips. Still, Meg began to fear for her equipment.

"I want to transfer the plates to the mules," she told Private Larson when Ben allowed a short break late afternoon. "We can't risk them breaking if the van tips over."

He glanced to where Ben and Mr. Pike

were having a heated conversation, the guide's face turning redder by the moment. "I'd have to check with the captain."

And was clearly reluctant to do so. His dusty boots tapped at the red earth as if he danced on coals.

"I'll ask Corporal Adams," Meg offered, and his sigh of relief was like a breeze.

Unfortunately, Corporal Adams was equally reluctant to approach Ben.

"I have endeavored to drive as carefully as possible, Miss Pero," he informed her, back straight and head high. "I would not want the captain to consider me lacking in doing my duty."

"And I would prefer to reach the canyon with my plates intact," Meg replied. She gave him her best smile and laid a hand on his shoulder. "Nothing ventured, nothing gained."

He grimaced, pulling away as if she had offended him. "That is all well and good, but I am hopeful of a promotion as a result of this expedition, and arguing with the commander is inadvisable to reaching that goal."

She could understand that. Some commanders took their frustrations out on their men. She didn't think Ben would act that way, but she didn't really know the man he'd become since West Point.

She stepped back. "Wait here. I'll ask." She moved toward Ben.

"I tell you you're wrong," Mr. Pike was saying as she approached. "You and Newcomb both. We should head west. Did you hire me as your guide or not?"

"I appreciate your experience and recommendation," Ben said. "But the decision on where to survey is mine. Scout to the east and report back. We'll be right behind you."

Their guide pulled his hat down and strode away.

Ben drew in a breath as he turned to Meg. "What is it, Miss Pero? Is this view particularly good?"

"No," Meg said. "Too many trees. And the terrain is only growing rougher. I'd like to transfer my plates to the mules. They're surer-footed. Your men would like your permission."

"Denied," he snapped. "The plates will have to make it to camp tonight. We'll distribute them to packs then if we must." He started to turn for his horse.

Frustration pushed her in front of him. "There are fifty plates to document the entire expedition. We can't afford to lose one."

Again, he drew a breath, as if struggling

with his temper. "We can't afford to lose any more time, either. I thought you understood that. Isn't it one of the reasons you gave for joining this expedition?"

Oh, the man was insufferable! "Yes, sir. Sorry to have questioned your unquestionable orders, sir. But if we reach your campsite with nothing but broken glass, don't blame me." She marched back to her horse, feeling as if the sun had lit a fire inside her. Corporal Adams averted his gaze as she passed.

"Never mind, Private," she said to Mr. Larson, taking the reins of her horse. "We will continue as we have."

He touched his cap. "Very good, ma'am. Thank you." As if he feared she might change her mind or countermand Ben's orders, he hurried back to the mules.

"You all right?" Dot asked as Meg led her horse to a fallen tree to allow her to mount.

"No," Meg said. "But short of appointing a new commander to this expedition, there's not much I can do about it. I was concerned about my plates. Captain Coleridge says there's no time to protect them."

"Maybe Corporal Adams can drive more carefully," Dot suggested.

Adams must have heard Dot, or felt guilty about refusing Meg, for the mules on the

84

van plodded along as they set out once more. Dot was forced to slow the wagon as well. Mr. Larson and Mr. Meadows let the mules behind them stop to graze. Ben and Mr. Newcomb had nearly outdistanced them all when Ben suddenly wheeled his mount and galloped back to them.

"Problem, Mrs. Newcomb?" he demanded.

Dot beamed at him. "Nary a one, Captain. You?"

His mouth worked a moment before he spoke. "I need this wagon to move faster."

"Happy to oblige," Dot said. "Just talk to your fancy corporal. I'm following him."

He glanced at Meg before focusing on the cook. "Of course you are. I have no concerns I can convince Corporal Adams to move along. Should I find another driver to spell you?"

Dot drew herself up. "I'm no greenhorn. I can outlast you and the horse you rode in on."

"Then keep up," he said. Turning, he galloped back to where Dot's husband waited, pausing only long enough to bark an order at Adams.

"Someone's a mite too big for his britches," Dot grumbled. But she called to the horses, and they continued at a faster pace along with the van. Meg could only hope her equipment, and her future, would survive.

They were all fighting him. Pike disagreed with the direction Ben had set; Dot and Meg held back. As he had feared, his men were all too willing to take Meg's side.

"I suppose you have an opinion on the matter too," he said to Hank as he rejoined him at the head of the column.

"I always have an opinion," the cartographer said. "But after living with Dot for twenty-five years, you learn to keep unimportant matters to yourself to maintain the peace."

Unimportant matters. Ben didn't see the pace or the direction as unimportant. They had work to do and a short time to do it. And he needed to know what had happened to his father.

For as long as he could remember, the Colonel had dominated his world. Tall, muscular, with a booming voice and commanding disposition, his father had led his troops, his friends, and his family. One look in those steely eyes, and men rode to glory, risking life and limb. He had commendations from every campaign, gifts from families he'd rescued from nature or hostiles. No one argued with the Colonel.

Perhaps that was why his father had taken Ben's choice of profession so badly.

"An engineer?" he'd scoffed. "There's no fame in that. No one remembers the builders. You rise in rank through courage, determination."

But rising in rank wasn't all that important to Ben. And building — whether roads to claim new lands, ramparts to protect civilians in time of war, or structures to house hardworking government employees — held so much more appeal.

He'd forged his own path for once, away from his father's influence, or so he'd thought until a conversation with the superintendent at West Point during his second year.

"What do you hope to achieve here?" Colonel Cullum had asked him when he'd ordered Ben to his office. He'd been a military engineer, one who'd served well during the war, and one the cadets could look up to. With his silver hair on top and dark beard below, he always seemed to be considering things from all sides.

Ben had stood at attention across the polished desk. "I want to become an engineer, sir."

"A noble profession," Cullum had assured

him. "It requires hard work, discipline."

"Yes, sir," Ben said, certain he was ready.

Cullum had smiled. "I would expect no less from your father's son."

At the time, he'd thought Cullum had known enough about his father to assume any son of Colonel Coleridge would have the same drive to succeed. It was only later he'd learned the truth about his appointment. His previous schooling, haphazard as it had been with the Colonel's constant movement, would never have qualified him for the prestigious academy. The recommendations he'd been told had earned him the recommendation from the district Congressional representative didn't exist. He'd been granted admission because he was the Colonel's son.

And that meant another man with better credentials, who had merited the right to attend, had been turned away. The matter still sat heavily on him.

"She has a way about her, that Miss Pero," Hank said, recalling Ben to the present. "Reminds me of Dot."

Ben shuddered theatrically. "I'm not sure the world is ready for another Dot Newcomb."

Hank grinned. "Sure would be interesting."

"I'm more interested in this survey," Ben assured him.

Hank shifted in the saddle. "What did you have in mind?"

"We'll follow Wheeler's model — establish a base camp and chart terrain."

Hank glanced back at the wagon and mules. "You didn't bring a naturalist or a meteorologist. Who's collecting samples?"

"I'll be looking at the minerals and noting weather. Private Larson and Private Meadows have enough knowledge to note basic flora and fauna on my direction."

"What if we find something new? Wheeler has."

Ben shook his head. "This is just a preliminary survey. Our primary objective is to locate a possible crossing point."

Hank nodded as if accepting that, but then he was a skilled cartographer, used to these surveys. His maps formed the foundation for many of the roads west of the Mississippi. By teaming him with Corporal Adams, who would keep everything organized and moving forward, Ben ought to have enough time to work on achieving their other objective.

They lapsed into silence, until the loudest sounds were the creak of the saddles and the call of a hawk circling overhead. Ben was just glad everyone kept moving. An itch between his shoulder blades made him feel as if someone was pushing at his back. He glanced around from time to time, but the only humans visible were the members of his team. The mules trotted readily behind Larson and Meadows. Adams grimaced as the van tilted over a rock. Dot's mouth was moving as she talked with Meg.

And Meg rode, head high, like a warrior queen going into battle. He faced front and kept going.

The sun was low among the trees when Pike rejoined them.

"All clear," he reported, more civil than when he'd left. "Follow that draw about a mile, and you'll find a plain that runs south toward the rim with a stream down the middle. Plenty of places to camp alongside."

All clear. No sign of any other inhabitants. It seemed Meg and Larson had been wrong. No one was on their trail or ranging ahead to cut them off.

Meg was right about one thing, though. He still felt as if they were being chased.

# 6

They reached the canyon by late afternoon
on the third day out from the fort. Though
she knew it was coming, Meg was unpre-
pared for the sight. Privates Larson and
Meadows had transferred her plates to the
mules and given her charge of them. One
moment, she was riding along, towing her
mules, trees clustered all around. The next,
the world opened up and dropped away.

Ben and Mr. Newcomb were mounted
side by side as she came abreast of them,
gazing with the same wonder she felt. It was
as if a mighty fist had struck the ground,
sending cracks spreading in all directions.
Banded cliffs, rough and rugged, dropped
thousands of feet to the Colorado River,
visible only in places as a thin line the color
of Ben's eyes. Other than the cry of the
wind through the pines, the stillness was
complete.

"I have to get a picture," she said, though

91

she suspected not even her father could have done this justice.

Ben turned from the view. "One shot. I'll have Corporal Adams stay with you. The rest of us will set up camp to the east. Private Meadows, after Miss Pero removes her plate, attach the other mules to your train."

As the private hastened to obey, Meg hurried for one of the packs that held her plates, fingers twitching and mind whirling. One shot? It would take dozens to capture every angle, each direction. But he was right. She had to ration her plates, or there would never be enough for the expedition.

Corporal Adams held the mule team steady as she entered the van and prepared the plate.

"Is everything all right?" he called from outside, just as she reached the final verse of "Amazing Grace."

Had he heard her? Her cheeks heated.

"Fine," she called as she slipped the plate into her stereographic camera. A solidly built box of fine-grain cherry with brass fittings and black leather bellows, the camera had cost her dearly, but she had never regretted it. Being able to take the two pictures of a stereograph at the same time all but guaranteed a good result.

"Might I be of assistance, Miss Pero?" he asked as she came down the steps. He eyed her camera as if he expected it to leap up at him.

"No, thank you," Meg said. "Just see to the mules and my horse. I'll be back shortly."

She pulled the tripod off the door and carried it and the camera closer to the rim. The ground crumbled easily under her boots, reddish stone cracking anew. How would she take the shot if she couldn't get close?

She craned her neck to see beyond the rim. That cliff didn't look so sheer. The ground broke away in terraces until it plunged for the river. How much better to get a glimpse of the water in the shot! Now to find a way down. She glanced around.

A short distance to the left, rocks jutted out from the rim like a giant staircase. Perfect! Holding her camera and tripod close, she eased out onto the upper rock. Pebbles skittered away from her feet to leap off and disappear into the void. The wind tugged at her hat, pushed on her camera. She could almost hear her father's voice.

*Get the shot, Meg. That's all that matters. Without the shot, you're no photographer.*

She sat on the rough ground and dropped

her legs over the edge. The next outcropping was five feet below her. Not too far. She rolled onto her stomach and shimmied over, drawing the camera and tripod after her.

She landed with a jolt that sent more rock flying, but she quickly righted herself and drew in a breath. Every inch closer opened new viewpoints, more vistas. Why hadn't she brought more plates!

Because her aunt and cousin wouldn't have allowed it. They begrudged her the plates she had. They would never have given her the money to buy more, and she'd needed what money she'd had to reach the fort.

She pushed away the thought of what lay behind and ventured closer to the end of the outcropping. The next step was a longer drop, with a narrower ledge at the bottom. But she could see more of the river. Just a little closer, and the light would be perfect.

*Get the shot, Meg.*

She lay on the ledge on her belly, stretched her arm down as far as she could, and let the tripod drop. It clattered against the rock but settled, and she could breathe again. Swiveling, she hung off the edge once more, feet feeling for any purchase. There! She eased herself over, camera clutched in one hand. She didn't dare turn, not until she was all the way down. Once she was down, she would be able to spot the handholds and crevices that would help her get back up. Anchoring her free hand on the rock at her waist, she bent one knee and reached down with her other foot.

Air.

Meg swallowed. She dared to glance down and saw only the dun of her riding habit turning rusty with the dirt. Where was the ledge? It couldn't be more than a few feet or so below her now.

She bent lower, felt deeper. It had to be here. Perhaps she should just let go and jump.

Trust that she would make it.

Taking a deep breath, she let go and stepped back.

The ground rose up to meet her, but the landing jarred the camera. She clutched at it to keep it from falling and nearly lost her balance. She caught one glimpse of the river before she pushed herself forward against the cliff. The rocks scratched her nose. That was better than falling. Too bad her pockets weren't deep enough to hold rope. Now she had a pocketknife that had been her father's and not much else. She took another deep breath, then sneezed at the dust and nearly overset herself again.

That was quite enough of that.

Squaring her shoulders, she turned, head high and thoughts determined. The sight before her took her breath away anew.

The near-ground undulated like wrinkled crimson fabric. Dusky green trees clung to any surface that wasn't perpendicular. Directly in front of her, the highest point was a fist of golden white stone, pointing to the heavens as if to remind her there was someone else above all this.

Her Creator.

She swallowed. She hadn't thought much about God since her father had been taken away. Papa hadn't bothered with churches, except for the occasional photograph of a worthy steeple. She'd always wondered why he'd chosen "Amazing Grace" to time plate preparation. She'd asked once.

"Who doesn't need a little grace?" had been his response.

Still, he'd always had a respect for the One who made such vistas possible. She felt that same awe slipping over her now. Some had called her work art, but this, this was true artistry, humbling her with its majesty.

"Halloo!"

The echoing call came from behind and above her, and for a moment she thought

God had deigned to speak. She shook her head at her own whimsy.

"Just a while longer, Corporal!" she shouted back. And then she went to work.

She set up the camera, angled it this way and that until she was certain she was catching as much of the grandeur as she could, that fist of rock to one side and the river far below. As the tableau settled into a satisfactory stereograph, she set the exposure. Now, if nature would just oblige by staying still.

Off to the left, closer to where the camp must be, something flashed.

Meg pulled her head out from under the hood and stared across the rugged slope. A bright spot flickered against the rocks, there and gone and there again, far too low to be caused by Ben or her other team members. It was almost as if the light had reflected off metal, a mirror, a piece of equipment, or the brass on another camera.

Was someone here ahead of them?

They had the tents erected, Dot was plucking the turkey Pike had shot for dinner, and still Meg and Adams hadn't returned. Ben stood on the edge of the campsite, arms crossed over his chest, gazing back the way they had come.

Where was she?

He turned to stride to the picket line, where Larson and Meadows had tied the horses and mules. Larson looked up expectantly from where he was examining a hoof on one of the pack animals.

"Saddle me a horse," Ben said. "I'm going for Miss Pero and Corporal Adams."

"Yes, sir."

Larson was quick. Cavalrymen had to be. They were expected to be able to mount at a moment's notice, shoot accurately from the saddle, and use a cutlass at a gallop. Ben might never follow in his father's footsteps, but he knew how to move quickly as well.

"If I haven't returned in a half hour," he instructed Larson as he mounted, "send Newcomb and Pike after me, and tell them to bring rope and their rifles."

Larson's eyes widened, but he saluted.

Ben rode back, keeping the horse well away from the rim. The sight of the canyon had shaken him. He'd read some of the reports from Powell's first expedition, heard the famed geologist describe the dangers of the place. The explorer had lost supplies and photographic plates to the rapids and had barely escaped with his life. Some of his men had fared worse. Fearing they might never survive the canyon, they'd set off on their own and had perished in the rough side draws. But even knowing all that hadn't prepared him for the depth, the height, the panoply of color and shape. And the incredible stillness, as if everything was waiting.

Men prided themselves on their ability to construct elaborate buildings that reached higher every year, mighty monuments that would stand the test of time. One look and the canyon made even the loftiest steeple a child's toy. This was true achievement, true glory.

Grand treachery.

He'd seen that immediately. The fissure existed for a reason. The ground bent easily to the trials of nature, the pressure even of a foot. He wouldn't risk a horse too close to the edge.

Even if Meg would risk her life.

He clucked to the horse and broke into a canter.

Adams was standing near where Ben had left him, clinging to the horse's halter and the mules' reins and muttering to himself. At the sight of Ben, he sagged with relief, then straightened and managed an awkward salute. "Sir."

Ben reined in and swung down from the saddle. "At ease, Corporal. Where's our photographer?"

Adams was so rigid he might have been carved from the stone of the canyon, but he managed a nod toward the crevice directly in front of him. "She remains at large in that direction taking her picture, sir. I asked if I might be of assistance, and she refused."

He sounded highly aggrieved by the fact. Ben tied his horse at the back of the van. "Call to me every few moments. If you don't hear an answer, take the animals east to camp and gather a search party."

His eyes were wider than Larson's. "Yes, sir."

Ben started for the rim. He was barely out of sight of the van when he heard the call.

"Halloo." Adams's voice echoed against the rock.

"Here," Ben called back. He eased himself out, heart starting to pound harder. He'd never considered himself anxious around heights, but the drop below, the sheer depth, sent a wave of dizziness over him. If he called to Meg, would he cause her to lose her balance and fall?

The very thought chilled him, but he refused to turn back. Not until he knew she was safe.

"Halloo!" Adams called.

"Here," Ben answered.

"Will you cease that racket?" Meg's voice floated up out of the abyss. He stopped, then nerved himself to peer over.

She was a good fifty feet farther out into the canyon, perhaps a dozen feet below him, and standing on an impossibly narrow shelf, head buried in the hood of the camera.

"Are you mad?" he shouted.

She yanked out her head and glanced up at him. Even from here he could feel her glare.

"Quiet!" The command ricocheted off the rock, and pieces clattered over the edge. "I'll be done shortly." She disappeared inside the hood.

Of all the willful, determined, ridiculous things she could have done. She might have sprained an ankle, broken a leg, fallen to her death. He couldn't speak for the enormity of it.

"There." She pulled out and sent him a smile. "Just a few minutes now."

He'd go insane.

"Halloo!" Adams shouted.

"Here!" His voice must have sounded as tense as he felt, for he thought Meg flinched.

He had to answer Adams three more times before she gathered up her equipment and moved back to the base of the ledge. By then, he was sweating. She must have heaved her tripod, for it sailed up and clattered onto the rock below him. He shifted as close to the western edge as he dared so he could keep her in sight.

Shoving her camera onto a rock partway up the cliff in front of her, she positioned her hands and began climbing. Her skirts parted to show breeches and boots beneath. He wasn't sure whether to be shocked at the display or impressed by her ingenuity.

Suddenly, rocks began sliding, and so did she. He was scrambling down to the lower ledge before she hit the ground.

"Halloo," Corporal Adams called.

"Help!" Ben shouted. "Now!" He righted himself, leaped over the tripod, and raced to the edge of the second ledge.

"Ow!"

He skidded to a stop. "Meg! Are you hurt?"

"I'm fine." The annoyance in her tone was somehow more reassuring than the words. "But could you please stand still? You're making it rain rock."

"Captain!"

Ben glanced back to see Adams peering over the edge of the first ledge. Ben held up a hand to hold him back. Then he dropped to all fours and crawled cautiously to the edge of his own shelf.

Meg glanced up. "I don't suppose you have a rope."

"Sorry. I'll come better equipped next time you decide to throw yourself off a cliff."

She made a face. "I didn't throw myself off. It was all very well planned. I thought I'd be able to spot the handholds, but I can't seem to find a reliable one."

"Allow me." Just the sight of her — face dusty, pale hair falling from its bun, eyes bright — steadied him. He stretched out on the ledge, reached over. A moment later, and something square and polished hit his hands.

"Take the camera," she said.

She'd be the death of him. "I don't care about the camera. I want you safe."

"I care about the camera. Please."

Thinking things he could not say aloud to a lady, he gripped the box and pulled it up beside him. Tempting to toss the thing into the canyon, but she needed it and so did he if they were to fulfill their commission. He set it carefully down on the shelf, then turned again and reached down.

This time her hands met his. He gripped them firmly and pulled. Rocks rattled as she scrambled up.

Everything in him demanded that he pull her close, never let go. He settled for holding one of her hands as they sat a moment on the rock. He wasn't the only one breathing hard. Too bad Larson wasn't near enough to hear them. He'd never mistake the sound again.

Ben closed his eyes, focused on the cool dry breeze that brushed his cheeks. She was alive.

*Thank you, Lord.*

"Well," she said after a moment. "That was an adventure."

"That was a gamble," he disagreed, opening his eyes. "You could have been killed."

She sent him a grin. "But wait until you see the shot. That picture alone could support me for a year."

He shook his head, releasing her hand. "Money won't mean much if you're not around to enjoy it."

"Spoken like a man on the government payroll." She climbed to her feet and went to fetch her camera. "The Army may take good care of you, Captain Coleridge, but some of us have to work to pay our room and board."

"Halloo?" Adams's voice shook with uncertainty.

"Coming," Meg called, cradling her camera as close as a newborn.

And Ben could only stand, pick up the tripod, and follow.

# 7

Meg thanked Corporal Adams for his concern before stowing her camera in the van.

"Captain?" he asked as Ben came up to her and offered her the tripod.

Something simmered in Ben's river-colored eyes. She'd frustrated him, perhaps even frightened him. But he didn't understand how important this work was to her. She accepted the tripod and packed it away. "I just need a few moments to protect the negative."

He snapped a nod. "We'll wait."

The quiet darkness of the stuffy van was almost welcome. A shame her thoughts were not as quiet. As she washed the plate in salty hyposulphite to remove any impurities that might cause the picture to decompose, then varnished the glass with shellac to protect it, all she could think about was Ben. He'd been so determined to protect her. It was a side of him she didn't remember from West

Point. Then again, the Academy had been a safe place, for him. It had been more difficult for her, prompting her to break off their association.

She simply didn't fit in his carefully constructed world.

It wasn't just the regimented Army life. She understood the need for discipline and order, particularly having grown up with her fly-on-a-whim father. No, it had become apparent that Ben Coleridge had been born to a family of privilege, and some considered her a poor match.

Certainly that aura of elitism had been evident for most of the cadets and instructors she'd met at West Point. They considered themselves gentlemen of the highest caliber and ladies shy, retiring creatures who giggled behind fans and cooed over the uniforms on the cadets' broad chests. Ben's classmates had had no idea what to say to or how to approach a woman who stood on her own, who was determined to accomplish more in life than to marry well.

She could have fought against their narrow views. She'd never been one to bend to society's dictates. But then she'd discovered the one person she could never gainsay.

Mrs. Colonel Coleridge.

That was how Ben's mother preferred to

style herself. That or simply the Colonel's wife, as if only one colonel mattered, and she was blessed above all women to be married to him. As if she had no identity, no purpose of her own. With her brown hair worn in a coronet braid, big brown eyes, and ample figure swathed in the latest fashion, she'd seemed gracious and motherly to all.

Except Meg.

"I don't recall a Pero in the regiment or at the Academy," she'd said after Ben had introduced Meg to her at the home the Coleridges were renting in the town of Cornwall, south from West Point. The elegant house with its white wrought-iron edging on the wide porch and horsehair furnishings in the pristine parlor had instantly alerted her that Mrs. Colonel Coleridge was used to finer things.

"My father isn't in the Army," Meg had explained. "He's a photographer here to take pictures of the cadets, faculty, and their families. But we're used to following the drum. Papa photographed the War Between the States."

Mrs. Colonel Coleridge's smile would have frozen the water on the nearby Hudson River. "How interesting. He took pictures

108

while my husband fought and his men died."

"Not everyone wants to be a cavalryman, Mother," Ben had reminded her, tucking Meg's hand in his arm, his support warmer than the wool of the uniform that had brushed against her.

"Certainly not," his mother had agreed. "Where would we be without sutlers and engineers?" She'd linked arms on his other side. "And you will make a fine engineer, so long as you focus on what is important." Her fond look had left Meg out entirely.

She shouldn't blame Ben's mother for trying to protect her son. Plenty of women hung about the towns near the military academy, hoping to find a promising fellow to marry. Mrs. Colonel Coleridge wanted the best for Ben, and Meg clearly didn't fit her definition. Perhaps if Papa had been a general or had perished on the field of battle, it would have been another matter. But then, perhaps Ben's mother would have considered no woman good enough to marry into the Colonel's family. When Ben had proposed, Meg had known there was only one answer. She refused to come between him and his career, much less his family.

There — the plate was dry, and she hadn't

sung a single line from "Amazing Grace." So much for focusing on her work. She slipped the negative into its frame and packed it carefully away.

Ben was standing by his horse as she came down the steps. Corporal Adams glanced between the two of them as if unsure where his orders came from.

Ben had no such trouble. "Follow me back to camp, Corporal," he said. "Miss Pero, do you need assistance to mount?"

She didn't trust herself to speak, lest she say something she'd regret. She certainly didn't trust herself in his arms. She glanced around and easily located a rock large enough to help her.

"No, thank you," she told him.

With a nod, he swung himself up into the saddle and started back even as Corporal Adams went to take his place on the bench.

Meg sighed as she settled herself into the sidesaddle. She didn't want to be miffed that Ben had come to check on her. He had made it easier to climb back up the cliff. He was only doing his duty, looking out for the expedition and all its members.

She eyed his back as she followed him through the trees, the van rattling along behind. His head was high, shoulders relaxed. He'd certainly grown into the swagger he'd shown at West Point. He'd become the man she'd always known he would — a leader like his father.

But she was no longer the photographer's daughter. She would always be grateful for what her father had taught her, but she was her own person, a photographer in her own right. She could contribute as much as the next person on this expedition.

She tapped her heel against the horse's side to urge the mare forward.

Ben nodded as she came abreast. "Something I should know, Miss Pero?"

"And how do you do and it's a very fine evening to you too," Meg said.

He kept his gaze forward, as if watchful for any movement among the trees. "Sorry. I didn't think you rode up merely to chat."

"I didn't, actually. I wanted to clarify my role."

He frowned. "You're the photographer."

"Oh, good. Photographers generally choose their shots based on what the expedition commander wants documented. You told me to take that shot."

He shook his head. "Take the shot, not risk your life."

"Sometimes, I fear, they are the same thing."

His jaw moved back and forth, as if he

111

couldn't decide which objection to state first. A day's stubble, golden against the tan of his skin, glittered with the movement. His skin would probably feel prickly when she kissed him.

*If* she kissed him. No, no, she wasn't going to kiss him!

"Perhaps we can come to a compromise," he said. "I'll tell you what we need documented, you choose the shot, and we agree on where you'll set up your camera."

Now it was her turn to hesitate before speaking. The restriction was like a rope chafing her ankle. But he'd said they'd agree, and she'd rarely had trouble being persuasive.

"All right," she said. "But there's one other matter to attend to. I saw something down on the slope."

He glanced her way. "Oh? Something else we have to shoot?"

She refused to bristle. "No. It was more of a flash, like sunlight off metal or glass."

He looked past her as if hoping to see it for himself. "You're sure it wasn't natural?"

She shrugged. "I suppose it could have been a reflection off water, perhaps near trees so the light would flicker as the branches moved. But it seemed too bright. Didn't you say another expedition was in the canyon?"

"Powell's. It's his second trip, so he knows his way. But he's on the river itself, and he should be much farther downstream by now. He set off in May." He swiveled in the saddle to look back at Adams and the van. "Corporal! Double time."

He broke into a canter, and Meg urged Stripe to follow, trying not to grimace at the cacophony behind her as the van picked up speed.

Ben only slowed when they approached the camp. Mr. Pike had located a flat space surrounded by trees with a stream cutting through a draw to the east. Once again, Dot had gathered rocks to surround the fire she'd built. The white canvas tents stood around the fire, the color, shape, and precise angles at odds with the sweep of trees and canyon around them.

Corporal Adams climbed down from the bench, and Private Meadows hurried to unharness the mules and lead them toward the picket line strung among the trees. Already the other horses had their heads in feed sacks while the mules grazed on the brush and grass. Meg dismounted and allowed Private Larson to see to Stripe and Ben's horse as Ben dropped to the ground and moved into the firelight.

Dot looked up from where she was roasting a turkey over the fire. "Miss Meg looks alive and well. What's the trouble, Captain?"

Her husband came out of the tent farther to the east and eyed Ben expectantly.

"Make setting up the theodolite your next priority," Ben told him. "Miss Pero spotted something down below, and I want to know what it was."

Mr. Pike appeared from behind another tent. "Shadows can play tricks on the eyes, particularly when the sun's going down."

"Shadows and I are old enemies," Meg said, trying not to take offense that he'd doubt her. "This was a flash of light."

Mr. Newcomb frowned. "Powell's expedition on the river?"

"If it is, something's wrong," Ben said. "I mean to find out. If Miss Pero is right, we may have to turn this survey expedition into a rescue party."

In the end, Hank couldn't get the theodolite erected before the sun was nearly down. Ben paced back and forth along the rim, rocks skipping off his boots to disappear over the edge. He tried his field glass, aiming the small monocular down the cliff, but the resolution wasn't sufficient to give him a good view, particularly in the fading light.

While Dot finished preparing supper, Hank worked patiently, leveling the six-inch-diameter instrument on the rocky ground, checking angles and inclinations. Meg alone seemed to appreciate Ben's agitation, for she came to block his path.

"Maybe we should try calling," she suggested. "If the other team is below and in trouble, they'll know we're here."

Why hadn't he thought of that? The moment she'd mentioned the light, his mind had seized on the idea and refused to let go. He couldn't tell any of them he hoped to find someone besides Powell.

He moved to the very edge of the canyon, cupped his hands around his mouth. "Youhalloo! Anyone down there?"

His voice echoed back to him, bouncing off the canyon walls like a ball.

"Halloo!" Meg tried, higher voice penetrating. "We're friends. Identify yourself."

The only reply was a collision of echoes.

He couldn't give up hope. The air currents in the canyon would be fickle, snatching away one sound to carry another close. Perhaps their quarry hadn't heard or couldn't answer easily. He strode to the fire, took a stick, and thrust it into the blaze.

"Corporal, fetch a blanket," he ordered.

Adams moved to comply.

Together, they stood in the twilight at the edge of the canyon. "Do you know Morse code?" Ben asked.

Adams nodded. "I took messages at my last post on occasion."

"Good," Ben said. "We'll use the blanket to send flashes of light. Start with H."

Adams raised and lowered the blanket quickly four times.

"E," Ben instructed.

The corporal gave a quick flap.

"L."

Fast, long, two fast.

"P."

Fast, two longs, fast.

Ben continued calling letters until Adams had finished the message.

"Help is here," the corporal said, lowering the blanket and blinking into the dark.

"Now let's see if anyone takes us up on the offer," Hank said.

The canyon below remained dark.

Ben wasn't aware he'd stood still waiting so long until Meg put her hand on his arm. The touch was kind, supportive.

"If the other expedition is down there and needs help," she said, "we'll find them."

Sitting near Dot, plate already loaded, Pike snorted. "In pieces, most likely."

Ben shook himself. "That's enough, Mr.

Pike. The rest of you, get dinner."

Adams moved off, Hank loping behind. Meg didn't leave Ben's side.

"Is there a reason to fear for Mr. Powell?" she asked.

He rested his hand over hers, unwilling to pull away from the touch. He wanted to borrow her hope.

"Reason enough," he told her. "On his first attempt to traverse the canyon two years ago, he and most of his men barely reached the end of the canyon alive. Congress funded him on this second attempt in hopes of gaining maps." He offered her a smile. "They even have a photographer."

She smiled back. "And you're here as well."

"Our survey should have started in June," Ben said. "We're months behind them. Or at least we should be."

"We'll help them," she insisted. "The flash I saw, it was very like what you did with Mr. Adams. It had a pattern."

His shoulders tensed. "What did it say?"

She shrugged. "I have no idea. I never learned that — Morris code, I think you called it?"

"Morse," he said. "It's used on the telegraph, and the Army and Navy send messages that way sometimes. I understand even some of the wilderness scouts have learned it. It was required study at the Academy."

The Colonel had been a big proponent, insisting that a member of the Signal Corps accompany his regiment during the war. His father could both read and transmit the code. Had that flash come from him? Who had he thought he was signaling? Why not answer now?

"Well, if it was a signal from Mr. Powell, he should have seen your answer," she said. "That should give him great comfort."

She was so certain. His spirit rose to meet her optimism. As if she sensed it, she batted her lashes at him. "Care to escort me to dinner while we wait, Captain Coleridge?"

"It would be my pleasure, Miss Pero," he said.

Together, they turned and strolled back toward the fire.

Dot had put together corn fritters and currants to go with the turkey. It was better food than Powell's team likely had after months afloat. Or what his father had living off the land with only an Army pistol for company.

Meg must have thought he wasn't eating fast enough, because she nudged his shoulder and nodded to the food on his plate.

118

Dot sat back from serving to glance sternly around at them all.

"Game will make itself scarce in a day or so," she predicted, "once they all realize we're a threat. I'd appreciate it if someone brought in a deer or a pronghorn before then."

"I'll do it," Pike said with a nod.

"Good. I'll see what can be done about gathering fruit. This time of year, I would expect raspberries, but I haven't spotted a bush yet."

"Miner's lettuce and mint too," Meg said before she dug into the food.

Pike was watching her. "Looks like someone's not so worried about what's in the canyon after all."

Meg stuck her knife into the slice of turkey. "Whether I eat or not won't change anything, Mr. Pike. Might as well eat."

Ben's mother had had a similar practical attitude when Ben was growing up. She had claimed never to worry when the Colonel was on campaign. She had had complete confidence he would serve well and return to her whole. Perhaps that's why his disappearance had so shaken her.

"She stays up far too late at night," his sister Diana had written him, "as if she could see him hundreds of miles away in

119

the dark. She picks at her food. She's trying to be brave for my sake, but I can tell she's imagining the horrors to which he must be subjected. Please, Ben, bring him home."

He'd promised Diana, himself, and the Army he would look into the matter. That was the secondary purpose of this expedition — to discover what had happened to the Colonel.

Once more, he forced himself to eat. If they did have to mount a rescue tomorrow, who knew when he'd have time for food again?

As if she understood he needed a distraction, Meg called him over after dinner to look at the scene she'd captured. The firelight illuminated the shapes on the glass plate, making it appear the wind moved through the trees on her picture. As always, the work was impressive. Even reversed on the negative, the photograph captured the awe, the loneliness, the sweeping glory of the place.

"Worth going out on a ledge?" she teased him.

He looked up from the plate to nearly slip into the glory of those spring-green eyes instead.

"No," he said. "No picture could ever compare to the loss of such beauty."

Her cheeks were turning pink in the firelight. "Why, Captain Coleridge, how you do go on."

He was leaning closer before he thought better of it.

"Captain!"

Hank's call pulled Ben's head up. What was he doing? Had he truly been about to kiss Meg within full sight of the entire expedition? Had he learned nothing in the last five years?

He rose to go to his cartographer's side.

"What have you, Mr. Newcomb?" he asked.

Led by Meg, the other members of the team crowded around as well. Hank straightened, smile turning up as he found himself the center of attention for once.

"I took one last look before the light was gone," he said. "I don't think that flash Miss Pero spotted was caused by a member of Powell's team."

Relief that the other expedition was safe after all vied with disappointment to have found nothing more. "Then why call me over?"

"Because I found something else." He nodded toward the theodolite. "It's mighty faint in the dark. Look in there, and tell me my eyes aren't playing tricks."

Ben bent and put his eyes to the scope, careful not to move the angle or inclination. The canyon leaped closer, gray, silver, and bone white as night fell. Still, silent. Lifeless. At first, he couldn't tell what had alerted the cartographer.

Then he spotted it, drifting on the breeze. Ben raised his head. "Is that smoke?"

Hank grinned. "My thoughts exactly. It's coming from under that overhang. Someone's been down there, Captain. And recently."

# 8

Ben and Mr. Newcomb were so busy talking neither commented when Meg slipped in behind them and peered through the theodolite. The thin telescope suspended among knobs and loops looked far less substantial and much more complicated than her camera, but the view was sharper. The canyon that had seemed so far away was suddenly much closer. In the fading light, it even appeared more like one of her photographs, all shades of gray. The only thing that was different was the thin smudge rising from under the outcropping just below them.

Meg raised her head. "Are we in danger?"

Ben and Dot's husband stopped in mid-argument over what to do next.

"Danger?" Ben asked, eyes narrowing.

He was like a cat ready to pounce, but she couldn't see the prospect of danger as quite so exciting. "Yes. Is the fire sufficiently doused to prevent it from spreading out of control?"

"No," Ben said immediately, as if seizing on the idea. "I'll go down and take a look."

She almost reached out to hold him close. Why? Surely it wasn't *that* dangerous. She'd seen no sign of flame, and the breeze had slowed.

"It's too dark," Mr. Pike pointed out. "You'll have to climb down and back in uncertain light. Good way to break your neck."

"He's right," Mr. Newcomb put in as Ben opened his mouth as if to protest. "No sense risking your life. That smoke doesn't look all that dangerous. It's drifting, not concentrated as it would be in a serious fire. And there are few shrubs close enough to burn. I doubt the blaze will spread."

Still Ben hesitated. "What if someone needs help?"

Mr. Newcomb shook his head. "If anyone was down there, he'd have answered our call. But we can keep watch tonight to make sure we're not needed."

Ben shifted on his feet as if ready to jump over the edge and race down the slope. The gallant, mad fellow!

Meg dusted off her hands, drawing all gazes to her. "Well, that's that, then. Dot, can I help you clean up?"

Dot glanced at Ben before looking back at Meg. "Sure. I never turn down help."

Ben roused himself. "Gentlemen, meet me at my tent in a quarter hour to discuss the plan of the day. Mrs. Newcomb, Miss Pero, please join us." He walked off before Meg could question him further.

Dot hustled back to the fire, and Meg joined her.

"Nice thing about the captain," the older woman said as she wrapped cloth about the remains of the turkey. "Not every commander sees fit to consult the cook."

"Or the photographer," Meg agreed. Still, she couldn't help wondering about his reaction to the smoke. If there was no danger, why the urgency to go down?

They all gathered a short while later in front of Ben's tent. Like the others, it was A-shaped, a tall pole in front and behind, typical Army issue. Through the partially open canvas flap, she sighted a campaign cot with a bedroll spread upon it. A traveling desk sat on top of the bed, papers secured with leather straps. On the ground nearby lay leather saddlebags that must hold his personal belongings. His rifle, canteen, and ammunition pouch hung in easy reach from the front pole.

Dot stood next to her husband to one side of the opening, while the three cavalrymen bunched opposite. Closer to the fire, Rudy Pike stood with his arms crossed over his broad chest, as if prepared to argue with anything Ben had to say. Meg slid in next to Dot.

"I plan to camp here for at least three days," Ben explained from where he stood directly in front of his tent, firelight playing over his muscular form. "We will conduct a preliminary survey, enough to give the Army a clear view as to whether we can drive a road through this area. Mr. Newcomb will handle the instrumentation for charting. Corporal Adams will assist."

Dot's husband nodded, and the corporal stood taller.

"Private Larson, Private Meadows, and I will collect mineral samples and note major flora and fauna," Ben continued. "If we spot something known to be edible, we'll bring it to you for confirmation, Mrs. Newcomb."

"Glad to help," Dot said. "Though after I identify it, I hope you'll let us eat it."

Private Larson chuckled, then quickly swallowed the sound when Corporal Adams glanced his way.

Ben turned to Meg, eyes bright. "Miss Pero, I want a clear shot in a circumference

— north, northeast, east, southeast, south, southwest, west, and northwest."

Eight pictures? That would make a dent in her supplies. "I could cut that down to four if I widen the perspective," she told him. "You might miss a few details at the edges, but you'd conserve the plates for later in the survey."

He nodded. "Good suggestion. Do what you can."

Why did she feel so warmed by his approval?

Mr. Pike spoke up. "What about me?"

"You'll be on patrol," Ben answered. "Ride in a semicircle around the camp at least twice a day, then determine our course west."

"And hunt for dinner," Dot reminded him.

"Exactly," Ben agreed.

Mr. Pike nodded. "All right. I can do that. Just none of you wander far from camp without me. This land may look flat, but it's full of draws and canyons. You climb into one, you might not climb out."

The night air felt colder.

"Any other questions?" Ben asked.

They glanced at each other as if daring someone to speak first. No one did.

"All right, then," he said. "Get a good

night's sleep. We start at dawn. Corporal, same watch schedule as last night."

"Sir," the three cavalrymen chorused.

As everyone moved to finish settling the camp for the night, Meg drew closer to Ben. "What are you hiding?"

He stiffened. "I don't know what gave you the impression I was hiding something from you, Miss Pero. It would be foolish of me to keep the rest of the team ignorant of an important detail."

Meg cocked her head, watching him. The firelight made it difficult to tell whether his color was heightening, and his stiff posture might only mean she had offended him.

"Yes," she said. "That would be foolish. So why the mystery?"

"No mystery," he insisted. "The Army sent this detail to conduct a preliminary survey to determine whether there's a viable route to cross the canyon. That's what we aim to do. May I see you to your tent?"

As it was less than twenty feet away, across the fire pit from his, she needed no escort. And his request wasn't nearly as friendly as hers had been earlier. It was almost as if he was trying to get rid of her.

"You've changed," she said. "The Ben Coleridge I knew was always frank about his intentions."

128

"And far too confident in his abilities to achieve them," he reminded her. "If you see a change in me, Meg, it's because I've come to realize I'm fallible."

She pressed a hand to her chest. "Never!"

His smile was gentle. "I'm afraid so. I do what I can under the circumstances, but I know my limits and I'm working to compensate for them."

She couldn't quite believe him. He'd been ready to dive off that cliff into the dark to learn about a simple plume of smoke. Besides, she'd long ago decided he'd inherited his confidence from his father. The Colonel had been a military legend. It was rumored he'd refused promotion to general because it could take him out of the field. With the commendations of his instructors behind him, Ben had seemed on a trajectory to eclipse him.

"Limitations, eh?" she said. "I'm certain your mother would argue that you had none. She thought you were perfect."

He quirked a brow. "Mothers are required to think their children are perfect. It's a regulation."

She laughed. "Maybe. I don't remember my mother, but from what Papa said about her, she was a practical sort. She'd never see him or me as perfect, nor make that a

129

requirement for accepting us as family. I always thought your mother, on the other hand, had higher expectations. What limitations do you see in yourself, Ben, that she somehow missed?"

It was a bold question. She no longer had a right to ask, if she'd had that right back at West Point. But something inside her yearned for him to answer.

He sighed. "I used to be too idealistic, too optimistic about the outcomes of every venture. I've learned to temper those expectations."

"How sad." The words were out before she could soften them. One of the things that had drawn her to him had been his enthusiasm, his cocky confidence that he could overcome any obstacle. If she had had a hand in dimming that bright light, she had much to atone for.

"I prefer to think of it as realistic," he said. "Now, you must excuse me. The first watch is mine." With a nod, he reached around her for his rifle and turned for the fire.

Ben thought she might follow him. Meg Pero was determined, if nothing else. But she seemed to accept his excuse, for she went to her tent, and he didn't see her again until morning.

It wasn't difficult staying awake for his watch. Their conversation kept repeating in his mind. She'd claimed his family thought him perfect. As if he was even close. The Colonel had had high standards, and Ben had done his best to meet them. But even his father would have pointed out the flaw in him. Had pointed it out more than once.

"You're overconfident, boy," he'd say. "A certain amount of bravado can carry a man a long distance. But sooner or later, strategy wins out. Think things through."

Perhaps if he'd taken that advice, he would have realized Meg wasn't interested in hearing his proposal or becoming his bride. He'd done all he could to plan ahead since then, always considering every angle before moving forward.

Yet what had he done this evening when Hank had spotted that trail of smoke? Thrown caution behind to be carried on the breeze. All he'd been able to think about was looking for his father. And he had no idea if Meg's flash or Hank's smoke had anything to do with the Colonel.

As he moved around the camp, the only sound a rough snore from the tent Hank and Adams shared, he forced himself to think things through. Could someone be camping just below them in the canyon?

Why not answer their calls? It was possible the sound hadn't reached that far, but a casual glance up the cliff might have given a glimpse of Ben and his team or at least the smoke from their fire. Had Hank discovered a would-be miner who distrusted any newcomer? An outlaw passing through and intent on going unnoticed? A native away from his tribe?

Or an injured man trying to survive?

The last possibility haunted him through the night, long after he woke Adams to spell him. By dawn, he knew what he had to do.

"I'm going down," he told Hank after they had eaten the corn mush and turkey Dot had prepared for breakfast and his men were seeing to the animals. "I want to know what we're dealing with."

Hank washed down his last mouthful with a slug of coffee. "All right. We can set up a harness from the van around you to anchor you, and you can play out the rope as you go down. Take your pistol and compass."

Ben raised his brows. "I understand the need to defend myself. But a compass?"

"You'll want to know which way to go if the rope breaks."

Ben grinned. "That's easy, Hank. I'll want to go up."

Dot glanced at them from where she'd set

a kettle of water to heat by the fire. "Not so fast, you two. You're forgetting something."

Hank met Ben's frown with one of his own. "What?" he asked his wife.

Dot leveled her spoon, yellow mush dripping to sizzle as it hit the flames. "Today's Sunday. Someone should conduct a proper service."

She was right, but the call of the unknown was stronger. "I believe the good Lord will forgive us if we do his will and help someone in need first," Ben told her.

Dot eyed him a moment, then went back to stirring her mush, perhaps a bit more briskly than before.

The cartographer was securing the rope to the leather harness around Ben's chest when Meg came out of her tent. The pale morning sunlight caught in her hair as she glanced around. But one look at Ben, and she was sweeping to his side.

"What are you doing?" she demanded. "Don't tell me that's what engineers wear to conduct surveys."

"Only when they're scaling cliffs," Hank said, tightening the rope. Despite himself, Ben flinched.

"Scaling cliffs?" She glanced over the edge, then back at Ben, face whitening. "You're not going down there."

133

Hank met Ben's gaze as if wondering why he would allow her to order him about. After all, Ben was supposed to be in command. When it came to Meg Pero, he never felt in command.

"Just an exploratory trip," Ben assured her. "I'll collect a few samples from the rocks, look for sources of water."

"And see where that smoke came from," she accused him. She turned to Hank. "Mr. Newcomb, can you rig another contraption like that one?"

Ben would not allow her over the edge, not until he knew what he was dealing with. He shook his head in warning, but the older man merely smiled at Meg. "Sure, but you're not going down there."

"Captain Coleridge should not go alone," she protested.

"I won't be alone," Ben hurried to explain before Hank could volunteer himself or one of the cavalrymen. "Mr. Newcomb will be holding the rope. He'll pull me back up at the first sign of trouble."

"Or at least the second sign," Hank agreed helpfully.

"Insufficient," she argued. "You saw what happened with me and the camera yesterday."

Hank regarded him with a frown, but Ben

couldn't give in this time. "You weren't harmed," he pointed out.

"But —"

"No," Ben said. "Stay here. That's an order."

"It's time you learned I don't take orders well," she retorted. "Mr. Newcomb —"

"Nope," Hank said. "I do take orders well."

"Fine," she fumed. "I'll stay put." Suddenly she brightened. "And I'll take a picture, with you in the shot. It can be the northern exposure." She bustled off toward the van, which was parked beyond the farthest tent.

"Now," Ben said, "before she comes back with reinforcements."

With a grin, Hank stepped back and played out the line.

Ben put both gauntleted hands on the rope and stepped back as well, until the heels of his boots were pressed in the crumbling edge of the canyon wall. Taking a deep breath, he pushed off backward and felt the sick drop into space. His body swung like a pendulum, and he hit the wall with both feet out, the thud echoing through him like a call along the canyon. Steadying himself, he started walking down.

About twenty feet below the top, the land

sloped less steeply, and he was able to turn and walk almost normally toward the shadow of the outcropping. Rock fallen from above crunched under his boots. To the right he spotted a well-worn track coming down from the eastern flank — a game trail, perhaps?

The arch of rock had left a cave of sorts beneath it, perhaps five feet deep and a dozen high. As he stepped out of the sunlight, the layers in the high rock wall became more apparent. That red spoke of iron, the faint strip of green was surely copper. He ought to take samples, but his gaze was caught by the circle of blackened rock on the ground.

A fire pit.

The silvery ash still had a stump of a stick protruding. Ben bent and removed one gauntlet to hold his hand over the coals. No heat. Cautiously, he flicked at the ash. No animal bones evident, so the fire could have been kindled by a native. They tended to reuse every part of their kills.

He rose and studied the surrounding ground, but the rock gave him no sign of who had been here, perhaps as late as yesterday afternoon.

He came out into the sunlight, glanced up toward the rim. Hank stood, one foot braced on the rock, rope clutched in both hands, ready to haul Ben up. Meg stood next to him, camera aimed down the slope. Between him and them lay a field of tumbled rock. Most was weathered a dull gray, attesting to the amount of time it had withstood the elements. But here and there patches of red or black showed vividly, as if someone had recently overturned the stones.

Why? Who else but an Army engineer would be out this way collecting samples?

He picked his way up the slope, carefully touching the tumbled stone with his bare hand. It wouldn't do to disturb a rattlesnake. He studied this rock and that, but none that had been turned over appeared any different from the other stones he'd seen so far.

Then something sharp pricked his fingers. Ben jerked back his hand and listened. No telltale dry rattle warned of a snake nearby. His skin didn't appear to have been punctured. Slowly, he reached down among the rocks and drew out the culprit.

It was a many-pointed steel star, the edges barely dulled. It looked just like one that adorned the spurs on a cavalry officer's boots.

# 9

Meg had planted her tripod beside Hank, screwed her camera into place, and aimed it down the cliff, trying not to think about the slender line of safety deployed over the edge. She had forced herself under the hood that draped the back of her camera. Normally, when the cloth fell, the rest of the world fell away with it. Sounds were dampened, smells minimized until the predominant scent was from the leather of her bellows and the faint whiff of iodine from the plate. Sight was restricted to what she could see through the lens, the world as imagined in her photographs. Too easy to imagine Ben's body, lying cracked on a rock, blue-gray eyes forever blinded.

She had shuddered and yanked her head out. Only when Ben had come out from under the outcropping had she found breath again.

Still, he took his time returning, pausing

here and there to touch the rocks.

"What is he doing?" she asked Mr. Newcomb.

His gaze remained on the slope below, as if he counted every second as she did. "Looking for the best samples."

All at once Ben stopped. Why? Was there something dangerous down there after all? A bandit hiding from the law? A mountain lion?

*Don't be silly, Meg. Mountain lions don't light fires.*

Hank straightened. "Here he comes."

Meg scrambled closer to the edge and peered over. Ben was climbing toward them, hand over hand along the rope, boots braced. She dashed back to the camera. Ducking under the hood, she waited until he crested the edge. His face was tight, mouth hard.

"Hold it!" she called.

He glanced her way but didn't pause as he jumped onto firm ground and began untying the rope from the harness. "Sorry, Miss Pero. You're here to photograph the terrain, not the staff." As if to make certain she didn't capture his likeness, he turned his back on her and started talking to Hank.

Oh! She was shaking as she pulled off the hood, but it wasn't just from frustration for once. He'd risked his life to climb down there. The least he could do was let her document his heroism after scaring the wits out of her.

She stalked up to him as Hank began coiling the rope. "So? What did you find? Was it worth your life?"

He eyed her. "I asked you the same question."

She stilled. "This is hardly the same thing."

"It's exactly the same thing," he said, cocking his head as if hoping to see her perspective. "You risked your life to take a picture. That's your profession — taking pictures. I went down the cliff to prove to myself there was no danger to my team. That's my profession — leading teams to achieve objectives."

Why did he have to be so logical? She puffed out a sigh. "Very well. I concede the point. But you were very stern with me yesterday, so I see no reason I shouldn't be as stern with you today. Fair is fair."

His mouth twitched. "And you saw fit to ignore my concerns, so I'll do the same with yours. Fair is fair."

The man was impossible!

"So do you want me to keep surveying the canyon after services?" Hank asked, laying the rope aside.

"Yes," Ben said, working the buckles on the harness. "I want to know if so much as a mouse moves on that slope."

"You found something," Hank surmised.

Meg tensed, not sure what to expect but knowing it must be bad.

"Campfire," Ben replied. "Cold now, but someone was there recently. I'd like to meet him. I have a few questions."

His reaction only raised questions of her own. A shame he was clearly not disposed to answer. Instead, he nodded to her camera. "I believe you have work to do as well, Miss Pero, after Sunday service. If you finish early, you could help Mrs. Newcomb with provisioning." He strode off, calling for the rest of the team to join him by the fire for Sunday worship.

Meg shook her head. She'd take her pictures, but she had other things in mind than gathering plants with Dot. When she had the opportunity, she intended to ask her questions. He might be the leader, but she had every right to protect herself and her equipment, from whatever he thought was coming.

It wasn't easy conducting a worship service with the rowel of the spur weighing heavily in his pocket. All he could think about was the Colonel.

The star had to have belonged to him. While ranchers might wear similar spurs, that particular star was a mark of a cavalryman, a rite of passage. Those new to the regiment had to earn their spurs. The Colonel would never have parted with his willingly.

So how had it reached that slope? And where was his father now?

He would gladly have relinquished command to investigate further. But he was the leader of this expedition. It was his duty to see to his team members' needs, even the spiritual ones. Larger expeditions like Wheeler's took along a chaplain or a soldier trained as a chaplain's assistant. Colonel Yearling, interim commander of Fort Wilverton, had deemed Ben's detail too small.

"Read a few passages, sing a few hymns," the lieutenant colonel had advised when Ben had questioned him about the matter. "Remind them of their responsibilities. Inspire them to lead lives of honor and productivity."

He hadn't felt up to the task then or now.

Corporal Adams must have requisitioned a Bible, for he handed one to Ben before stepping back into place with the others around the fire. The black leather binding felt stiff in his hands as he opened it to Psalms. Even here, his father intruded, for Ben found himself thumbing to Psalm 144, the Colonel's favorite.

"Blessed be the Lord my strength," he read aloud, "which teacheth my hands to war, and my fingers to fight."

Larson and Meadows nodded, even though neither could have seen much of war yet. They would have been too young to fight in the War Between the States. Before Ben had joined West Point, the classes of 1861 and 1862 had been graduated early to serve, some on one side, some on the other. He was thankful he'd never had to face a friend across a battlefield.

"My goodness, and my fortress," he continued. "My high tower, and my deliverer."

Now Dot was nodding too, her hand reaching for Hank's where he stood beside her.

"My shield," Ben read, "and he in whom I trust; who subdueth my people under me."

Meg shot him a glance. Did she think he expected her to be subdued under him? His mother had played that role with the Colonel. Really, everyone had played that role, even some generals above him. Ben had never wanted that in a wife. Better someone

143

who stood beside him, encouraging, challenging, helping him to grow.

Meg certainly challenged him. Was she still smarting from his refusal to let her climb down the cliff with him? A shame he couldn't tell her his reasoning, but even Hank and the cavalrymen didn't know about his other charge. His superior in Washington had been adamant.

He finished reading, sang along as Corporal Adams led a few hymns in a squeaky tenor, then dismissed them all to their duties. He wasn't sure why he was disappointed when Meg went off to her camera without another glance his way.

But work proved no easier than worship. He had his own routine that had proved efficient on other surveys. Divide the area into a grid with one-foot squares. Start in the northwest corner. Take rock samples, note flora and fauna. Move one square to the east and record any differences. Continue to the edge of the grid, drop down a row, and continue back across. He set Larson to start a similar pattern in the southeast corner, knowing they would eventually meet, and had Meadows run samples back to Adams for further testing and archiving.

It was slow, methodical, painstaking work, the results of which would allow the Army to determine whether to build roads, construct outposts, and encourage settlement. The information could help people start new lives or safeguard them from danger as they traveled through to richer lands beyond. He never knew what he might discover — a new species of beetle, a hardier form of wheat, a vein of copper. He always started expecting great things.

Today, the work seemed more tedious than expectant. He wanted to be down in that canyon. Surely he could learn something more. Perhaps that trail led not to a meadow frequented by pronghorn but a trapper's cabin. His father could be staying there.

He snorted at the fantasy, and Meadows glanced his way with obvious concern. Was Ben so desperate for news he'd clutch at any possibility like a drowning man a rope? Or was it duty that drove him?

He'd told Meg leading teams was his profession. That was true enough. But he also had a responsibility to his mother and sister, who were waiting for any word from him. He had no answers, only more questions. Most in the Army would have considered this a futile quest. The general directly above his father had listened to his mother's pleas with solicitous attention and an unforgiving attitude.

"He told Mother it was only to be expected," Diana had written. "That the Colonel had died as he had lived — on the field of battle. But there wasn't a battle, was there, Ben? He rode out of the fort and never returned. Why didn't he just send a scout? That's not like him. Why won't they listen to us?"

One official had listened — Ben's commanding officer in the nation's capital. After serving under Wheeler on a survey in Nevada Territory, Ben had suddenly been reassigned to the Monuments Division in Washington. He had done his best to work on testaments to the country's leaders and accomplishments, but his heart remained out West. Then Colonel Katlin had called him into his office.

"There's a need for a survey leader in Arizona," he said. "I promised your father I'd keep you here long enough to win promotion to major, but after recent events, I can't in good conscience continue to comply."

It hadn't been easy to stand at attention when every part of him was fuming. How dare the Colonel interfere in his life again? Had he no faith Ben could win promotion on his own? He'd made captain, hadn't he?

"I'd appreciate the recommendation, sir," he'd said.

Katlin had leaned back in his padded leather chair. "And I'd appreciate information. The survey starts from the same fort your father left. Help me discover what happened. For now, keep the matter to yourself."

He'd needed no further encouragement. A day later, he'd headed West.

Yet what had he accomplished? The Colonel was still missing. No one at the fort had been able to shed any light on his disappearance. Colonel Yearling seemed content to let matters rest. If the truth was to be discovered, it was all up to Ben.

He called a halt when the sun reached its zenith, sent them all into the shade of the trees, where Dot had cups waiting.

"Located some lemonade-berry," she reported. "Couldn't cool it like I'd prefer, but it'll keep you going until dinner." She glared at Pike, who had ridden in after an easterly sweep. "That is, if we have dinner."

"Pronghorn hide in the heat too, you know," he said, hitching up a suspender. "I'll find a rabbit or two."

"Or four," Dot retorted. "We have a hungry boy to feed."

Meadows turned pinker than the sun had

left him.

Meg appeared to have forgiven Ben for their earlier disagreement, for she moved closer and perched on a rock near him, tin cup in one hand. "I took shots to the north, west, and south. I'll have to wait for the eastern exposure until later this afternoon."

He nodded. "The light should be better in an hour or two."

"Or four," she said, mimicking Dot.

He chuckled and took a sip of the tart liquid. It was thicker than real lemonade, not much more than mashed berries and water, but easier to come by on the trail. "Talk to Dot about gathering plants outside the sample grid. Man doesn't live on meat alone."

"Don't tell Mr. Pike," she teased.

With the temperature high over the next few hours, Ben set the team to sedentary tasks — writing up the notes from the morning's survey in duplicate, mending gear, and testing rock samples for useful ore. He checked hardness against the Mohs scale by scratching each sample against sharpened quartz, evaluated cleavage with a chisel, peered through a magnifying loop to spot crystallization. The samples were sandstone, mostly, tinted red from iron, as he had suspected, with limestone chunks.

Once again, the work failed to capture his attention.

He set aside the samples and moved in next to Hank, who was sketching the terrain to the east in his journal.

"See anything in the canyon?" Ben murmured.

Hank glanced up at him. "Nope. Nothing unusual, that is. Hawk, skunk, few chipmunks, and a female mountain goat with a kid across that game trail. Whoever was there has moved on."

The observation dampened his hope of finding a trapper's cabin. But where had the person gone? And why had he been here to begin with?

He forced himself to finish the first survey before dinner. Pike had brought in a brace of rabbits, which Dot had made into a stew with beans. He and his men reviewed their findings, and Ben talked to Hank and Pike as well. Everyone had been fruitful, and he felt useless.

As they headed for bed and he prepared to start his watch, Meg sat beside him once more.

"What's wrong?" she asked, ever forthright.

"Nothing," he said, resting his rifle across his knees. "It was a good first day."

"So why are you so tense?" she challenged.

He could not have been so obvious. "I just want to make sure we remain on schedule."

She shook her head. "You've been on edge since we spotted that smoke in the canyon. Come on, Ben. It would do you good to talk. A burden shared is lighter. Ask the mules."

His smile rose despite himself. "I'm not a mule."

"Do tell."

Why was it so easy to laugh around her? "All right. I'll admit to being as stubborn as a mule on occasion. But I'm an Army officer, Meg. The only person I should share concerns with is my commanding officer."

"A shame he isn't here." She scooted closer. "But I am. And I promise not to tell."

"Or record it in a photograph?"

"Don't push me that far."

The urge to tell her was strong. Hank and Dot had known his father professionally, but, of anyone on the team, Meg alone had interacted socially. She knew the potency of the Colonel's personality, the effect he had on people, the reason men died at his command. She would understand the importance of Ben's secret commission. And she might have insights into what he could tell

150

his mother and Diana. He'd just have to go carefully.

He ran his hand over the cool metal of the rifle. "You remember my father."

She inched closer, until her skirts brushed his trousers. "Absolutely. Those eyes could cut through steel."

They could indeed, though he remembered them bright with pride more often. "I forgot. Your father photographed him, didn't he?"

She nodded, firelight flickering over the planes of her face. "Papa was delighted with the opportunity. He kept telling people he'd *shot* Colonel Coleridge."

Ben smiled. "He had reason to crow. The Colonel didn't sit for many portraits, painted or photographed. He was a man of action."

She laid a hand on his arm. "I'm so sorry you lost him, Ben."

One step at a time now. "That's just it. I'm not sure I have. He just disappeared."

She pulled back her hand. "But it's been two months. Surely if he was alive, we'd have heard by now."

"Out here?" He waved to encompass the trees, the plateau, the canyon. "There are dozens of places to hole up."

She sucked in a breath. "The outcropping,

the fire. You think that was your father."

He reached into his pocket and drew out the star. "I found this on the slope."

She took it from him, angled it to the light. "What is it?"

"The rowel of a spur. The Colonel wore two, one on each boot, held in place by brass bands shaped like an eagle's head."

She glanced up, eyes widening. "How many other people have them?"

"Most of the cavalry officers in the area wear spurs. But those officers are all accounted for, and I imagine their spurs as well. No one else from the fort has come out this way in months."

She looked down at the rowel again, turning it slowly in her hand as if she thought the points might prick her. "I don't understand. What would the Colonel have been doing on that slope? Why didn't he report back to the fort? How could he have left this behind?"

"All that," Ben said, "is what I want to know."

She nodded slowly, handing the star back to him. "Of course. I'd want to know if it were my father. If there's a chance he's alive, we have to find him."

Ben cocked his head, hope plucking at him. "We?"

"Of course." She grinned. "You didn't think I was going to let you have all the fun, did you?"

"Of course." She grinned. "You didn't think I was going to let you have all the fun, did you?"

# 10

She always loved learning other people's stories. The great portrait artists of the past had depicted their subjects with something that showed their work — a globe for an explorer, a quill for a writer. She wanted more from her pictures. When she photographed people, she tried to weave in their emotions — hope, sorrow, excitement.

Now Ben's smile pulled her in as surely as his tale. The Colonel had always been kind to her. From the moment he had appeared in the doorway of her father's studio, even before Ben had introduced her to him, he'd gone out of his way to talk to her as if she were an equal. It was his wife who had insisted that Meg would never be the kind of woman suited to stand at Ben's side.

"So, what do we do?" she asked now. "I take it you found no other clues by the fire?"

"None," he confessed, voice sharp with frustration. "And I don't understand why he wouldn't have started back to the fort unless he was injured. And if he was injured and awaiting rescue, why not answer our hails?"

She shivered. Could anything less than violence or treachery have made a man like the Colonel relinquish a part of his spur?

"I don't know, Ben," she said. "But I'll do whatever I can to help you discover the truth."

He laid a hand on her arm. "Thank you."

Two little words, one small touch. But they opened a flood of emotion. She wanted to throw her arms around him, promise him all would be well. She wanted to feel his arms come around her, sheltering, protecting. There was nothing quite so splendid as being held in Ben's strong arms.

But she had no business being in his arms when she had turned down his proposal.

She stood, removing herself from his touch, and he glanced up at her.

"One thing, Meg. The others don't know about the search for my father. I'm under orders, but I'm not at liberty to share them widely."

That he would share them with her was more honor than she'd suspected. It seemed he was still willing to confide in her, even after the way they had parted and years of

155

going their separate ways. The thought pleased her more than it should.

"I'll keep the matter to myself," she promised. "Will you need Mr. Newcomb on the theodolite tomorrow?"

He cocked his head as if surprised by her abrupt change in thought. "No. Why?"

"I want to scout for the best place to take a shot," Meg said. "I imagine I'll need to scan every inch of the canyons around here."

His smile edged up. "I imagine you will."

Meg nodded. "All right, then. I'll report anything I discover, sir." She snapped a salute as sharp as any Corporal Adams had given.

He laughed. "Why do I feel I ought to be saluting you instead? Sleep well, Meg, and thanks again. It's good to have someone to confide in."

To confide in. To share hopes, dreams. They'd had all that once, and she'd turned her back on it. Was it possible they could still be friends?

The thought persisted as she lay in her bedroll next to Dot's, trying to find a comfortable spot on the narrow, Army-issued cot. When she and her father had been part of an expedition to explore the Columbia River Gorge, some of the men had cut brush to cushion their sleep. This area didn't carry enough of that sort of springy plant. Besides, truth be told, it was her thoughts and not the unyielding wooden poles bracketing her that threatened her sleep more. In her mind, the scenery of West Point replaced the red rock of the canyon.

She'd tried to capture the Hudson River by dawn's rosy light, and Ben had been allowed to rise early and help her with her equipment. She had been carrying her father's equipment since she was eight, but she'd wanted an excuse to bring Ben along, so she hadn't protested the offer. They walked in the murky morning light through trees turning crimson and gold with the coming fall, until she had a good perspective across the river to Garrison's Landing.

"What's special about this spot?" he'd asked, glancing around.

"Not much at the moment," Meg said, adjusting the tripod. "But I'm told when the sun rises, it will set the Hudson on fire. That's what I want to capture, the reflection in the river."

He shook his head. "Your camera lens is so small, but you see more than most people."

His praise warmed her. "It's a focus more than anything, the ability to hone in on one thing in the entire picture and bring it to life."

He propped his foot on a rock. "A shame I didn't meet you sooner. I might have chosen a different path."

Somehow, she doubted that. Confident, inquisitive, loyal, he was meant to be a leader. "The Colonel wouldn't have been happy if you'd become a photographer."

He chuckled. "He's still not happy I decided to become an engineer instead of a cavalry officer."

About to put her head under the hood, Meg had paused. "Why *did* you want to become an engineer? I can see you riding for glory."

He'd grimaced. "Glory or death. Too many of my father's friends and troops have been killed over the years. But that wasn't the reason I shied away from the cavalry. I want to blaze trails, chart roads, build bridges. I want to give men chances I've taken for granted — homes, occupations, families."

Even now, she heard the fervor in his voice. He wanted to make a difference. Finding a way across the canyon could help hundreds move into new territory, establish outposts, communication. Her photographs seemed rather small beside all that.

But she was up at dawn the next morning anyway.

As yesterday, Dot had risen ahead of her and already had coffee brewing. Her cast-iron bake oven was nestled deep in the coals with more heaped on the lid. The tangy scent of cinnamon drifted on the breeze.

"What are you making?" Meg asked, venturing closer even as Private Meadows paused on his way to water the mules and sniffed the air as if he hadn't breathed in days.

"Cinnamon rolls," Dot proclaimed, and the young private grinned.

So did Meg. "Good use of those cinnamon sticks of yours."

Dot nodded. "I'll put a pot of cornmeal mush on as well. That ought to stick to the ribs." She glanced at the sky, which was heavy and tinted with the red of sunrise. "Looks to be coming on rain."

"Or hail," her husband said cheerfully, ducking out of his tent. He joined Dot and patted her back. "Morning, sweetheart."

"Morning, darling." Dot beamed as he sat beside her.

Meg turned away to give them a moment of privacy, or at least as much as the crowded camp allowed. If she hadn't been along, very likely the couple would have

159

shared a tent, but Dot took her chaperone duties seriously.

Private Larson was just as serious about his duties. He had a new grid laid out before the others finished eating, explaining the location and orientation between bites of Dot's succulent rolls.

"Excellent work," Ben told him, and Larson puffed out his chest.

Mr. Newcomb was also accommodating when Meg asked to use the theodolite.

"I'll be manning the wheel today," he told her, showing her the odometer and recording device mounted on an iron-rimmed wheel. She knew the instrument could be pulled by the mules or walked along by hand to measure distances.

"Where are you charting?" she asked.

"That craggy edge," he said with a fond look toward the rim. "Happy hunting, Miss Pero."

Meg started happily enough. The theodolite involved two round glass plates, each of which could be rotated or clamped in place, mounted inside a telescope-like device. Mr. Newcomb had already leveled and centered the instrument. All she had to do was rotate the upper plate, and she could see from one side of the canyon to the other. She turned it so that she was looking at the eastern

160

edge, bringing the rugged cliffs with their eroding rock bases into sharp contrast. But though she moved the view slowly from east to west, she caught no sign of human occupation.

"Any luck?" Ben asked her privately after ordering the midday halt. Everyone else except Mr. Pike, who was out hunting, had gathered around the fire, where Dot was once more handing out cups, this time with coffee. The sun had yet to appear out of the clouds, the air felt cool and moist, and Meg thought she heard a distant rumble of thunder.

"No luck at all," she told Ben. "But I'll keep looking later."

Ben cocked his head toward the fire. "Come take a rest."

With a nod, she rose from her place behind the theodolite, stretching tight shoulders, and followed.

Mr. Newcomb glanced up as Meg and Ben joined the others. "I know you had a plan for the afternoon, Captain, but it may have to wait. There's a storm coming. You can feel it in the air."

He was right. Meg's skin was turning clammy, and her hair refused to stay confined to its pins. Across from her, Dot's graying hair stuck out like a halo around her face.

Ben nodded. "I feel it too. Finish your coffee, then bring in the equipment and make sure the animals have shelter. First sign of rain, call to quarters."

The team downed their drinks, then split up to obey.

Mr. Newcomb put the wheel away in the wagon, then came to take down the theodolite and stow it likewise. Meg helped Dot secure the food supplies in boxes and leather packs. The cook also piled some of the wood under the van.

"Might as well keep it as dry as we can," she told Meg.

Her stereographic camera was already in the van, but she went to retrieve her other camera from the tripod. She'd have to use the plate soon or the chemicals would dry, leaving the picture blurry. She had just unscrewed the camera from its base when the first fat drops began plopping down around her, hitting the dry ground so hard they raised puffs of dust.

"Quarters!" Corporal Adams squeaked, and everyone began diving for the tents. To the west, the sky split with lightning.

Meg stared at it. Oh, for such a shot! But her camera would never capture that sudden flash, that jagged fork of light. Would it? She had a plate in the camera. Why not try?

Indecision made her hesitate. The wind rushed past, pushing her so hard she swayed on her feet. The rain followed, slicing across the clearing in a curtain of cold. Gasping, she seized her camera, but her wet fingers slipped on the wood.

Thunder shook the ground. Her camera started to fall. Meg lunged for it and managed to catch it, but now she was the one falling.

Strong arms caught her, pushed her upright.

"This way!" Ben shouted against the pounding rain.

Sheltered against him, she stumbled for the tent.

Dot's eyes were wide as Meg burst in, Ben right behind.

"Looks like we got a gulley washer," the cook said, shifting over to make room for them.

The canvas bounced with the rain, and the wind pressed against the fabric, causing the poles to tilt. Thunder rolled again, deep and hard. It was all Meg could do not to hide her head on Ben's shoulder. She'd thought she'd seen nature at its most grand. This seemed like nature at its angriest. And she wasn't entirely sure how they were to survive.

Ben made himself smile with complete confidence at the two women under his command. Dot grinned back. Was there anything that frightened her? He would have asked the same about Meg, except, at the moment, her face was white, and she clutched her camera close.

"Always an adventure," he said. "Too bad cameras aren't made for the rain, or you could have captured quite a shot."

That took the edge off. Her shoulders came down, and her lips turned up just the slightest. "I know. I wish the exposure didn't take so long. Can you imagine catching that flash of lightning over the canyon?"

"Nature at its finest," Ben agreed.

Her lips trembled. "I was thinking nature at its angriest, actually."

Dot nodded. "Let's hope Pike had the good sense to find safe ground. Too high, and he could collide with one of those bolts. Too low, and he could be swept away in a flash flood."

Meg's color, which had just begun to return, fled once more. "Flash flood?"

"Usually down a draw," Ben explained. "We saw no signs of past inundation in the survey yesterday. We should be safe here."

"Good thing too," Dot said. "This close to the rim, we could be washed right over."

The day darkened around them as the storm moved closer. Meg was breathing hard, and all Ben wanted was to hold her. The best he could do was sit so his shoulder brushed hers.

"Little chance of that," he assured them both. "The worst you'll have to do is put up with me until the storm passes."

The thunder crashed directly overhead. Meg jumped. Ben gave in to his instincts and slipped an arm about her waist. "I'm glad you were able to bring in both your cameras in time, Miss Pero. I didn't damage that one when I grabbed you, did I?"

She sucked in a breath and bent to check, just as lightning brightened the tent and sent their shadows dancing wildly around them. Even Dot glanced about with a shiver.

The cook had mentioned a flood. Had the Colonel and his guide been caught in a draw with a storm coming in? Had they been swept over the edge into the canyon, their horses and equipment lost? Powell's first survey had indicated towering walls in places along the canyon. Impossible to walk out. With no tools and likely few trees where his father and the guide might have fallen, they wouldn't have been able to build a boat and float out either, much less make it through the roaring cataracts that had cost Powell so much.

Still, why not climb out after the flood was over, or, failing that, respond to calls from above now? How could a flood have deprived him of the star of his boot and nothing else? His thoughts just led him in a circle.

"Everything seems to be in working order," Meg announced. "But the plate will have to be scraped and recoated before I feel comfortable shooting with it."

Dot nodded. "That's a shame, but at least it's still usable. There's sure to be lots more to see the next six weeks before we start back. What's the plan from here, Captain?"

Was she trying to take his mind off the storm as well?

A sudden blast of wind bowed the tent, and he leaned against Meg to keep from hitting the wet canvas. Every touch would just pull water deeper into the fabric. A silky curl caressed his cheek. It was almost as if she were in his embrace. He couldn't seem to move away.

"Why don't you sit beside me, Captain?" Dot asked. "More room on my side of the tent."

He glanced up, guilt tugging at him, to find Dot regarding him, amusement sparkling in her gray eyes. Bless the woman for her attention to duty. Ben shifted across the tent. As if she hadn't noticed their proximity, or been affected by it, Meg busied herself pulling her bedroll away from the damp wall.

"I suspect you've weathered plenty of these storms," she said, and he wasn't sure whether she meant him or Dot.

Dot seemed to have no such trouble marshalling her thoughts. "Oh, sure," she said. "I've always liked watching storms — those black clouds, the sudden rain, the roll of thunder. Hank and I were at Fort Arbuckle one year. Now, *they* have storms. Twisters, they call them. Big silos of swirling wind, picking up most anything in their path — dirt, bush, cow or two."

Ben shook his head. "Cow, eh?"

"Yes, sir. Seen it myself. Very affecting. Now, that would have made a picture, Miss Meg."

Meg finally smiled. He felt as if the sun had come out and caught him in its benevolent rays. "A very fine picture indeed. But I'm glad we don't have that kind of storm around here."

"Flash flood and cougar are bad enough,"

Dot agreed. "Wouldn't want to lose any of the animals."

That set Meg to fiddling with the camera again. Ben racked his brain for a way to get Dot off calamities.

"How did you and Hank meet?" he tried.

Dot's gray eyes turned misty. "My mother died when I was young. My father was a sergeant in the infantry. I'd followed him from one assignment to the next since I was a girl. I was already helping the cook at the fort where we were assigned. Your father served there at the time, Captain."

Ben started. "I didn't know you and Hank served with the Colonel before San Francisco. That must have been one of the times he left Mother behind."

"When your little sister was born," Dot agreed. "Hank was visiting with a survey detail. He was eating with the commanding officer, and he said he wanted to thank the chef for the fine dinner. Chef." She snorted.

"You," Meg guessed.

Dot nodded. "I tried to send the real Army cook, but he was a kind fellow, and he wanted to see me praised. So out I went, saucy as you please. One look at Hank, and I knew. Hank said it wasn't so much the look as my cooking. He always claims I can

168

make most any miserable hunk of meat edible."

One look. It had been that way for him. One look across the dance floor, and he'd known he had to learn more about the woman with the presence of royalty. One week in her company, and he'd wanted a year. A month of talks and walks, dances and photographs, and he'd wanted forever. He'd thought he'd put it all behind him, but one look across the tent, meeting that green gaze, and his heart was pounding as quickly as the first time he'd approached her.

But this time, it would take more than one look to compel him to trust his heart.

## 11

The storm passed as quickly as it had come. Meg's agitation lingered a little. Something about the ferocity of the rain, the roar of the thunder, tightened her shoulders and quickened her breath. The canyon made her feel small; the storm made her feel vulnerable. But with Ben nearby and Dot chatting away as if nothing was truly wrong, she thought she had acquitted herself well. Still she didn't take a deep breath until the sun broke through.

"Assemble!" Ben commanded as he exited the tent.

She stepped out among the steaming canvas with the others. Dot's cooking tripod had fallen. So had the one for Meg's camera. She hurried to right it and found it otherwise unharmed.

Private Meadows kept glancing at the sky as if he expected a lightning bolt aiming for him. But he, Private Larson, and Corporal

Adams stood at attention as Ben moved closer.

"All survey documentation was protected, sir," Corporal Adams reported.

"Survey equipment is in fine shape," Mr. Newcomb put in.

"Camera equipment too," Meg said.

"All animals present and accounted for," Private Larson added.

"Wood's wet," Dot said with a glance toward the pile they'd shoved under the wagon. "Going to be a smoky fire tonight."

Ben was looking over his men. "Privates, did you stay out with the animals?"

Meg could see why he asked. Both men were soaked, the wool of their uniforms darkened and sagging. As if he noticed her looking, Private Larson inched his chin higher.

"Yes, sir," he told Ben. "We tried staying in the tent, but I could tell the mules were fractious. Best way to calm them is to show them a united front. We didn't have time to pull out the ponchos."

Private Meadows nodded.

"Well done," Ben said. "Go change out of those wet clothes."

The two looked at each other, then directed their gazes over each of his shoulders. "No, thank you, sir."

171

Ben frowned. "Are you disobeying an order?"

Private Meadows visibly swallowed.

"No, sir," his companion said. "Leastways, not on purpose."

Corporal Adams took a step forward. "May I have your permission to speak privately, sir?"

Ben moved closer. The three cavalrymen spoke quietly to him.

"What's that all about?" Meg murmured to Dot.

Dot chuckled. "They probably don't own a spare uniform. Army can be stingy that way with the enlisted men. Any other time, we'd just bundle them in blankets while their clothes dried by the fire. But with you along . . . ."

"They're embarrassed," Meg realized. She raised her voice. "Captain Coleridge."

Ben glanced over his shoulder at her. "Miss Pero?"

"Perhaps you and I could take a walk, determine what else you want to photograph here before we move on."

"You bet," Private Meadows said. Then, as if he realized he was supposed to be standing at attention still, he snapped his mouth shut and turned his gaze forward.

"I'd be delighted," Ben said. He nodded

172

to his men, who scrambled for their tent.

Dot rose from where she'd been trying to resurrect the fire. "Reckon I'll come along."

Ben held up his hand. "No need. We'll walk the perimeter. You should be able to see us at all times. Just don't mention that to my men."

Dot nodded as she tucked up her skirts and sank back on her haunches. "Best get to it, then. With this wet wood, it will be a while until dinner anyway."

Ben joined Meg, and they set out.

"That was kind of you," he said, leading her through the trees on the east side of camp. The canyon on their right looked darker in places, where rain had dampened rock and drenched soil. Even now the sun was drying what was left of the water, steam rising like mist and obscuring the bottom. Everything smelled moist and clean.

"I never intended that my presence should impact the others," Meg told him, touring around a damp bush where raindrops sparkled like silver. "And you need each of us in fit condition."

"True." His hand brushed the pistol at his waist as if making sure of it. "There are too many dangers out here."

As if to prove it, the ground beside her shifted, pieces tumbling down. She scrambled back and bumped into Ben. He steadied her, hands on her upper arms, body close, and once more she found it hard to breathe.

"Hey!" Dot shouted from the camp. "Look for dry wood while you're out there."

Ben's smile said he knew what Dot was doing. He shifted Meg back from the cliff and calmly put himself on the outside edge of their walk.

"I'm not sure anything's dry out here," he said.

Doubtful. Her boots were turning red in the mud. Still, she lifted an overhanging bush with one foot to peer into the slightly drier reaches beneath. A chipmunk dived away from her view.

Ben was quiet as they turned to the north, away from the canyon.

"Thinking of your father?" she asked.

He nodded. "It would take something like that storm to fell the Colonel."

She was a little ashamed of her own reaction to the noise, the relentless wind and rain. But surely the Colonel had survived worse. "Did you see any other indication of human occupation during your survey today?"

"Nothing significant," he said, lifting an aspen limb to allow her to walk under. "Larson found a patch of grass much shorter than the others in the area, and the ground appeared more disturbed even though we hadn't pastured the mules there. The grass might have been cropped by a horse, or a pronghorn."

She stopped. Ahead, the ground cracked into another side canyon, smaller than the one where Ben had found the rowel from a spur. The pine was sparser here, with grass springing up everywhere between. She could see the Colonel and his guide camping here overnight. But what had stopped them from continuing? Or returning?

"Dot mentioned cougar when we were in the tent earlier," she said.

"This is the sort of habitat they favor," he allowed, pausing to pick up a fallen branch that had been sheltered against a pine. "But they're usually wary of people. Besides, if the Colonel and his guide were attacked by a cougar, why would I have found his spur on the slope?"

Because it had broken off as he'd fallen to his death? She couldn't say the words aloud and extinguish the hope that burned in him.

She turned to him with a smile. "Perhaps we should discover where you want me to photograph. Tomorrow is our last day at this site if I remember your timetable correctly."

"It is." He turned to her as if glad to have something else to discuss. "We should have the survey completed by tomorrow evening even with this setback. Let's find your shots."

They continued around the perimeter, and Ben identified a view to the west he wanted captured and an exposure along the draw to the east of them. The latter would take some maneuvering. What had been a trickle of a stream when they had crossed two days ago was now a rushing freshet, and the ground closest to the canyon was loose and crumbling. Not the best place to set up her tripod. Perhaps things would be drier come morning.

They managed to find a few more downed branches that had escaped wetting and carried them back toward camp. They returned to find Dot alone by a roaring fire, smoke billowing off over the canyon.

"Hank's looking for dinner," she explained. "Corporal Adams is tidying the wagon. Seems things shifted some. Doesn't bother me, but he likes things organized." She shrugged as if the behavior perplexed her.

"And our two modest cavalrymen?" Ben asked, glancing around.

"Changing back into their uniforms," Dot

told him. "They'll still be a bit damp, but better than they were." She wrinkled her nose. "They don't smell so good, though. There's something about wet wool."

Meg tried not to notice when the two privates joined them by the fire a short time later, once more dressed in their navy coats and light blue trousers. They'd attempted to comb their hair. Private Larson's was slicked to his head, but Private Meadows had a cowlick on the crown that stood up like a feather. Meg resisted the urge to pat it down as she would have done a little brother. The young cavalryman was embarrassed enough as it was.

"That was some storm," Meg said, holding her hands to the fire as Larson slowly rotated in front of the blaze as if trying to finish drying on all sides.

Private Meadows wiped his nose with the back of his hand. "Never liked lightning storms. They can start fires."

Two sentences? That was the most she'd heard from him in days.

"That they can," Ben agreed, as if just as eager to encourage Meadows.

"Have you seen a wildfire?" Meg asked the private.

"Not wild, ma'am." As quickly as his urge to talk had come, it apparently left. "Excuse me." He headed for the picket line.

Ben shook his head. "I'll check on Corporal Adams."

As he left, Meg turned to Dot, who was giving the beans she'd started cooking a stir.

"That Meadows is a quiet fellow," Dot remarked. "Never can get more than a few words from him."

"I wish I knew his story," Meg said with a sigh.

Private Larson kept turning like a weather vane on a barn. "I know a little. He hails from Tennessee. I heard he lost his pa and older brother in the Great Rebellion. They fought for the Union."

"He couldn't have been more than a boy," Meg murmured.

Dot snorted. "He's still a boy."

Larson paused in his turning. "He's nineteen, Mrs. Newcomb. He was thirteen when he ran off to help fight like his pa and brother. He was sent home, but there was nothing left. While he was gone, the family farm was burned, the rest of his family with it. He had to work for five years as a farmhand before he was old enough to sign up. To tell the truth, I think he came West because he wanted a new start."

She wanted to follow the private and hug him close, vow that the future would be brighter, but she feared she'd only embarrass him anew. Besides, who was she to predict what the future held?

"Thank you for telling us, Private Larson," she said. "Small wonder he doesn't like lightning."

"Flames neither," Larson said, beginning to rotate once more. "We had a small brush fire at the fort before you came. Couldn't get him to come out from under the bed even though Colonel Yearling mustered the whole fort to fight it. The colonel gave him kitchen duty for a week."

He stopped to eye Meg. "Don't let on I told you that."

"I won't," Meg promised.

Dot dumped more beans in the pot as if intent on giving Meadows an extra helping.

But her look hardened when Hank returned a little later, empty-handed.

"Sorry," he told her. "Most of the animals went to ground with the storm. We'll have to make do."

"Salt pork and beans it is, then," Dot proclaimed.

Larson groaned while Meadows, who had returned from dealing with the mules, looked crestfallen. Even Corporal Adams, who had joined them with Ben, seemed disappointed, his thin lips dipping.

179

Meg shifted closer to Dot. "Any bacon left?"

"A little," Dot admitted, and all three of the cavalrymen brightened.

"You probably know this trick," Meg said. "My father taught me. Cook one or two pieces and soak the salt pork in the grease. It improves the taste."

"Sounds good to me," Dot said. "Maybe fry up the dried apples to go with them." She nodded to Meg. "You're a handy one to have around, Miss Meg."

"Yes," Ben said, "she is."

Once more her cheeks were warming, but it had nothing to do with the blaze and everything to do with the man who was watching her across the fire with eyes as deep and fascinating as the Grand Canyon.

They broke camp two days later. Ben helped Larson and Meadows load the equipment and remaining supplies into the wagon and onto the pack animals, returning Meg's plates to the van. They'd accomplished what they'd set out to do — to document this location — noting flora and fauna, collecting mineral specimens, and mapping the terrain. He and Hank had taken barometric readings to confirm altitude, showing them to be at more than eight thousand feet above sea level. Meg had shot several fine photographs — they'd viewed the negatives together, her head close to his. It was time to move on.

But he'd learned nothing more about his father.

He had trained the theodolite down the slope one last time before snapping it into its wooden case and securing the straps to hold it stationary while they were traveling. He'd sighted no movement, heard no calls for help. Though he knew the members of several tribes had been noted in the area previously, it was as if he and his team were the only people within miles.

Pike had rejoined them after the rain. His clothing soaked, his hat battered, the guide reported the area to the west clear and the east open.

"How'd you make it through the storm?" Larson asked.

Pike eyed him. "You call that sprinkle a storm?"

Larson looked away. Adams looked impressed. Ben shook his head.

Now Pike ranged ahead to locate their next campsite. Ben and the rest followed more slowly. At least that gave him time to study their surroundings. The pines were thinning, and low bushes crowded the way, brushing the horse's legs. He didn't trust the soil he could no longer see. Far too easy to ride into a skunk hole, fail to notice a dip. It was never wise to risk the horses. He reined in and held up his hand before climbing down. "Dismount!"

Hank followed suit. Glancing back, Ben saw that Meg had stopped as well to slide from her saddle. Adams got off the bench to hold the leaders on the photography van, and Dot reined in her team on the wagon and jumped down as well. Larson and Meadows halted the mules and waited for guidance.

"We'll need to walk and lead the animals," Ben called. "The ground's too rough."

With nods, they all started forward again.

He felt his way along, blazing a trail for the others to follow. At times, he had to veer a bit to avoid a pitted area. More than the slow pace, the silence of the canyon weighed on him. Had his father died alone, hearing nothing but the faint rush of the river far below? Or was he out there somewhere, injured, waiting for rescue?

"Hold up!"

Meg's call had him turning once more to find Hank at his heels. She had left her horse with Dot and was approaching quickly on foot, wading through the brush that clung to her skirts. The shadow from her broad-brimmed hat reached only below her nose, making her lips look pinker than usual.

And it appeared he knew just how pink they usually were.

"Spot a picture worth taking?" Hank asked as she joined them.

"Too many," she said. "But that's not why I called. The wind's blowing behind us for once, and the mules are a little close."

Ben glanced back again. Dot was waving her hand before her face as if to bat away the ripe odors. A rare north wind was pushing dust toward them along the plateau. The passing of the mules was only raising more. Already he couldn't see the last of the pack animals.

"I don't want us separated," he told her and Hank. "Have Dot and Corporal Adams drop back behind the train. I'll speak to the privates."

Meg nodded and turned to go. Hank went with her, leading his horse. Ben remounted and retraced his steps to where Larson was standing beside the team on the west.

"Sorry about the dust, Captain," he said. "This wind came up out of nowhere."

"Like any wind around this canyon," Ben allowed. "Keep pushing south, setting the trail for the rest of us through the brush.

183

Pike should be back shortly with an idea of where we'll camp."

"Yes, sir."

"I'll tell Private Meadows." Ben maneuvered his horse through the mules to the east. He found the youth stationary, gaze out over the side canyon.

"Something wrong, Private?" he asked as he rode up.

Meadows flinched, ears turning red below his Army cap. "No, sir. Sorry." His gaze drifted out over the canyon again, eyes wide in wonder.

Ben smiled. "It is a grand sight."

Meadows nodded.

It struck Ben that his youngest private might have thoughts as deep as that canyon.

"What do you think of it, Private?" he asked.

Meadows swallowed, and for a moment Ben thought he'd give no more than his usual one-word answer. Then he turned to Ben.

"Never saw anything like it. I'm from Tennessee, near the Mississippi. Pa used to say the land was flat enough a ball wouldn't roll unless pushed. He sure would have marveled at this."

"We're all marveling," Ben assured him. "And the work we're doing will help others

184

come and marvel as well. Now, return to your post. We're moving the mule train to the front of the column while this wind blows."

"Sir." With one last longing look, he turned for the pack animals.

Ben glanced out over the canyon. Knobs of whiter stone stuck up here and there. The red stone below was dotted with the green of brush and tree. So vast, each vista more beautiful than the last. More rugged too. Some places a mule might have made it down and back again, but no wagon could have navigated the steep slopes. He could only hope Powell was having better luck below.

Because, despite his encouragement to Meadows, he was having no luck above, reaching either of his objectives.

# 12

The rough edge of the canyon forced them inland for the next while. The brush gave way once more to pine forest with plenty of grass between the trees and an occasional shrub. Larson and Meadows slowed the mules, allowing them to stop and graze here and there until the others caught up to them. The sunlight slanted down to highlight the nutty brown of a fallen tree, the vivid red of wild raspberries. Meg caught Larson eating a handful. He stopped, red staining his fingers.

"They aren't poisonous, are they?" he asked. "I mean, they kind of look like the berries we picked back home."

"They're raspberries and quite edible," Meg assured him. "Where is home, Private Larson?"

"Pennsylvania, ma'am. Chambersburg."

She caught her breath. "The town the Confederates burned? I remember how the

Union rallied to send aid. My father sold portraits to contribute money for rebuilding. Please tell me you didn't lose your family like Private Meadows did."

"No, ma'am." His gaze went out over the grazing mules as if he saw something far less peaceful. "Most everyone survived that night, thanks to some Rebels who refused to obey orders. We still didn't have anything to return home to. Pretty much the whole town was gone." He raised his scruffy chin. "But we showed them. The town's coming back. And many of us enlisted to make sure nothing like that ever happens again. My pay goes home to help my ma and little sisters."

If he could focus on the good, so could she, though her mind conjured images of conflagration. "You have sisters?"

"Six of them," he said with a grin. "If you ever get to Pennsylvania, Miss Meg, I'd be proud to have you take their picture."

"And I'd be proud to take it," Meg told him. She'd much rather think about composing that shot — the private in his dress uniform, brown hair combed, smile bright, framed by six little girls in pinafores, gazing at their brother in admiration — than to remember the horrors of the War Between the States. The fighting had ended more than six years ago now, but the wounds would take much longer to heal.

She glanced back at Ben. Though they could have ridden, he continued walking, as if satisfied with the leisurely pace for once. With Hank at his wife's side, it was easy for Meg to drop back next to him. The wind pushed at her as if urging her forward, deeper into the unknown. Her spirit rose to meet it. The war was over. The country was expanding, just as Ben had predicted. Who knew what they might discover through the trees? A fertile plain perfect for farming. Ben's wagon road across the canyon. The secret to his father's disappearance.

Ben's head turned from side to side, gaze sweeping the way as if he watched for any potential danger. Sunlight and shadow striped the planes of his tanned face. He must have taken time to shave that morning, for that firm chin showed little sign of stubble. How warm his skin had felt to her touch once when she'd dared caress his cheek.

She forced her gaze forward. "You're particularly quiet. Penny for your thoughts."

He shook his head. "Sorry. I was wondering how all this came to be."

"Why, Captain, I would have thought a West Point graduate could tell me all about it," she teased. "The action of water and wind on stone or some such."

"The Colorado River and its tributaries carved these canyons," he agreed. "But they are more than geologic wonders. There's always a reason for God's creation. What was he trying to tell us? What are we to learn from all this?"

Meg reared back. "God didn't put this here for us. We just stumbled upon it."

"Did we?" He focused ahead, as if he could still see the canyon in all its majesty. "Or did he have it ready when we needed it?"

What a strange idea. She couldn't remember hearing anything like it. Of course, she hadn't heard all that many ministers pontificate. The way they'd kept moving, she and Papa had attended church sporadically when she was growing up.

Certainly, her aunt had as narrow a view of the Creator as she did everything else. The few times Meg had attended church with her, Aunt Abigail had been more interested in Meg's behavior than in anything the minister had said. It seemed Meg didn't sit up properly, appear pious enough. Ladies were not to frown when the minister spoke, for all it was Meg's habit as she carefully considered his words. And ladies certainly didn't sing with any sort of gusto. She was to be quiet, still, unremarkable. If that was what God wanted, why create something completely remarkable!

No, it made much more sense to her to consider God a distant being. He'd set things in motion. It was up to them to see how those things played out. The only time she'd truly prayed with all her heart was when she'd realized her father was ill. God hadn't given her any indication that he was listening. He certainly hadn't acted. How could Ben assume God cared enough about them to plant this canyon for their pleasure?

"You're in an odd humor," she said.

He shrugged. "Perhaps I need to think about something other than my father's disappearance. We're moving away from where I found the only clue. And I can't go back. I have a duty."

And he'd do it despite his own longings. That was the difference between him and her father. Papa's good intentions had never lasted long. He had craved the excitement, the movement, the change. There was something to be said for predictability.

Particularly when it came to income.

"I have a duty too," she said. "I need more stereographs. I can see shots in every direction. The train's moving slowly. Mind if I stop at the first good view of the canyon and set an exposure?"

He hesitated. "I don't want you to fall behind."

Meg raised her brows hopefully. "It will only take a few moments."

The jaw she had been admiring looked as hard as the stone of the canyon. "It's not safe being out here alone."

"I can protect myself," she reminded him. "Papa taught me to use a gun. Besides, we haven't seen any sign of predators."

"Yet," he said darkly.

He was being difficult again. She would not resort to harsh words. She forced herself to count to ten, then pasted on her sweetest smile. "Well, if you're concerned, you could wait with me."

His eyes narrowed, and she could only hope he was considering the matter. It wouldn't do to push him further. She'd seen that in West Point. Ben Coleridge had a stubborn streak as wide as the Colorado.

But then, so did she.

"Very well," he said. "One shot. And then we catch up with the others."

Meg beamed at him. "Thank you, Captain. I'll make sure it's worth waiting for."

She had her opportunity a short while later. They had run into a denser group of trees and were picking their way along. She'd lost track of direction, but she'd seen Ben consulting his compass from time to time and knew he was keeping them on a steady heading.

Suddenly, all vegetation stopped, and the world dropped away once more to reveal another view of the canyon. Meg stopped to stare. Everywhere she looked was red. And so many shades! Fiery at the base of the cliffs rising to brick and vermillion with maroon in the distance. Despair welled up inside her.

It must have shown on her face, for Ben paused to frown at her. "Meg? What's wrong? Isn't this the shot you've been waiting for?"

"Yes," Meg said, voice catching. "But look at it. The colors, the textures. And all I have is black and white!"

His mouth quirked. "Quite a challenge, but I believe you're up to it."

She had to be. Determination building, she turned to hail Corporal Adams ahead of them and went to prepare her plate.

Ben helped her plant the feet of the tripod and level it on the soft soil. Dot and Hank pulled up to watch and rest the mules.

"Now, that's a picture," Dot said, gazing out at the sculptured cliffs.

"Not yet," Meg said. "But it will be." She plunged under the hood.

Darkness wrapped around her. Sound faded. All she could see was the glory before her. She turned the camera slowly, looking for the best angle, the right light. The canyon called to her, drew her closer. Such beauty! Such majesty!

Had God known she needed this, not only for a picture that would produce income for her future but to fill her empty heart?

Perhaps it was Ben's words, perhaps this view through her lens, but for the first time in a long time, she wondered whether there truly might be Someone who cared.

At that moment, the sun broke free, setting the cliffs on fire. She caught her breath, adjusted for the change in light, and set the exposure.

Normally, while she waited, she pulled her head out from under the hood. But now she wanted a moment more alone with her thoughts. Though her lens was fixed on a narrow portion of the canyon, she felt as if her world was widening. Or perhaps she was widening.

*Thank you, heavenly Father.*

The prayer came from her heart. Was she mad to think she heard a response? More awed than by the view, she drew in another breath and brought herself back into the light.

"Got it?" Dot asked, brows squeezed together in concern.

"I think so," Meg said. "I hope so. You only get one chance at glory."

Ben smiled. "I have a feeling you're wrong. But saddle up. We need to catch the pack train."

She was a wonder. That artist's eye had pinpointed one of the best views looking northeast along the canyon: the rugged cliffs that seemed to go on forever, the snaking curve of the river far below. He could understand her frustration on seeing it. God had pulled out every shade of red in his paint box. But if any photographer could do it justice, it was Meg.

She seemed to be delighted with her work. Dot was asking questions, so Meg dropped back to chat with her as they followed the rim to the southwest. With the way more open here, they had all remounted. Hank was the logical person to ride beside Ben. He wasn't sure why the cartographer's company seemed less satisfactory than usual.

"We're going to have a problem," Hank said.

Ben frowned. "Oh?"

Hank grinned. "There are too many places to take a picture. What will she do when she runs out of plates before she runs out of canyon?"

Pike rejoined them midafternoon, when Ben had called a halt to rest the animals. The sun had risen high and with it the temperatures. The breeze had evaporated, leaving the musky scent of the mules hovering like an unseen cloud. Flies buzzed about, accompanied by the sound of slaps as his men fought off their attack. They'd have to break out the mosquito netting to sleep tonight.

"Might want to be careful with that." As he reined in, Pike nodded to the canteen Adams was using. "Couldn't find a good source of water for the next little while. We'll be camping dry tonight. We'll need to make do."

"What about meat?" Dot asked. "Salt pork will be mighty salty without anything to wash it down with."

"I spotted a few pronghorns to the north," Pike said. "I'll see what I can do. Follow the rim another two miles until you see a lone pine. That's where we'll camp tonight." Clucking to his horse, he moved off.

"Not much for conversation," Hank commented.

Dot shook her head. "Never was, from what I hear. The only person he kept company with was Willy McCoy. I think he feels the loss keenly."

Meg frowned, but Ben stiffened. He knew that name. It had been on the report about his father's disappearance.

"McCoy?" he pressed.

"The guide who went out with the Colonel," Dot explained.

Meg's brow cleared, and she gazed off after Pike, who was disappearing through the trees. "It seems Mr. Pike has a reason to be terse."

Perhaps. It was hard to imagine the taciturn Pike being close to anyone. Still, the guide might have his own ideas of what had happened to his friend and the Colonel. Maybe Ben had another opportunity to learn the truth about his father after all.

He didn't have a chance to talk to Pike privately until later that evening. The guide had returned with a pronghorn, which he'd skinned, gutted, and prepared so Dot could roast it over the fire. The rich scent hovered in the air. Meadows licked his lips. Dot served the meat with apples and currants in a sauce that hinted of cinnamon.

Still, he couldn't quite enjoy the feast as

much as Meg and the others when all he could think about was cornering Pike.

While the others finished cleaning up after dinner, he had his chance at last. Ben took Pike aside. The only one who appeared to notice was Meg, who looked up from drying a plate to nod encouragement. Had she too wondered what their guide might know? Funny how her thoughts so often aligned with his.

The night's camp was near the edge of the canyon again, but already darkness wrapped the landscape in mystery. Ben and the guide stood at the extent of the fire's glow, the night air cooling rapidly.

Might as well start out officially. "No surprises on your reconnaissance?" Ben asked.

Pike pursed his lips. "Nope. Everything was pretty much as I expected. There's usually a pond at the neck of the peninsula we crossed. I was thinking we'd camp there, but I found the ground dried up. Too late in the season. A shame we didn't start sooner."

"A shame I couldn't get here sooner," Ben agreed. "You'll scout ahead for a water source?"

"Tomorrow," Pike promised.

Ben nodded. "Good. We can make do in many ways, but water's not one of them."

"For any of us," Pike said with a look to the rest of the group.

Ben shifted a little closer. "By the way, I understand Mr. McCoy who disappeared with the Colonel was a good friend of yours. My condolences."

Pike looked away. "Part of the job. He knew what he was getting into, same as me."

Something in the guide's tone poked at him. "And what was he getting into? He and the Colonel were only supposed to be confirming the safety of the route to the canyon for the survey team."

Pike snorted. "Safety? No such thing out here. An hour after they passed, a rockslide could have closed the trail behind them. A day, and they could have been surrounded by natives, who don't generally take kindly to a fellow wearing a cavalry uniform."

Surrounded by natives? That made no sense. If there had been rumors of an uprising, someone else in the fort would have heard about it.

"We haven't seen any signs of natives," Ben pointed out.

"Nary a one." Pike almost sounded disappointed. "But never fear, there's plenty out here that can kill a man. Cold, heat, flash floods, wildfire, cougar, failure to find meat or water."

198

He'd thought of the same risks when trying to decide whether to bring Meg with them. "There's a beauty too," he told Pike. "You can't deny that."

Pike shook his head. "This canyon might be beautiful to some, Captain, but it's no fit place for man or beast, I don't care what the Army says. You'll see that for yourself soon enough, and then you can tell them to build their road somewhere else."

# 13

Meg woke up to a blowing wind that whistled through the branches of the tall pine at the edge of the camp and rushed through her tent every time she or Dot opened the flap. It tugged at her hat as she sat near the fire to eat the hardtack and leftover meat Dot had served up.

"No mush or coffee this morning," the older woman said. "Can't risk using up more water."

Adams sighed.

"It's not just us," Larson put in. "The mules will need to be watered tomorrow at the latest."

"Thirsty mules don't move," Meadows agreed, pausing to yank a hunk off his hardtack with his teeth.

Meg smiled at him, and he hastily looked away as he chewed the thin, dry bread.

"I'll find you water," Pike promised, rising and dusting his hands on his already dusty trousers. "Don't get too comfortable here. The captain asked me to keep looking. I'll be back by midday." He loped for his horse.

"Adams, Larson, Meadows, report," Ben commanded, coming out of his tent.

The trio scrambled to stand and salute.

"I finished transcribing Mr. Newcomb's journal into the second set of records," the corporal said in his precise voice.

"Excellent," Ben said, and Meg thought the stiff-backed clerk relaxed a little.

"The animals are fed and healthy, sir," Larson said when Ben looked to him next. "There's plenty of forage hereabouts. Mr. Pike says he'll find us water."

Ben nodded, then turned to Meadows.

"No corn mush, sir," he said, a mournful note in his voice.

Ben's mouth quirked, but he didn't go so far as to smile, and Meg liked him better for it.

"Form a grid while we wait," he told his men. "Five by five with the last square at the cliff edge. We should be able to sample that much before Pike returns."

"Yes, sir," they chorused.

"I'll take what measurements I can," Hank said. "Miss Pero, care to help with the surveying?"

Adams looked over in surprise. So did

Meg. The lanky cartographer was smiling at her as if he had full confidence in her abilities. Since they wouldn't be making this their next formal camp, she probably shouldn't waste a photograph. And Dot wouldn't need help with cooking.

"I'd be delighted, Mr. Newcomb," she said.

"Mr. Newcomb, Miss Pero," Dot complained in a singsong voice. "We're going to be working together for another six weeks. Might as well get comfy. His name is Henry, but he prefers Hank."

"Now, Dot," Hank started.

"It's all right," Meg assured him. "I was born Margaret, but all my friends call me Meg. I hope you'll be one of them, Hank."

He nodded.

"Oh, stop turning pink, ya big galoot," Dot said, slapping him on the back. "Meg will think you got sunburned."

Adams turned abruptly away from them. "It seems I am unneeded this morning, sir. Might I assist on the survey?"

"Always glad for another pair of hands," Ben said. "You can help take barometric readings. Dot, pack up and be ready to move when Pike returns."

They all split up then. Meg followed Hank to the edge of camp.

"Give me a moment," he said.

She perched on a rock, letting the early morning sun bathe her. Tipping back her chin, she breathed in the dry air.

He knelt and snapped open the brass catches on the sides of the wooden case, then swiveled back the leather straps that secured the instrument inside. Lifting the metal cylinder with all its screws and apertures, he settled it into place on the tripod, pivoting the center scope out and pointing it into the canyon.

"Does it balance easily?" Meg asked, thinking of her camera.

Hank was eyeing the spirit level on one side. "Mostly. Usually just takes a few turns of the screw." He suited word to action, then rotated the instrument and leveled the other side as well. After several rotations, he nodded and looked up. "Done. Take a look."

Meg rose and pressed her face to the eyepiece. The lone pine came into view. She fiddled with the focus. A black beetle with an iridescent shell was scurrying up the cracked bark.

"You borrowed this while we were at the other camp," Hank said. "Do you know how to use it?"

"Only as a telescope," Meg admitted. "I know it can be rotated horizontally and vertically."

"To measure angles and estimate distances in a straight line," Hank said. "Mainly, we want to calculate the depth of the canyon. To do that, I need a set of numbers."

She pulled back from the instrument. "What numbers?"

"Did you notice the notations around the circumference? Those measure portions of the circle. I'll calculate certain points and triangulate to extrapolate."

He was quickly outdistancing her. "And how can I help?"

"The hardest part for me isn't the calculations," Hank said, one boot scuffing at the ground. "It's writing in the journal. I'm supposed to describe the near-ground, foreground, and background. Overall terrain, any outstanding features, color. Corporal Adams is forever complaining about my lack of detail. I thought with your eye, you might do better."

"I'll try," Meg promised.

While Hank peered into the theodolite and noted various angles in the expedition journal, she took up the other leather-bound book. The cartographer had sketched the canyon at their previous stop — she recognized the formations, the perspective. She thumbed back a few pages to see how he had described the terrain before. A loose page fluttered free. She caught it before it could be lost to the canyon.

Dot's face smiled up at her. Hank had captured the wistful look she got when talking about her cinnamon sticks. A stray hair curled about one ear.

"Why, Hank," Meg said. "This is very good."

He glanced up, then turned red as he plucked the pencil drawing from her hand.

"I'm no artist," he said, tucking the picture into his shirt. "And I should have been focusing on my work instead of my sweetheart."

"I think it's lovely that you still call her sweetheart," Meg assured him with a smile.

From the fire came a yelp. Dot leveled her wooden spoon at Meadows, who was cradling his fingers.

"What did I tell you about sneaking sugar?" she demanded.

"That's my gal," Hank said with pride in his voice.

As if she thought otherwise, Dot sent him a look that would have roasted a bison whole. Meg bit her lip to keep from laughing.

"We best work," Hank said, turning to the theodolite once more. "Before she finds another use for that spoon."

Meg paged to a blank spot in the journal and took up the pencil. "Perhaps I should say aloud what I'm planning to write so you can see whether it will meet Corporal Adams's approval."

Hank nodded absently. "Sounds good."

Meg trained her gaze down the slope in front of them. "Directly ahead of the theodolite, sheer drop, perhaps twenty feet. Soil appears rocky, amber in color. Next forty feet or so, steep slope to another drop, redder soil, shrubs growing more thickly, looks like bricklebush. Can't see much beyond, so it's likely pretty sheer. Not even a glimmer of the river, but the opposite side is rugged all the way to the top with greater striation."

She glanced at Hank to find him staring at her. "Sorry. Too much detail?"

Hank shook himself. "No. That was great. Have you done this before?"

"No," she said, turning her gaze back into the canyon. "But maybe I should have. This is fun."

And it was. She noted each transect of the canyon, going from east to west. She spotted bighorn sheep leaping from rock to rock, the rams with their milky-colored horns curling around their heads. A hawk soared past their spot with a cry of protest at finding them near its hunting ground. She counted at least six bushes of wild raspberries just out of reach down the steep slope. And she determined four views that would have made superlative stereographs.

She was disappointed when Pike returned and Hank had to start packing the theodolite and his journal.

"There's a spring at the end of this plateau," the guide reported when they all gathered around. "It'll take you the rest of the day to reach it, and it's rough going, all downhill. But if we leave the rim and strike due south, we should be able to make it before dark."

"That's a lot of terrain with no survey," Hank said with a look to Ben.

"We can't survey if we can't keep watered," Ben countered. "Mount up and ride in ten."

She would never get used to the commands. Meg moved, however, to comply.

Pike was right about the terrain. She kept having to duck under tree branches, shift as her horse swayed over uneven ground. She was just thankful Stripe seemed as surefooted as the mules. Still, even with four mules in harness in front of him, Adams eased the van along. Good thing her cameras were well secured and her plates better cushioned now. She wished she could say the same for her.

They had a reprieve at one point when they came out onto a grassy plain with odd humps here and there, as if a giant child had scattered his blocks in a fit of pique.

"Old Indian village," Pike said as if he noted them glancing around curiously.

"Then there has to be water," Ben maintained.

"If there was, I couldn't find it when I came through earlier," the guide said. He clucked to his horse and led them on.

Meg cast a longing look at the peaceful site before following.

The sun was low in the west, slicing through the trees, as they approached the canyon once more. A steep-walled scarp, golden red in the dying light of the sun, stuck out into the larger canyon to form a smaller side canyon directly below them. A stream cut through the valley beyond, on its way to join the Colorado, but Meg couldn't spot any way down. Once again, Ben's hopes for a wagon road were about to be dashed.

"Spring's over there, near the rim," Pike said with a nod to the west. "Best we set up quick."

"Agreed." Ben swung down from the

saddle and began issuing orders. Hank, Adams, Larson, and Meadows obeyed. Meg helped Dot unpack the cooking gear and erect their tent.

Every time she glanced up from her work, Ben was somewhere else — assisting Hank in setting up their tents, corralling the mules so Larson and Meadows could picket them, swinging a bucket into the stream to bring up water. When Adams called him over to look at one of the van wheels, he went readily and quickly identified the problem.

"Nothing wrong with the wheels," he told the clerk. "But the ground's soft enough that the van is sinking. Grab Larson, and we'll move the heavier items into the tents, so we have a chance of pulling the van out in the morning."

The heavier items? Those would be her cameras and plates. Meg finished tying off the tent lines and went to help.

By the time Dot had a fire going with wood Larson and Meadows had gathered, Meg was sagging. Dinner was once more hardtack and salt pork, but at least Dot had water for coffee and tea to wash it all down.

"I'll take first watch," Ben told his men. "I'll wake you when it's time."

The three horse soldiers headed for their bedrolls, obviously trying not to look as tired as they felt.

"I'll take a shift," Hank offered, but Ben waved him toward his tent.

"Thank you," Meg said, rising. Was that creak her dried-out boots or her weary bones?

Ben glanced up at her, eyes smoky gray in the firelight. "For what?"

"For taking care of us all. Everyone needs someone to count on."

He nodded. "Get some sleep, Meg."

She was glad to join Dot in their tent, though it was more crowded than usual. The boxes with her developed plates had been shoved down the center, pressing her and Dot's cots to either side. Her cameras nestled up against the end of the tent. She could only hope it wouldn't rain that night, for she had no room to move anything away from the walls. She had to crawl over the foot of the cot to get into bed as it was.

"Will you be all right?" Meg asked Dot through the makeshift wall between them.

"I can do anything for one night," Dot replied. "See you in the morning, Meg."

"Sleep well," Meg said. "Or at least as well as you can."

She must have been as tired as she felt because she fell asleep immediately. It was still dark when she woke to the sound of movement.

"Morning already?" she asked, glancing up before she remembered she couldn't see Dot.

But she could see someone. Outlined by faint moonlight, a darker shadow hunched near the open flap of the tent. She could just make out a head, broad shoulders. And two arms that appeared to be wrapped around one of her plate boxes. Cold doused her.

"Dot?" she called.

"What? Huh?" Dot's voice on the other side of the boxes was thick with sleep.

Meg screamed.

Hand raised to rouse Adams for his shift, Ben jerked around at the piercing sound. Clouds crossed a crescent moon, giving little light to the area. He could barely see across the small clearing where they'd camped. He could still make out a shadow darting out of Meg's tent.

"Stop!" he ordered, running toward it, but the figure disappeared among the darker wall of the trees.

Meg's scream had woken the others. Hank called; Adams stumbled out of his tent, pulling a suspender up over his shoulder; and material rustled as Larson and Meadows scrambled to rise as well.

"I'll follow," Pike shouted, dashing past from the direction of the picket line. "You see to the ladies." He disappeared into the night after their phantom.

Adams lit a lantern just as Meg ducked out of her tent, Dot right behind. Ben was at their sides in a heartbeat.

"Are you all right?" he asked.

"No," she said, and his heart sank. "That is, I'm fine, but someone was in the tent with us."

Anger licked up him, like fire to kindling. Who would be so brazen as to attempt to trouble the two women? Or had their surprise visitor known who was in the tent? Ben glanced to the cook, who was rubbing her eyes with her fists. "What did you see?"

"Nothing," Dot said, lowering her hands. She glanced at Meg. "Sorry."

"Probably a nightmare," Hank said, joining them.

Meg drew herself up, but Ben put a hand on her arm to stop what was likely a protest. "It wasn't. I saw someone leaving the tent. Pike must have seen something as well because he's in pursuit."

She relaxed beside him. "Thank you for believing me. He had his arms around one of the plate boxes, but he let it go when I called."

Dot rubbed an ear. "Loudest call I ever heard. Like to wake the dead."

"I'm not concerned about the dead," Ben said. "Dead men don't rob tents." He turned to his men. "Privates, check the animals. Make sure none are missing. Corporal, inventory the supplies. Hank, make sure of the equipment. Dot, are you armed?"

"Always."

He smiled at the quick answer. "Good. You and Meg get some coffee brewing. Dawn's still a while away, but I doubt anyone will be sleeping any more tonight."

Meg shot him a look of gratitude bright even in the dim light, then wiggled back into her tent to reach for a coat. Ben pulled out his pistol and went to follow Pike.

He found the guide returning from the trees to the east.

"Report," Ben demanded.

"Lost him." Pike's voice was rougher than usual, frustration lacing the words. "He went over the rim like a sure-footed mule. No way to follow in the dark."

Much as he would have liked to do otherwise, Ben had to agree. "Did you catch a glimpse of him?"

213

"Not enough," Pike said, starting back for the camp. "You?"

"Only a shadow," Ben admitted, falling into step beside him.

Pike kicked out his foot, and Ben heard a rock bounce over the rim.

"Probably a native looking to steal something," the guide grumbled. "Who else would be out this way?"

Who indeed? Yet Ben couldn't be so quick to assume the thief was a native. Though he'd only been in the area a short while, his other assignments had put him in contact with a tribe from time to time. Few members had been thieves. Most just wanted peace.

"Miss Pero all right?" Pike asked as they neared the camp. "Must have given her quite a scare."

That scream would be with Ben a long time. "She wasn't physically hurt. Neither was Dot. But I don't like strangers wandering into our camp uninvited."

"Funny he got past you," Pike said. "But then, natives can move like the wind."

He didn't like the idea that anyone could get past him. He hadn't fallen asleep. How had he missed their nocturnal visitor?

"It seems we need to be able to chase the wind in the dark," Ben said. "This doesn't happen again."

Pike shifted. "You think it might?"

"I'll take no chances. Tomorrow night, we double the guard. Consider yourself conscripted, Mr. Pike."

# 14

She couldn't have gone back to sleep if
she'd tried. Meg drank down the coffee,
welcoming the dark, burnt taste that nearly
scalded her mouth. The men moved about
the camp, checking food, equipment. She'd
already looked through the box the
would-be thief had grabbed and the rest of
her plates. None had been damaged. Everything seemed accounted for.

But then, why would a thief have even
known to try? Had he simply snatched up
the first box he noticed in the tent closest
to the rim, hoping it might contain something valuable? Why not choose the tent
closest to the plateau instead? Wouldn't that
location have made it easier to escape?

For that matter, why was a thief out here?
It wasn't as if he'd have many to rob or any
to sell to.

Dot had been pawing through the boxes
and sacks that held her supplies. "Didn't

216

get the cinnamon," she declared, holding up a tin can still half full of the bark-colored sticks. She sank back on her haunches. "And there's the saleratus. Phew!"

"Nothing missing," Ben summarized a short time later as most of them gathered around the fire. "And nothing damaged. That's good news."

"We were fortunate this time," Adams agreed.

"And there won't be a next time," Ben said grimly. "From now on, I want a two-man patrol from sunset to sunrise, opposite directions around the camp, meeting north and south. I'll team with Private Larson, Private Meadows with Hank. Pike and Corporal Adams, take the last two hours before dawn."

Pike's lip curled. "Is that really necessary? Our culprit's gone and not likely to come back after hearing Miss Pero's scream."

She would not apologize. "It woke everyone, didn't it?"

"It sure did." Hank rubbed an ear as if the sound was still ringing.

"The well-being of every member of this team is my responsibility, Mr. Pike," Ben said. "I won't have this survey disturbed again. You heard my orders. If anyone wants to sleep between now and dawn, you have my permission. I'll be up. Dismissed."

Meg poured him a cup of Dot's black brew and handed it to him. "Here. I have a feeling you're going to need this."

He accepted the tin cup with a nod of thanks, and their fingers brushed. Warmth traveled up her arm. Meg pulled back.

"If you want to return to the fort," he said, gaze on the fire, "I'll send Pike with you. We can survey here until he rejoins us."

He wanted her gone? Even if she hadn't needed the commission from the work, the possibility of capturing a noteworthy stereograph, she would have been disappointed. But maybe he was trying to protect her again.

Meg cocked her head. "Why should I leave? I still have forty photographs and more than a dozen stereographs to shoot."

Ben tossed back the coffee. "Good. Let's get to it, then."

Meg leaned back as well as she could on her rock. "Sorry, Captain, but that's one order I can't obey."

He turned his gaze on her at last, firelight making his frown look particularly fierce. "Why?"

"It's still dark," Meg said with a laugh.

That won a chuckle from him. "So it is. Very well, Miss Pero. At ease until it's light."

If only it was that simple.

Between the coffee and the jolt to her nerves at discovering a stranger in the night, Meg could not be easy. She helped Dot with breakfast, starting the cornmeal mush, then mixing the saleratus into the flour and water so that the dough for Dot's famous cinnamon rolls would rise. She also gathered wood for the fire around the edge of the light.

And she peered into the shadows beyond, wondering if anyone was peering back.

What a horrid thought. She didn't like the feeling of being watched, being studied. Surely Mr. Pike was right. The thief knew they'd be on alert now. He wouldn't return.

Would he?

She felt as if the darkness were reaching for her, trying to draw her closer. She squared her shoulders, glared out into the night.

"I'm not afraid of you."

She was ashamed how glad she was that no one answered.

Still, dawn was a long way off. She yawned more times than she could count. She tried to busy herself with her cameras, but even that could not keep her attention for long. Her bedroll was calling. But if Ben and the others were determined to stay awake, she'd stay awake too.

Just when she thought she wouldn't make it another moment, the sky began to brighten. Meg rose and went to the edge of the firelight, gazing out over the shadows of the canyon. Dawn peeled away the night, spreading rose and gold across the eastern horizon. Darkness fled back into the depths of the canyon. Even the air felt new. Meg drew a breath and went to join the others for breakfast.

If she had thought the night had been long, the day seemed far longer. Even after Dot's cinnamon rolls had been gobbled up, tempers remained near the surface. Larson shouted at Meadows for giving a mule too much water, and the quiet private came close to shoving him before carrying his bucket to another of the pack animals. Dot ordered them all to gather items they needed washed, then complained about the growing pile. Adams muttered over the survey report as he sat scribbling by the fire. Pike grumbled at everything and everyone.

And Ben kept hovering.

She didn't notice at first. It was only natural that Ben should make his rounds and instruct his team, from Hank at one side of the camp to Larson on the other. The private was busy laying out the grid.

Their campsite sat on a point spearing out into the canyon. Ben had instructed Larson to cover from side to side and back a good one hundred feet from the rim.

"That ought to take a while," Meg commented as Larson paced off the spaces.

"A few days at least," Ben said, watching him.

"What do you want me to photograph?" Meg asked. "You're not studying a square this time. It's a triangle."

"North, south, east, and west," Ben said. "And any major formations in the area. Take Pike with you."

Meg grimaced. "Must I?"

Ben turned to eye her. "No one works alone, particularly after last night."

It was a logical approach, but he was already deviating from it. Meg nodded to where the cartographer was setting up the theodolite. "Hank does. Unless Corporal Adams or I am helping, of course."

"That's different. Hank is an old hand at this. He can take care of himself."

Meg drew herself up. "I can take care of myself, Captain Coleridge. The only reason I screamed last night was to alert the rest of you. I thought you'd want to catch anyone breaking into the camp."

That jaw was firming again. She could see

221

it through the stubble.

"You're right," he said, and the admission eased some of the tension in her shoulders. "I want to know everything that happens on this survey. It's my goal that everyone returns to the fort, safe and healthy."

Unlike his father. She decided not to say the words aloud. But she began to understand his stance. He'd already lost one person he cared about. He wasn't going to lose another.

"I won't stray far, I promise," she said.

"I'd prefer you not stray at all. And I must insist you have a partner."

Those eyes were implacable. Better not to argue the point, not while everyone was so on edge. "Fine," Meg said. "I'll take Private Meadows."

He crossed his arms over his chest. "Can't spare him."

She gritted her teeth. "Hank, then."

"I need him on the theodolite."

"Dot," she bit out.

"Will be washing today since we have ample water."

"Corporal Adams."

The clerk must have caught his name, for he clutched his notebook closer and turned away from them.

"Indisposed," Ben said.

Meg blew out a breath. "Then it will have to be you."

He recoiled. "Me?"

"Yes. Mr. Pike has no appreciation for my work. I can't trust him to protect the camera. He might even stumble into the shot. I have too few plates as it is. I won't risk wasting them. I'll go prepare a few now. If you want any work done today, Captain, you'll join me."

Ben shook his head. He couldn't spend the morning staring at the glory of the canyon. The grid was almost established. Larson and Meadows could note the flora and fauna, but they wouldn't recognize the difference between slate and basalt. Minerals were his specialty. He knew the weights, the colors, the properties and best uses.

The Colonel had only been moderately amused at his skills. "Well," he'd said after hearing Ben had taken top marks in the subject at West Point, "at least you'll be able to spot fool's gold."

That had been important to the Colonel. He'd served near San Francisco during the Gold Rush and had seen too many men desert for the hope of striking it rich. He realized the folly of pinning his future on something that wasn't real. So did Ben.

Pike was the logical choice to accompany her. He knew the area better than any of them, he was a good shot, and he could be spared from other duty. Indeed, the big man seemed restless. He'd already spoken quietly to Dot twice, with the second conversation ending with Dot ordering him in no uncertain terms to find her meat or face her wrath. He'd been out on the survey grid too, advising Larson as if the private had never attempted a grid before when Pike was clearly the novice. He'd even breathed down Adams's back as if reviewing the journal notes for grammar and punctuation like a schoolmarm.

No way around it. Pike was a difficult fellow to get along with, and Meg didn't need him distracting her from her work any more than the others did.

But Ben couldn't have Meg working alone, and, truth be told, he preferred to be at her side. The realization was enough to make him think twice.

But ultimately agree.

"Prepare your equipment," he told her. "I'll join you shortly."

She nodded and hurried off, skirts flapping about her boots.

He went to find Pike.

It appeared to be Hank's turn for a dose

224

of the guide's advice, for Pike was standing at the cartographer's shoulder, frowning at the theodolite.

"Heard those things aren't reliable," he was saying as Ben approached. "Had a map to Prescott once — led me straight down a box canyon."

Hank's eye twitched before he applied it to the telescope. "Maybe it wasn't the map but the person reading it that was at fault."

Pike bristled, but Ben stepped between them. "Mr. Pike, I believe Mrs. Newcomb asked you to hunt. We need meat, and you're the best one to bring it down."

The deserved praise didn't move the guide. "I can go out later. After last night, I figured I should stick closer to camp."

And continue pestering the rest of the team? "That's an order, Mr. Pike."

The guide eyed him a moment, then turned and stomped toward the picket line.

"Thanks," Hank said. "One more piece of helpful wisdom and he might have been wearing this theodolite."

"I'm disappointed in you, Mr. Newcomb," Ben said, and the cartographer swallowed his smile. "I'd think you'd have more respect for government property."

Hank grinned.

Ben turned for Adams, who was still working by the fire. Beyond him, he saw Pike riding out to the north.

Adams's thinning hair had already darkened under the brim of his hat as the day warmed, and he was beginning to sport a beard.

"I'll be helping Miss Pero with the photography," Ben informed him. "I'll have Larson and Meadows bring over anything of interest. Note it in the journal for my attention later. If you find a mineral specimen you can't identify, bring it to me."

Adams's brown eyes were guileless. "Yes, sir. I am delighted to be of assistance to you and the lady."

Feeling as if the clerk saw right through him, Ben went to find Meg.

She must have finished preparing her plates, because she was pacing off the ground looking south into the canyon, tripod leaning against a tree and camera balanced on a flat-topped rock. She stopped suddenly and pointed. "Look, you can see the river."

He edged closer, and a pebble tumbled over the rim to bounce its way down the slope. Golden scarps jutted out to the right, straight ahead, and left, and the rugged cliffs seemed to go on and on into the distance. Far below, a ribbon of blue flashed in the light. "What do you know?"

She bustled past him to retrieve her tripod. "Step aside if you please."

A step or two in either direction would have sent him plummeting. Ben eased back beside her. "Maybe we should set the tripod on more solid ground."

She planted it where he had been standing. "Two of the three legs are on rock," she informed him, swiveling the top plank and her slender form this way and that as if trying to find the perfect angle.

"You're not," Ben said, making a grab for her as her foot reached the edge.

Her eyes widened, and she hung for a moment in the air. Ben hauled her back.

Right into his arms.

She stared at him. Her eyes were greener than the pines, offering rest more surely. Golden lashes fluttered. Petal-pink lips parted. Her breath brushed his cheek.

"Are you going to let me finish setting up?" she asked.

Setting up. The picture. Right. That was why she was in his arms. He released her.

"Only if you promise to be careful," he said.

"I'll promise if you will." She picked up the camera and attached it to the tripod. Then she dove under her hood.

With most of her out of sight, he could breathe again.

"I'm careful," he said. "I plan every part of the survey."

"Where's the fun in that?" she asked, swiveling toward the edge again.

Ben put himself between her and the rim. Her hip brushed his.

"You're in my way," she complained.

"You're out of rock. Even you can't take a picture in midair."

"Oh!" She pulled out from under the hood, hair wild with static. "Ben! What an inspired idea. Just think of the view!" She glanced around, then pointed again. "There, that tree. If you could just give me a boost . . ."

Ben stared at the pine perched precariously over the precipice. "No."

"Please? You'll be famous. I'll be famous. They'll name this Coleridge Point after you."

"No," Ben repeated. "You said you only have so many plates. I won't risk one, the camera, and my photographer."

She slumped, lower lip out in a pout. "Fine. We'll just take a boring, everyday photograph no one but the Army will care about."

"You never took a boring, everyday photograph in your life," Ben said. "With nature as your canvas, your picture will be nothing short of spectacular, even if you took it blindfolded. And no," he hurried to add, "I will not blindfold you either."

"Spoilsport." She gave her skirt a twitch before diving back under the cloth.

Over the course of the next two hours, she shot south, east, and west. Adams brought him two samples that he easily recognized as limestone. The sun was high when Ben called for the midday break.

He carried the camera and tripod back to camp for her, but she continued past the fire to stop at the northern edge, gazing into the trees, hands on her hips.

"No," she declared. "I won't shoot north. You'd get nothing but trunks."

Ben nodded as he accepted a cup of water from Dot. "Agreed. You can help Hank this afternoon."

Hank brightened, and Adams frowned.

Dot scowled. "I need Meg to help with dinner. I can't wash and cook at the same time."

"Since when?" Hank asked.

Dot aimed a kick at the pile of shirts and unmentionables the team had brought out earlier to be washed. "Since you all got so dirty, ya big galoot. I'll finish the washing.

229

Meg can start dinner."

Meg took a step back as if to distance herself from the fight.

"Someone else can help with dinner," Hank said. "Meg knows how to record the terrain better than anyone I've met."

Dot's look darkened further. Adams turned away and marched for the van.

Ben had had enough. "Meadows," he called, and the private came over. "Help Mrs. Newcomb with dinner."

His private swallowed, but he saluted. "Yes, sir." The gesture appeared to be aimed more at Dot than Ben. With a look of commiseration to Ben and Meadows, Meg went to help Hank.

Ben thought that would settle the matter, but his cook muttered to herself as she slung a shirt into the hot water and used a spoon to slosh it around. Perhaps she would have preferred the talkative Larson as assistant, but Ben needed the more experienced soldier on the survey.

Dot's attitude wasn't improved when Pike returned to report he'd had no luck.

"Took a shot at a deer," he said, "but she got away. Guess it's salt pork again tonight."

"I wouldn't sound so pleased about it," Dot told him.

Meadows roused himself to speak. "Chuck

in bacon like Miss Pero said."

Dot rounded on him. "I know my business, Private. See you mind yours."

Meadows ducked his head.

Ben was never so glad for sundown. The salt pork might be briny, but anything Dot cooked was at least palatable. Conversation was sporadic. He caught sight of Meg's chin heading for her chest more than once. His feet dragged too as he moved toward his bed. Hank had offered to take the first watch with Larson, and Ben had gratefully accepted. He paused at the tent flap to glance back at the camp.

Dot and Hank were in deep conversation near the rim. The cook stuck her finger twice into her husband's chest before shoving back the flap on her tent and disappearing inside. Hank shook his head and started on his rounds.

Now what was wrong? He had a strong feeling that nature and their midnight visitor were about to be the least of his worries.

# 15

Meg stood on the very edge of the point the
next morning, fascinated by the play of light
and shadow across the canyon. Every movement of the sun, every passing cloud,
changed the view and brought new aspects
into clarity.

"How's the journal coming?" Hank asked.

The cartographer had requested her help
again that day. Since she'd already taken
the three photographs she and Ben had
agreed upon, she had time enough. She
stepped back to where the leather-bound
journal rested on a rock, the breeze finger-
ing through the pages. "Sorry. I was about
to describe the far field."

Noting something on his own pad, Hank
nodded.

Meg picked up the journal with one hand
and arranged her skirts with the other as
she sat on the sun-warmed rock. Though
she'd tried to dust off her riding habit each

232

morning, the dun-colored material was beginning to show its wear. Iodine contributed rusty specks on the sleeves. The gray spot below her waist showed where bromide had sloshed as a plate went into the bath. The hem had darkened to brown from contact with the soil. She was just glad Dot had washed her other camisole yesterday. The clean cotton felt cool against her skin.

Pencil in hand now, she stared across the river at the red and gold cliffs rising beyond. Their camp was high enough here that she could see the farther plateau, which appeared to be more of a prairie. At the very least, she couldn't spot many trees. She duly noted that in the journal.

"You and the captain would make a good match."

The pencil bit into the paper, and Meg hastily raised it. "Match? What are you talking about?"

Hank glanced her way with a frown as if confused by her response. "He's an officer of fine character; you're a young lady of considerable talent. Why wouldn't you hit it off?"

Meg forced herself to bend back over the journal. "Too many reasons to enumerate." She set about describing the texture and color of the far cliffs.

"He's a good man," Hank said when she raised her head again. Had he been watching her? His usual good-natured grin gave nothing away. "Look how well he treats his men. Most officers I've worked under were a lot more demanding."

She could imagine. Some of the men who had hired her father had been unreasonable, expecting far more work far too quickly and for far too little money.

"I find no fault in his leadership," Meg said, "except for the fact that he sometimes refuses my requests."

"Can't have everything," Hank allowed, fiddling with his theodolite.

Meg grinned at him. "Why not?"

He chuckled.

Behind them, a pot clanged.

Hank winced. "Something's got Dot's back up."

Meg glanced in that direction. The cook was shoving her gear about, jaw working as if she was talking to herself. She'd finished the washing yesterday. A few shirts still hung here and there from the trees, flapping like flags. She had plenty of wood stacked nearby.

"I noticed," Meg said. "Do you think it's because Mr. Pike hasn't gone hunting yet?"

Hank glanced to where the guide was sitting a little way from the cook, whittling at a stick with his big knife. For some reason, Pike had shown a preference for Dot's company the last couple days. Maybe, like Meadows, he hoped to be able to scrape some sugar off the cone.

"Could be," Hank allowed. "She can do a lot more with a turkey, goose, or pronghorn than salt pork."

"Maybe we should send Meadows out instead," Meg said. "He looks bored."

The private was standing at one side of the grid, scratching at his back, while Ben and Larson bent over a plant as if arguing about its species, and Corporal Adams cast Hank and Meg sour looks.

"Do you think he can even shoot?" Hank asked.

"Can't most boys his age shoot?" Meg asked, gaze going out over the canyon again.

Hank laughed. "Don't let him hear you call him a boy. He can't be much younger than you."

She glanced at Meadows again. His beard was coming in, much more slowly and patchy than Larson's or Adams's, and with a few streaks of brown among the gold. "Maybe he just seems younger. Now, I really should concentrate."

"Yes, ma'am," Hank said with a salute.

They continued at their tasks in companionable silence the rest of the morning and into the afternoon, until Ben called the mid-afternoon break. As had become the habit, everyone gathered around the fire. Dot had dried apples soaking in a pot of water. She kept poking at them with her spoon, shoving them deeper.

"What have you for us today, Dot?" Ben asked cheerily.

Dot didn't meet his gaze. "Working on dried apple pie. Might take a bit."

"How about some water now?" Pike asked.

Dot skewered him with her gaze, then jerked her head to the west. "Spring's over there. Help yourself."

Adams picked up a tin cup and stalked off. Larson and Meadows exchanged glances, then took a cup each and followed. Muttering to himself, Pike trudged in their wake.

"Something I can help with, sweetheart?" Hank asked.

"Nope," Dot said, gaze once more on her bobbing brown apples. "And I'd appreciate it if you'd all just let me be."

Ben nodded to the east, and Meg and Hank rose and joined him closer to the tents. "Anyone have any idea what's troubling our cook?"

Hank shrugged.

"Could we have offended her in some way?" Meg asked the cartographer.

"She gets this way sometimes," Hank said. "Has ever since we were married. Never can get her to tell me why. She'll settle down on her own. She always does. Best we do as she says and leave her be."

Meg wanted to believe that. But she felt as if she and Dot were becoming friends. Surely she should do something to help.

She and Hank finished with the canyon later that afternoon. By then, Hank had noted all his calculations, and she had, in his opinion, adequately described the indescribable view.

"What now?" Meg asked the cartographer, rubbing her neck, stiff from looking up and down all day.

"Now we reposition," Hank said. "I'd like to see what's on the other side of that." He pointed to the westernmost outcropping.

"So would I," Meg said.

They shared a grin.

"Not like that!" Dot shouted. "Ain't you never skinned a rabbit before?"

Poor Meadows had been assigned to assist the cook with dinner again. Mr. Pike had brought in something, rabbit by the sound of it. The skinning knife trembled in Meadows's grip.

Hank sighed. "Best see what I can do." He nodded toward the outcropping. "There's still enough time for a photograph."

Meg laughed. "Indeed there is. Good luck, Hank."

"You too."

She didn't need luck. She just needed the right angle, the best perspective. She went to ready her stereographic camera and a plate.

Adams was standing at the back of the van as she approached.

"Will you be taking a picture?" he asked.

Meg let down the steps. "Mr. Newcomb suggested I try farther along the rim."

"Well, at least you're doing your job for once and not mine."

Foot on the bottom step, Meg paused. His perennially red face had darkened, his eyes narrowed.

"I serve on this expedition, same as you, Corporal," she informed him. "If my help is needed, wherever, I give it. If you have issue with that approach, I suggest you take it up with Captain Coleridge."

He wrinkled his sunburned nose. "I very much doubt the captain would take my side over yours. A pretty face can do more than years of loyal toil when it comes to promotion and favor."

Meg held her ground, gaze even with his. "A pretty face isn't any good for convincing gentlemen to take a lady seriously. Only being the best at what you do can achieve that goal. Be the best. Make them notice you."

He frowned as if he hadn't expected her answer or had never considered the matter before. "That is rather difficult for a man of letters. I wasn't trained for this sort of wilderness work."

Meg cocked her head. "Then why join the Army?"

He dropped his gaze. "I had intended to become a solicitor, but the man I apprenticed under was more interested in lining his own pockets than helping his clients. When he was jailed, fingers were pointed in my direction as a potential accomplice. The safest thing was to put myself out of reach." He glanced around at their rugged site. "Though this wasn't entirely what I had in mind."

"It seems you have intelligence, knowledge, and a desire for advancement," Meg said. "Use them. Talk to Mr. Newcomb. Learn why he prefers my work to yours. And do not," she added, raising a finger at the sly look that came over his face, "imply that it has anything to do with beauty."

He stepped back and saluted her. "Yes, ma'am. Do you need any assistance with your photography?"

"No, thank you," Meg said. "And you have an appointment with Mr. Newcomb."

With a nod, he hurried off.

Meg shook her head as she went to prepare the collodion. Some days she couldn't win. Gentlemen in power, who could decide whether to hire her and what to pay her, took her pretty face as a sign she wasn't competent. Others assumed she'd been hired simply for her looks. The only way to show them the error in their thinking was to be the best at her profession. And that was what she intended to do.

When she stepped out of the van a few minutes later, Ben and Larson were hard at work on the grid, Hank and Adams were in deep discussion, and Meadows was frantically working over the fire while Dot stood nearby, arms crossed over her chest and foot tapping on the dry ground. Pike paced the perimeter, rifle cradled in one arm. There was no reason to bother any of them. Hank knew where she was headed. She caught his eye, and he nodded. Cradling her camera close, she set out.

It was easy going through the trees, with little underbrush. The golden soil crunched beneath her boots. Through the pines on her left, she caught glimpses of the canyon, so she kept her bearing.

A little way along, the trees opened for a fine view. She ventured closer to the edge. The west held an excellent perspective down the canyon, farther than any she'd seen so far. Straight ahead, the gold and red striation of the opposite cliffs showed to advantage. Both possibilities. And to the east . . .

Meg caught her breath. Another outcropping jutted into the canyon, the rocks gilded by the setting sun. In the center was a massive hole, allowing her to see back down the river to vermillion cliffs. Oh, what a shot!

She set up her camera, checked the angle once, twice. Her fingers trembled on the material as she lifted the hood. This could make her future. She focused on the farther canyon, like a scene through a heavenly window. One more adjustment and . . .

The view went black.

Meg jerked out from under the hood to meet Pike's amused gaze. The guide was standing directly in front of her camera, blocking any chance for a picture.

"Straying a little far afield, aren't you?" he asked.

"Attempting to take a picture," Meg informed him. "Get out of my shot."

He didn't budge. "Captain was concerned. He wants you back at camp."

"Happy to oblige," Meg said, jaw tight, "as soon as I get the shot."

He made a face. "It's a big canyon. One picture ought to be as good as another."

"If you don't move, now," Meg said, "I will shoot you where you stand."

She'd meant with the camera, but Pike clearly took her words literally. Paling, he stepped out of the frame.

Meg dived back under the hood. The light was fading, the canyon dimming in the distance. It would be a good shot, but not the amazing picture she'd hoped for. She took the shot.

"Done?" Pike asked as she emerged from the hood.

"A few more minutes for exposure," Meg replied.

He hefted his rifle higher, betraying the damp circles under the arms of his broad-cloth shirt. "We're exposed enough out here. Good wind could knock us both over."

"You're welcome to wait in the trees," Meg said.

His eyes narrowed. "If you can take it, I can take it."

There was no if. Her father had taught her well. She knew her capabilities. She knew her intentions. She just wasn't sure of his.

Ben winced as another clang echoed from near the fire. Larson handed him the last mineral sample of the day.

"What's bothering Mrs. Newcomb?" Larson asked.

Whether from respect or fear, none of his men called Dot by her first name. Ben could only hope it was his own respect for her that made him hesitate to return to the fire now.

"I'll speak to her later," he promised.

They finished recording their finds and moved back into camp. Hank was already near the fire, but on their arrival, he excused himself and drew Adams and Meadows off toward the spring.

"I told them to wash," Dot said before Ben could question her. "Last thing we need is dirt in the food." She slammed down the lid on the pot she'd been stirring.

Larson backed away. "Best I go wash too." He scurried off faster than a rabbit.

Ben eyed his cook. Her back was hunched, her face tight, her fingers cramped, as if she

243

were holding on to something tightly. "What's the problem, Dot?"

Dot tossed her spoon into another bowl. "Problem? One scrawny rabbit to feed seven people. Red dust falling into everything. Strangers disturbing my sleep. It's enough to give anyone fits."

Ben crouched near her. "Not an old campaigner like you."

Dot narrowed her eyes. "Who you calling old?"

Ben kept his smile in place. "Certainly not you. I merely wanted to point out that you have more experience than most of us. We rely on you for guidance, as an example. When you're upset, we want to set matters right."

Her body relaxed, her look softened. "That's mighty nice of you, Captain. But you can't fix what's wrong with me." She sighed.

"Give me a chance," Ben said. "I might surprise you."

Her smile appeared. "You might at that. I can see why Meg favors you."

Something zinged through him, like a bee making for its hive. He glanced up, suddenly realizing that Meg wasn't in sight. "Where is Meg? I thought she was helping Hank."

All sunlight vanished from Dot's face.

"She sure was. You'd be smarter to keep her to yourself."

Ben's look came back to her. "I have no hold on Miss Pero."

She snorted. "Men. Why are you all so blind?" She picked up her spoon and leveled it at him. "She's pretty and smart and knows her craft. You could do far worse."

Ben rose. "And Miss Pero could do better. How soon to dinner?"

"Another quarter hour." She eyed Ben. "Well? Go and wash."

Bemused, Ben went.

Hank, Adams, Meadows, and Larson were all standing beside the spring talking. Ben's shoulders felt lighter when he saw that Meg and Pike had joined them. Her color was high, but he wasn't sure whether that was from exposure to the sun or some emotion.

"Dinner in a quarter hour," he reported. "I suggest you don't want to be late."

Hank scratched his neck. "That's sure enough."

"I also suggest Mr. Pike return first," Ben said.

His guide frowned. "Why?"

Hank grinned. "Dot's the least angry at you. You brought her meat."

"Not enough meat, according to Dot," Ben warned. "But I did take that into con-

245

siceration."

Pike shook his head. "You're all afraid of her."

"Yes, sir," Meadows said with a shudder.

"I'll go back," Meg said, hitching her camera closer. "I'm not afraid of Dot. I'd like to know what's troubling her." She started through the trees. Ben was about to go after her when Pike stepped in front of him.

"Captain, a moment."

Ben shifted to give him his full attention.

Pike tipped his chin in the direction Meg had gone. "I noticed her leaving camp by herself, so I followed. She was clear out on a ledge, taking some fool picture. She could have fallen, met a cougar or bear or a pack of coyotes. I thought you wanted everyone to go in pairs."

"That was my order," Ben said, frustration building. "Thank you for reporting to me. I'll speak to her."

Pike nodded and headed for camp.

"Mouth runner," Larson muttered.

Ben turned on him. "You have something to say, Private?"

Hank shook his head, Adams's eyes widened, and Meadows shrank in on himself as if expecting Ben to reprimand their comrade.

246

Larson raised his scruffy chin. "Yes, sir. I don't much like the way Mr. Pike talked about Miss Meg. If he was so all-fired worried, he could have just checked on her. No need to report her to her commanding officer."

Ben hid his smile. "I appreciate your insight and candor, Private. Finish up and return to camp."

"Sir."

As the three cavalrymen ambled off with Hank, Ben bent to rinse his hands in the cool spring water. What was it about Meg that inspired loyalty, support? Pike had gone to her rescue, Larson had defied authority to champion her.

And he was about to court disaster to warn her.

# 16

Meg stored her camera and set the plate into its solution, then went to the fire. Dot busied herself with the stew she'd made, the savory scents hanging in the air.

"The rest of them are washing," Meg told her. "They're a little afraid to return. You certainly have a way with the gentlemen."

Dot slammed down the lid. "No, I don't."

So forceful. How could she get through to her friend? Meg propped her chin on her hand. "I don't know. They do what you ask, even Mr. Pike."

Dot dropped her gaze to the fire. "They're afraid I'll spit in their food."

Meg shuddered. "Well, I certainly hope they're wrong."

"Maybe." Dot glanced up with a shadow of a smile. "They're wrong. I wouldn't do that. But they don't take to me like they do to you. Even Hank likes you better."

Her sigh could have felled one of the pines.

Meg dropped her hand and straightened. "Now, you listen to me, Dot Newcomb. Hank is your husband, committed to you heart, mind, and body. And if you think I would stand between a husband and a wife, you don't know me."

Dot restacked the plates, the tin rattling in her grip. "I never said you'd do anything wrong. But Hank would have to be blind not to notice you. Who wants an old dull moth when a pretty butterfly flutters near?"

"First off, you're no dull moth," Meg started, thinking of the drawing Hank had made that showed the beauty inside Dot.

Dot held up her hand. "I am. I always have been. I never thought to find a husband as handsome and clever as Hank. From time to time, I've wondered whether he regretted choosing me. But I never questioned his loyalty. Then that old Rudy Pike had to go and mention how much Hank admired you, and I couldn't get it out of my mind."

Meg glanced to where the men were coming out of the trees. "I don't much like Mr. Pike at the moment. Perhaps he means well, but the relationship between you and your husband is none of his affair. Nor mine. If you're worried about Hank, talk to him."

Dot nodded, then began ladling stew onto plates as the men seated themselves around. Meg went to rinse the photographic plate and set it to dry before joining them. Ben and Hank both looked up with a smile of welcome.

Meg sat and accepted her plate, with a sidelong look to Hank. Could Dot have reason for concern? Surely he wouldn't form an attachment to Meg. Then again, Ben hadn't been the only cadet to approach her at West Point, and there had been several men since who'd attempted closer acquaintance. She'd let them all know she wasn't interested. She certainly would never have taken up with a married man! She'd thought Hank's attentions no more than a compliment to her abilities. He'd even encouraged her to consider Ben.

She watched him as they ate. He grabbed an extra biscuit and tossed it to Meadows, warning him that growing boys needed to eat. He praised Larson for how well the mules were behaving. He assured Adams he'd be glad for the man's help the next day. He joked with Pike about the lack of hunting opportunities. And he swapped stories with Ben about another expedition they'd been on. In short, he treated the

250

other members of the group no differently than he treated her.

Dot was worrying about nothing. She might not have noticed that Hank was treating Meg kindly if it hadn't been for the poison Mr. Pike had dripped in her ear.

That Dot wasn't the only one he'd attempted to influence was evident as soon as dinner ended. Ben rose and nodded to Meg.

"Miss Pero, we need to talk."

The other men exchanged glances. Adams eyed her speculatively, as if he couldn't decide whether this request denoted favor or discipline. Larson and Meadows hastily excused themselves as if they suspected she was in for a scold. Pike smirked at her across the fire as if he knew it.

Meg handed Dot her plate with a word of thanks, then stood to follow Ben toward the canyon edge. Twilight crept up all around them. As if the canyon too were headed for sleep, its colors darkened, dimmed. Quiet wrapped around her. It did not bring peace with it.

"What's wrong?" Meg asked.

"I understand you disobeyed orders," Ben said, gaze out over the canyon.

"I did no such thing," Meg informed him. "Hank suggested I see about pictures to the west. He knew where I was going."

"But he wasn't with you in case you needed help," Ben pointed out.

"So you sent Mr. Pike." Meg shook her head with a tsk.

"Apparently he spotted you leaving camp," Ben said.

"And followed," Meg confirmed. "I might have known he'd bring you the tale. He couldn't be content with interfering with my photograph."

Ben turned his gaze to hers, smile tilting up. "He interfered with the shot? I knew the man was fearless, but I didn't think he was suicidal."

"Did he tell you I threatened to shoot him?" Meg demanded. "I meant take his picture, but I'm fairly sure he understood it another way."

Ben laughed. "Very likely, and I suspect you knew he would. Why are you fighting us, Meg? We just want to keep you safe."

Her fists balled at her sides. "You sound like my aunt after Papa died. 'You're just a woman, Meg. You shouldn't be traipsing about at the back of beyond. You should settle down, have children.' Maybe I don't want to settle down."

"That," he said, "you made abundantly clear."

She hadn't meant to remind him of their

past, but she found herself ready to meet it head-on. "I'm sorry if I hurt you, Ben. I thought maybe I could settle down with you, but I'm not suited to be an officer's wife. I have a profession, one I love and am reasonably good at. Besides, I've lived through an expedition before. You don't have to protect me."

Her hair must have come partly undone because he reached out to stroke a lock back behind her ear. "Even if I want to?" he murmured.

Those blue-gray eyes were warm enough to melt the tensions clinging to her. How easy to cling to him instead, allow him to protect her. But that protection came at a price, and the price was too dear. She raised her head, and his hand fell.

"You're the leader of this expedition," she told him. "It's your responsibility to take care of all the members of your team. I understand that. But you let Pike go off scouting alone, send Meadows for water, leave Hank with the theodolite, Larson with the grid, and Dot at the fire. I only ask for the same professional courtesy. I took appropriate precautions. Hank would have raised the hue and cry if I hadn't returned in a reasonable time. And you know my scream can carry."

He shook his head. "You've made your point. Continue with the precautions you stated, and you'll get no more complaints from me."

Why did the breeze smell sweeter? "Thank you, Ben. I promise to be sensible."

"Well, let's not take things to extremes."

She smiled, then sobered as she remembered her conversation with Dot. "There is something else you can do for me."

He stilled, and she wondered what he expected her to say. "Oh?" he asked.

"Talk to Hank. Dot has it in her head he doesn't love her anymore. That's why she's been so grumpy. Advise him to make it up to her."

He recoiled. "I'll do no such thing. The relationship between husband and wife is sacred."

"I agree, but sometimes people need a little help."

"Not from me." He stepped back from her. "I lead by example, and I'm no kind of example in love and marriage. You should know that better than anyone."

His cheeks were turning pink. She could tell even in the dim light. Hers felt warm as well.

"I didn't turn you down because of you," she insisted. "You are a fine man, Ben Coleridge. I simply realized I wasn't ready for marriage. But I don't like seeing one struggle. If you won't talk to Hank, I will."

She turned past him to do just that. Ben caught her arm. "Be careful, Meg. I know many men who wouldn't appreciate hearing about their failures."

"And that's one of the many faults of the breed," Meg replied. "Now, excuse me. Dot is my friend, and I intend to help her, whether you like it or not."

She thought Ben might follow, perhaps even argue some more or issue an order she would have to refuse, but she reached Hank's side where he was checking his cartridge box by his tent, with no further protest from Ben. The cartographer looked up as she approached. Then his smile faded, and he stood.

"What's wrong, Meg?"

"Do you love your wife?" Meg demanded.

He reared back. "Of course. Why would you even ask?"

"Because Dot's wondering. She thinks you're tired of her."

He ran a hand through his hair. "Of all the fool . . ." He pointed at the canyon, shadow on shadow now. "You've seen that view. Would you ever grow tired of it?"

"No," Meg allowed with a frown.

"Why?" he challenged.

"It's vast and marvelous and it changes every hour of every day," Meg said.

His hand fell. "And so does my wife. I bore easily, Meg. Life with Dot is never boring."

"Then I suggest," Meg said with a smile, "you tell her that."

"I'll do one better," Hank said. "I'll show her."

What was she doing? Ben watched as Meg spoke earnestly with Hank near the cartographer's tent. Hank grimaced and pointed with great animation. She'd complained about Pike's interference with her photography, then gone on to interfere in something far more important — a marriage.

He blew out a breath. Who was he to say whether it was the right thing to do? His one attempt at courtship had led Meg to kindly refuse his suit, claiming he'd misunderstood.

That her tender smiles had been meant in friendship.

That the kiss they'd shared had been only for fun.

That the time they'd spent together had served to stave off boredom before she headed off on her next adventure.

256

Now she said she had been serious in their courtship, only to realize when he proposed that she wasn't ready for marriage. Who was he to counsel anyone on love?

Whatever she said must have had some effect, for Hank clapped her on the shoulder and went to talk to his wife. As if she didn't see him coming, Dot began storing the plates and supplies.

To give them as much privacy as the camp allowed, Ben called for his men and Pike to join him and confirmed sentry duty for the night before they all turned in.

He and Meadows took the first shift, circling the camp and watching for any other movement. The moon wouldn't rise until later. They kept the fire going so it would be easy to spot any change in their surroundings.

Unfortunately, it was still too hard to ignore his own thoughts.

What was it about Meg? There was no denying her beauty, but he'd met pretty girls before and after he'd courted her. His sister Diana had made sure of it. Having lived at forts and towns from one side of the country to the other, Diana knew how to make acquaintances. She'd always brought her friends home to meet Ben and their mother. But after Meg and her father had left the area, his sister had made it her mission to match him up.

"Something has you moping," she'd said when he'd visited their house south of West Point. "I know the cure. We'll host a party."

"A party isn't going to make me feel better," he'd told her.

"Well," Diana had said with a toss of her honey-blonde curls, "it might make me feel better."

She'd trotted out every friend and acquaintance, from local belles to distant cousins in the area for the summer and taking in the spa nearby. None had touched his heart. Friends since then had introduced him to sisters, even mothers, with the same result. It seemed there was only one woman for him, and she didn't want him.

"All clear," Meadows murmured as they met to the north of camp.

"All clear," Ben agreed. If only that included his own path.

The next day, they fared better. Dot still banged the pots, but the sounds were less jarring, as if the force had faltered. She offered Larson and Meadows seconds at breakfast, winning a smile from the shy private. Following worship service, Hank and Adams worked on the expedition notes, freeing Meg to take pictures. Pike insisted on accompanying her, which she allowed with a look to Ben.

After starting Meadows and Larson on the grid, Ben went to check on his cartographer and clerk. Adams was bent over the travel desk, neat hand compiling various observations. Hank was sitting on a boulder near the edge of the canyon, legs splayed and paper spread between them.

"Everything all right?" Ben asked him quietly.

Hank smiled at him. "Fine. I should have the map sketched by the end of the day. How much longer on the grid?"

"Should be done by midday tomorrow. I'll have Pike scout ahead for the next campsite."

"Good." Hank bent back over his work, one large hand holding the paper in place against a rising breeze. When Ben couldn't make himself move away, the cartographer looked back up. "Something else?"

How to phrase it? He'd argued with himself half the night and finally justified the interference as a way to make sure all his team members were in fighting shape. He had been certain the Colonel would have approved. Now he wasn't sure what to say.

"Dot seems in a better mood today," he ventured.

"Better," Hank acknowledged with a look to his wife. "But I'll see what else I can do." He returned his gaze to Ben. "You ever have a sweetheart, Captain?"

Adams glanced up as if just as interested in the answer.

"Once," Ben admitted cautiously, vowing not to confess more.

Hank nodded. "Then you know you should never take her for granted. Seems I was guilty of that. Dot deserves to know I love her. She should never have to question my devotion."

Had Meg somehow imparted all that in a few moments? Ben could only shake his head in amazement. "Dot's fortunate to have you," he told his friend.

"I'm the fortunate one," Hank insisted. "I hope your sweetheart feels the same way one day."

Adams flushed and dropped his gaze. Ben tipped his hat and moved on. His sweetheart had no reason to question his love. She didn't think it was love at all.

Still, he kept an eye on his cartographer throughout the day. Hank made sure to sit closest to Dot at the midday break and thanked her for the water she served him.

He asked her opinion about the weather, what kind of camp they should look for next. As she started working on dinner, he wandered out of camp to return with an armful of wild cabbage and mint. Dot took them from him with an exclamation, set them down carefully, then threw herself into his arms.

Ben looked away with a smile.

Was that his problem? He'd been a cadet with little income of his own, and it wasn't proper for a gentleman to lavish gifts on a lady in any regard. Should he have brought Meg flowers from the garden his mother tended? As independent as Meg was, she might have laughed at the gesture.

Then again, Dot was pretty independent herself.

The idea refused to leave him as he returned to work that afternoon. He tested the hardness of the mineral samples and thought about how hard it would be to win Meg's love. They had both grown, in their careers, in their confidence. Would she be any more amenable to marriage now?

He helped Meadows and Larson categorize a few odd plants, one the exact shade of green as Meg's eyes. He must be mad to think about approaching her in the middle of a survey. Yet surely they could determine

261

their own minds without jeopardizing the work.

Was he willing to risk looking foolish again?

Wouldn't winning Meg's heart be worth any effort?

Dinner was swiftly approaching when he made the decision. Heart thumping as hard as it had when he'd told the Colonel he wanted to be an engineer instead of a cavalryman, he headed out of camp for the field of wildflowers he'd seen riding in. He gathered sunflower-like goldeneye; brushed aside butterflies to collect the tall, spiky purple blooms of lupine; and snapped off feathery goldenrod, until his fist could hold no more. Then he approached the van, where Meg had been working.

He paused a moment at the foot of the steps, willing himself to knock at the door. If she told him she could never think differently about him or marriage, he'd lost nothing but his pride.

And if she approved, oh, what he might win.

Raising his head, he reached up and rapped. No one responded. Deflated, he glanced around the van and counted heads. Most of his team were gathered around the fire. He could see Adams's balding pate down by the stream. Where was Meg?

He rapped again. He knew enough about photography to understand it was never wise to let in light at the wrong time. Then again, those chemicals and the heat could prove a dangerous combination.

"Meg?" he called, concern tightening his throat.

From inside came a jagged sob.

Flowers falling from his hand, he leaped up the steps and yanked open the door. Sunlight speared through the darkness to show Meg standing beside the counter, cradling one of her plates. She raised her head, and light glittered on the tears streaking the dust on her face.

Ben went to her, plans forgotten. "Meg, sweetheart, what's wrong?"

She held up two jagged pieces of glass. "Someone broke my plate."

## 17

Meg sucked back a sob. Her picture, her glorious picture of the beautiful window in the sky, destroyed. Who could have been so cruel?

"Easy," Ben said, taking first one then the other piece of broken glass from her fingers to lay them on the counter beside her. "Plates break. You told me how easily back at West Point."

She could scarcely think. "I was so careful. All the jostling over the rough ground, all the packing and unpacking. We haven't lost one until now. And I promise you, I was very, very careful with this one."

He glanced down at the pieces as if trying to match up the broken negative with the terrain around them. "A stereograph?"

She nodded. "Oh, Ben, it was one of my best. I had such high hopes." Tears were coming again.

He took her in his arms, held her gently.

She allowed herself to lean against him, soak up a little of that strength. Just when she'd thought her future was made, it all slipped away again.

"I know the moments you create never come twice," he murmured. "But you have more plates. You can take another shot at the same location, maybe produce an even better picture."

He knew just what to say to soothe her wounded heart. Her father had always claimed the best picture illuminated not only the subject but the photographer as well. She felt as if she had laid bare her soul, only to have it trampled. Why would anyone destroy her picture? Was Adams so vindictive? Was this her thanks for trying to help him?

Then another thought struck.

"Pike." She pulled back to meet Ben's gaze. "It had to be. He was the only one who knew what I shot that day."

Ben shook his head. "Even if he thought you'd threatened to shoot him, breaking something behind your back doesn't sound like Pike. He'd tell you face-to-face, let you know just how angry he was."

She couldn't argue with that. Pike certainly wasn't afraid of confrontation. Adams, on the other hand . . .

No, she could not make herself believe it of him.

"Then who?" she asked Ben.

"I don't know," he said. "You're sure it was intentional?"

Doubt tugged at her. Could the plate have had a crack that had deepened when exposed to the chemicals? Or had it reacted to the changes in temperature from the day to night? It was possible, but none of the others had broken.

"It must have been," she said. "I finished the negative yesterday and set it aside to show you when we had time today. When I returned to the van before dinner, I found it like that, as if someone had snapped it in two."

He peered around the van's crowded interior. "Nothing fell on it?"

"No." She wrapped one arm about her waist to ward off the chill that was building despite the stuffy space. "It seems to have been deliberately smashed. Why?"

He shook his head as if just as mystified. "I wonder, could our mysterious visitor have returned?"

"Surely we would have noticed," Meg protested.

Ben retrieved the two pieces of the plate. "We've been busy. You were away from the van most of the day. It's possible someone sneaked in."

"And broke one plate?"

"Some tribes refuse to be photographed," he said with a look to the pieces in his hands. "Perhaps a native thought you had caught his likeness in this."

She couldn't make herself believe in his phantom, for all she'd been the one to first sight the fellow. But believing one of her teammates would destroy her work was equally as repugnant.

"This might not be the only act of vandalism," Ben said. "Come with me. We'll check each tent."

Meg nodded, following him out of the van. As she reached the ground, her boot squished against something. Looking down, she saw wildflowers strewn across the golden soil. How had those gotten there? Her unknown nemesis would hardly have brought her flowers in consolation. She hurried to catch up to Ben.

Most of the team members had already gathered around the fire, ready for dinner, when Ben reached them, Meg right behind.

"We have reason to believe our midnight prowler paid us another visit," he told them, glancing at each in turn. "Check your tents, the supplies, and the animals. Make sure

267

nothing's missing or harmed. Report back in ten."

As the men moved away, Dot rose from the fire. "Need me to check our tent, Meg?"

"No," Meg said with a look to Ben. "I'll do that while you look through the cooking supplies."

As if determined to protect her, Ben followed Meg to her tent and waited outside as she searched in the boxes still stacked down the center and the packs holding her and Dot's clothes and personal items.

"Nothing seems to be missing," she told him.

"I'll check my tent," he said. "See if Dot needs help."

With a nod, Meg returned to the fire. She sat beside Dot and dug through the various boxes and burlap sacks that held the cooking supplies. Meg wasn't entirely surprised to find the flour, salt, dried fruit and vegetables, cornmeal, coffee, and tea intact.

"Sugar cone looks thinner," Dot said, sitting back on her heels. "But that could be Meadows. The boy has a sweet tooth something fierce."

"And I don't know anyone who'd make off with hardtack," Meg concurred.

All the pots and pans, cutlery, and plates were accounted for as well. It was the same story with everyone else when they reported in. All supplies, equipment, horses, and mules were as expected and in good condition.

"So it was just my plate," Meg said with a frown at Ben.

"All this for a plate?" Pike complained with a curl of his lip. "You're welcome to mine."

"Not that kind of plate, and you know it," Meg threw at him.

When he frowned as well, Ben stepped between them. "That's enough. The reason I asked you to look over everything is that one of Miss Pero's photographs was damaged beyond repair. It was part of the official record for this expedition."

Adams straightened. "As such, there are stiff penalties for misuse." He glared around at the others as if suspecting each of having a part.

Interesting. Was he agreeing so readily to keep them off his trail, or had she reached him with her suggestion as to how to handle Hank? The two had been working well together lately.

"If anyone has any knowledge as to how this happened," Ben continued, "speak with me privately. Now, eat dinner and turn in. Those on watch, look lively. I'm still not convinced our visitor won't return."

It was a quiet dinner. Everyone kept peering around as if wondering whether a traitor sat among them. Meg didn't notice anyone approach Ben for a private word, which likely meant no one felt the need to unburden himself. Dot didn't speak to her until they were in the tent and snuggled in their bedrolls.

"You know I wouldn't do something like that?" Dot asked.

"I know," Meg assured her. "Even if you were mad about Hank."

"Oh, I wasn't mad at you," Dot said. "And even if I was, I'd just put too much salt or a handful of pepper in your food."

Meg laughed. "So long as you didn't spit in it."

She thought she might have trouble sleeping that night, what with the broken plate and Ben's suggestion that their midnight stranger had returned. Instead, Meg fell asleep immediately and didn't wake until she heard Dot dressing to go out and start breakfast. The air that came through the flap as Dot opened it was crisp, cool, and scented with pine. Meg waited only until the canvas fell back in place before rising as well.

Her father had taught her early on the importance of weight. Horses and mules could only carry so much, even when teaming to draw a photography van. Cameras, plates, frames, and processing chemicals were heavy, and food was almost as necessary. That meant clothing must be kept at a minimum.

Unlike the cavalrymen, however, she had a spare riding habit, with skirt, breeches, and bodice, this one in navy with brass buttons in two rows down the front. Time to let the dun habit air out a while. She brushed out and twisted up her hair under her hat before exiting the tent.

Ben was waiting by the fire. He smiled at the sight of her, and her face felt warm in the cool morning air.

"No disturbances in the night," he said as if she could have missed the noise it would have caused. "But I want that picture replaced. After breakfast, show me where you shot it."

"You might not want to go there," Pike put in from where he was drinking some of Dot's black coffee. The cavalrymen were checking the mules and horses.

"Why not?" Ben asked Pike as Meg accepted a cup Dot had poured.

"It wasn't stable ground, Captain," he

271

said. "She was lucky to get her picture the first time and come back in one piece."

That excuse would likely deter Ben. He certainly took her safety seriously. To her surprise, he merely nodded to Pike. "I'll keep that in mind. I trust Miss Pero to know her limitations."

Well, that was a first.

She kept glancing at him as they set out after breakfast. His floppy felt hat shaded his eyes from the early morning sun, the gold castle emblazoned on the crown glittering in the light. Though his uniform had seen better days, he walked with all the confidence of a man who knew his abilities and his worth.

He had insisted on carrying the camera and tripod. The box and hood rested in his capable hands, the long poles of the tripod bundled under one arm. She'd brought two plates with her this time. The light wouldn't be the same, but she wanted to make sure everything else went well.

"This way," she said, directing him through the trees.

They came out on the rim, and Ben stuck out the tripod to block her way forward as if thinking she would walk right into thin air.

"I see what Pike meant," he said, craning

his neck to peer over the edge. "That's a steep drop. You're sure this is stable?"

"I thought you trusted me," Meg challenged. She juggled the plates so she could point to where she wanted the tripod erected.

"I trust you," he assured her. "I'm not as sure about the terrain. What was it about this spot that drew your attention?"

As he planted the tripod in the dirt, Meg nodded down the canyon. "That."

He stared, lips slightly parted, and it was rather gratifying, even if she'd had nothing to do with the creation of the great window in the sky. She could only hope her stereograph would inspire such awe.

As Ben ranged along the rim, looking for an easy way down, she laid one of her plates aside and finished setting up the camera, then pulled the hood over her head and shoulders. Once more the world fell away to open up through her lens. As she had feared, the morning light anointed the end of the canyon but left the foreground in shadow. She could take the picture anyway, hope it turned out.

Meg pulled out from under the hood and waited for Ben to come back her way.

"Done?" he asked.

"No," Meg said. "I need to come back at

sunset. If you really want to make up for the lost picture, you'll let me."

Ben shifted on his booted feet. They had much to do if they were to stay on schedule. They had to finish the grid and begin packing up. Tomorrow Pike would lead them to the next base camp. And sunset was no time to be wandering near the edge of the canyon. One misstep . . .

Why did he have such a hard time refusing that winsome smile?

"I have a better idea," he said. "I want a closer look at the cliff across the way. Come back to camp with me now, and we'll collect Hank and my men and do a quick survey. That ought to put us here at the time you need."

"Oh, Ben, thank you!" She threw her arms around him for a hug.

She was soft against him, sweet. How many times had he held her, dreaming of more moments to come? It was the most natural thing in the world to lower his head now and kiss her.

Tenderness welled up so strongly he could only tighten his embrace, gather her closer, shelter her from whatever lay ahead. Why had he not pressed his case before, helped her see the future they might have together?

She pulled away, breaking the kiss, and he had no choice but to let go, even though everything in him demanded that he hold on.

She stepped back, eyes wide and cheeks fiery. "Why did you do that?"

*Because I never forgot you. Because I cannot forget you. Because I'm a fool.*

"I don't know," he told her. "You can slap me if you like."

She frowned as if considering the matter. "No. I don't think that will be necessary. It wasn't unpleasant."

Ben started laughing. "Such high praise, Miss Pero. You'll turn a fellow's head."

She began unscrewing her camera from the tripod. "Carry the extra plate, if you please."

"I'll carry the camera and tripod," he said, stepping closer again.

"No, thank you." He'd never seen that back so stiff. "I can see to them."

With a shake of his head at his own stupidity, he picked up the plate, then followed her back to camp.

Larson and Meadows seemed glad for a change of scenery. Adams was willing to cease scribbling, and Hank was interested in seeing what Meg had discovered, so they packed up what they needed and prepared to return to where Meg had tried to replace her picture. The corporal drove the van, so Meg would have her chemicals handy. Pike started to come with them, but Ben told him to stay with Dot. Neither looked pleased with the idea.

Meg walked along, chatting with Hank, as if nothing had changed. She'd said his kiss hadn't been unpleasant. Hardly encouragement. But not entirely discouragement. Why did he never know where he stood with her?

"I want a grid one deep all along the edge," Ben ordered when they reached the rim again, and Larson set about laying it out while Adams climbed down and saw to the mule team.

Meadows and Hank were standing beside Meg, gazing at the outcropping.

"A picture frame," Meadows said.

"Bit crooked," Hank said, tilting his head to one side as if trying to set the formation at right angles. "But it is a wonder. What do you think, Captain? Rock developed unevenly, leaving a hole?"

Ben shook his head. "More likely that window held softer material that was weathered away by wind, rain, snow, and ice. Easy, Private." He seized the hem of Meadows's blue uniform and hauled him back from the edge. "I'm not in that much of a hurry to see the bottom of the canyon."

He set Larson and Meadows to collecting samples while Adams and Meg described the terrain in the expedition journal and he and Hank examined the opposite cliff. More trees clung to the fragile surface, which told him there must be soil and perhaps ledges of flat ground. Possibility for a switchback trail, perhaps? Still, those were never easy on wagons.

Hank was less impressed. "Just as rugged as the rest of it," he proclaimed after closer inspection. "Looks like we keep going."

Ben reluctantly agreed. His thoughts should have been on their work, but he kept glancing back to watch Meg. She was perched on a rock, face turned to the canyon and pencil moving across the page. She was as focused on the landscape before her as her camera, determined to record every little curve and outcropping. She'd have made an excellent engineer.

The sun was low when Ben ordered a halt. Meg had recoated her plates and set up her camera. Now she was bent under the hood, as still as the canyon.

"About done, Meg?" Ben called.

"Not yet." Her voice came back muffled.

"What's she waiting for?" Larson asked

Meadows.

Meadows shrugged.

Hank hefted the mineral sample Ben wanted tested further. "Think I'll start back."

Ben nodded. "Meadows, go with him."

"Sir." The two started for the trees.

Larson kicked a rock and sent it bouncing over the edge. The rattle echoed around them. Adams shuddered.

"Meg?" Ben called.

"Not yet."

A moment more, and the sun touched the window, turning it to gold and spearing through it to land beyond. He heard the click and whir of the machine.

"So, that's what she was waiting for," Larson mused. "One touch from heaven."

And why she'd been heartbroken to have lost the picture. It was one shot in a million, and she'd captured it not once but twice.

"I'd be honored to carry your camera, ma'am," Larson said when she emerged from the hood in the golden light.

She slipped the plate out of its frame. "Thank you, Mr. Larson. I'll carry the plate."

"Only one?" Ben asked with a nod toward the other unused plate.

She sighed. "There wasn't time. The light fades too quickly. Now, if you'd let me come back tomorrow evening . . ."

"No," Ben said. "But I'm sure there will be other worthy sights along the way."

Her sigh said she doubted that.

Adams and Larson had the mules harnessed by the time she finished processing. At one point, Ben was certain he heard her humming. "Amazing Grace"? Well, that hole in the sky had been amazing. How could he ever tire of seeing all the variety in God's creation?

"Satisfied?" he asked her when she climbed down a short while later, plate tucked under one arm.

Her smile was his answer.

She followed him to the front of the van, where Adams sat waiting.

"Take the lead," Ben instructed. "We'll be right behind."

"And drive carefully," Meg added.

Adams sniffed. "I am always careful, Miss Pero."

Ben hid his smile. Then he noticed Larson staring toward the trees behind the van.

"Something's there," the private murmured.

The hairs rose on the back of Ben's neck. Their unwanted visitor, perhaps?

"What do you see?" Ben asked.

"Not sure," Larson said. "Low, kind of brown, fast."

Ben's stomach dropped as he caught sight of it as well. "Cougar."

# 18

Meg heard the word and stiffened, heart starting to race. Was that a streak of tawny gold among the trees? She sensed eyes on her every move.

The mules seemed to feel the same way. They shifted in their harness, setting the van to rocking. Holding her plate close, Meg clutched at a wheel with her free hand with the insane notion she could keep them safe and still.

Ben pulled the pistol from his belt, movements slow and steady. "Hold on to them, Corporal. The cat's probably just curious. Photography chemicals must be a novelty."

But surely not one the cougar would find palatable.

"At ease, now," Ben said as if he were dismissing his men to an evening of relaxation. "We don't want it to know we're concerned."

"I'm afraid it's much too late for that,"

Adams said, reining in the shuddering mules. "Permission to leave as fast as possible, sir?"

"Denied," Ben said. "Cats of any size chase prey that runs. Stay close together and make no sudden movements. Be as loud as you can."

She'd heard that. The big mountain lions preferred to take on strays, and size and sound made them unsure.

Larson saluted. "I'll do my best, sir!" he shouted.

"Excellent, Private," Ben shouted back, urging Meg behind him.

How hard could it be to shout? She'd called to her father often enough, trying to get his attention away from his camera and onto something more important like food and rent. She'd been known to bellow "Amazing Grace" when trying to keep herself awake after a long day photographing. She had certainly belted out a fairly decent scream the other night. Yet now the words seemed locked in her throat with her breath. On the bench, Adams looked as scared as she felt as he attempted to keep the team calm.

From out of nowhere, words popped into her mind and out of her mouth.

"The Lord is my light and my salvation;

whom shall I fear? The Lord is the strength of my life; of whom shall I be afraid?"

Had she heard it in some church service? Sung it in some hymn? Either way, Ben caught on immediately. With a grin, he shouted, "But they that wait upon the Lord shall renew their strength; they shall mount up with wings as eagles; they shall run, and not be weary; and they shall walk, and not faint."

Oh, for such strength now. She'd never thought these open woods could feel so confining. She wanted to pelt through the trees, hide behind a wide trunk. But both tactics would only encourage the cougar to give chase.

"The slothful man saith, there is a lion without, I shall be slain in the streets," Adams contributed.

Well, maybe that wasn't the best way to take her mind off their stalker!

"Turn the van, Corporal," Ben ordered. "Larson, Meg, when the bench is facing the other direction, climb up on either side."

Larson nodded and stepped back to give Adams room.

"What about you?" she asked Ben.

He kept his revolver trained in the direction they'd last spotted the cat. "I'll be right behind you."

Somehow, the corporal managed to turn the jittery mules. After tucking the plate behind the bench, Meg stepped up beside Adams and braced herself against the wall of the van. Larson did the same opposite her. The van bounced, and she could only hope that meant Ben had jumped onto the rear steps. "Back to camp now, Corporal," he called. "Give them their heads."

The corporal eased up on the reins, and the mules took off.

The van rattled and shook over the rough ground, every vibration reverberating up her body. A crash inside told her something had fallen. She could see her plate wedged in tightly, but right now, she couldn't afford to care what happened to it. Though she knew cougars rarely attacked so large a group, she felt as if their lives depended on reaching camp safely.

From the back of the van, the pistol barked.

"Ben!" she cried, even as Adams flinched.

"Keep going." Ben's voice was firm and in command. She tried to find a similar control of herself.

"There it is!" Larson cried, and, for a moment, she thought the cougar had leaped ahead of them. Then she saw it too. The white triangles of the tents poked up ahead.

"Slow, Corporal," Ben called, and Adams reined in the mules.

The van rocked again as Ben jumped off his perch to come around the van at a confident saunter she could only envy.

"Ho, the camp!" he called. "Cougar! Bring your rifles."

A moment later, and Hank, Meadows, and Pike had joined them. They raised their rifles to point out into the trees. Meg pulled out her plate and went with Larson and Ben to cross beyond them. Ben and Larson went to fetch their own rifles.

Meg picked up her skirts with her free hand and dashed into the circle of the fire, where Dot stood, heaping on the wood, her cook pots pulled away from the heat.

"Cougars don't trust the flames," she told Meg. "Seen too many wildfires, I suppose. Stay still and try to look bigger than you are."

Easier said than done. Meg mimicked Dot, widening her stance to spread her skirts, holding her plate with two hands so she could point her elbows out. She still didn't feel much bigger, but the fire was another matter. It crackled as it climbed, sending shadows leaping up the trees around them in the twilight.

Ben, Hank, and the guide dropped back

to camp, their gazes watchful, their guns trained, while Meadows and Larson went to help Adams release the team. The horses must have sensed the cat as well, for they snorted and pulled at the picket line. The remaining mules grunted and shuffled closer together. As the firelight flickered over the nearest, Meg saw their eyes showing white.

"We could lose them all if that cat gets much closer," Hank said to the others. "They'll yank themselves off the picket and run as far and fast as they can."

"We will hold them," Adams promised, and Meadows and Larson nodded.

Ben stepped forward. Meg wasn't aware she'd started after him until Dot caught her arm.

"Scat!" he shouted into the darkness. "Shoo! We're ready for you." As if to prove it, he aimed his rifle into the trees and fired. The sound echoed, rolling along the canyon. Was that rustling in its wake the sound of branches as the big cat moved away as well?

The three cavalrymen set about soothing the animals, and everyone else remained vigilant until darkness wrapped the camp. Meg slipped her precious plate into a saddlebag for safekeeping. The animals eventually quieted some, and Dot served

286

supper. The men took turns eating and watching the woods, rifles at the ready. They all kept the fire high and their voices loud, just in case. Meg's ears started to ache with the sound.

Ben seemed the least affected. It had been the same after he'd kissed her. She'd been amazed, delighted, and just a little terrified to feel those familiar emotions crowding around her. Yet he'd joked about it, offered to let her slap him as if he'd insulted her. Why did she struggle to understand this man?

Though his rifle was always in easy reach, he talked and joked now. Larson and Meadows stopped staring into the darkness. Hank slipped his arm around Dot's waist as she huddled against him.

"My father was passing through Illinois in 1858," Ben said, poking another log into the fire with his boot. "He stopped to hear one of the debates between Lincoln, who was running for the senate, and Stephen Douglas, his opponent. Lincoln told a story about an old woman whose cantankerous husband got into a brawl with a bear. If her husband won, she'd be safe from the bear. If the bear won, she'd be safe from her husband. Not knowing which was worse, she rooted for both."

Larson let out a guffaw.

Meg knew how the woman had felt. She didn't know whether to draw closer to Ben or run as fast as she could in the opposite direction.

"Well, I'm not rooting for that cat," Pike said, eyes on the trees and finger on the trigger of his gun. "Can't track it, much less hunt it, in the dark."

Ben leaned forward, and the firelight highlighted his cheekbones. "We don't need to hunt it. The important thing tonight is to keep the cat out of camp and away from the horses and mules. Dot, commandeer whoever you need to assist you on kitchen duty. I want this place spotless — nothing to draw it in."

Dot nodded. "Count on me, Captain. That cat will get no meal on my watch."

"Or mine," Pike said, and the other men nodded.

"If you think I can sleep, you're all mad," Meg said.

Ben smiled. "Then we'll keep each other company. We'll sleep out in the open tonight, two or three on each side of the picket line, one awake while his companions sleep. For now, Dot, you have the command."

Dot had already been heating water on the edge of the fire. Now she set Pike to washing and Larson to drying. She and Meg bundled all the food into sacks and confined it in boxes to minimize the scent. Meadows dug a hole and buried the remains of dinner deep. Then Dot swept a flaming branch over the area as if hoping to mask any remaining odor.

"It won't be so bad sleeping out," the cook said as she and Meg carried their bedrolls closer to the picket line a short while later. "Nice night for it."

In all the hubbub, Meg hadn't noticed. Now she looked up. Thousands of lights clustered above her, glittering against the black of the sky.

"That's a shot," Ben said, stopping beside her to look up as well.

"Someday we'll have a camera to capture it," Meg said, feeling as if the sky were tugging her closer. "Color too. Just think of the pictures we can create."

"You already create beauty," he said.

Meg smiled. "No. I just re-create it, and I know I never completely do it justice."

They positioned themselves around the picket area, close enough that the horses and mules could see them but far enough back to avoid most of the flies. The horse soldiers had confined the animals in a rope triangle anchored to trees. Pike, Hank, and

289

Adams faced southwest, the direction from which the cat had come.

"I see the strategy of Mr. Pike and Hank," Meg told Ben. "But Adams?"

Ben glanced at the scrawny corporal. "You wouldn't know it to look at him, but he's a crack shot, according to Colonel Yearling."

Meadows and Larson took the northeast, and Meg, Dot, and Ben faced the camp and rim. Meg didn't have to ask why she was stationed at the least likely advance. She certainly wasn't a crack shot, except behind the lens of a camera.

She started to spread her bedroll next to Dot's, but the cook promptly repositioned hers between Meg and Ben.

"Keeping watch for a cougar doesn't offer much opportunity to compromise my reputation," Meg pointed out.

"Just doing my duty," Dot said with a satisfied nod. She climbed into her bedroll. "Wake me when it's my turn to watch."

With Ben sitting up, Meg might have gone to sleep as well, but she couldn't be easy. The horses and mules couldn't seem to relax either. They remained on their feet, shifting this way and that, grunting and snorting, as if keeping watch from all directions. The ropes picketing them had never seemed so fragile.

Meg edged around Dot to sit next to Ben, and he nodded as if glad for her company. The brass on the rifle lying across his knees flashed in the starlight as he shifted. Behind him, Stripe lowered her head over the picket line and blew softly against Meg's hair.

Meg reached up and stroked the velvety muzzle. "Isn't there anything we can do to ease their fears?"

"Yes, ma'am." The answer was from Larson on her left. "They like it when you sing to them."

The derisive snort was likely Pike's. His gruff voice confirmed it. "I'm not singing to a bunch of mules."

"I have heard it done and done well." That precise protest had to be Adams.

"I tell you we can do it," Larson insisted. She heard a murmur as he must have spoken to Meadows. When the song began, she was surprised to hear Meadows's soft tenor.

Oh, Shenandoah, I hear you calling,
Away, you rolling river.
Yes, far away
I hear you calling.
Away, I'm bound away
Cross the wide Missouri.

"Might as well say the deep Colorado," Pike called.

His teasing didn't stop the young private. The horses and mules stilled, and Meg felt as if even the stars dipped closer to listen.

My girl, she's gone down the river,
Away, you rolling river.
And I ain't going to see her never.
Away, I'm bound away
Cross the wide Missouri.

The private had lost his family to the war. He'd left whatever lay behind to join the Army and head West. Was there a girl gazing across the Missouri, waiting for his return?

In the dark, something caressed her hand. She turned her palm to meet Ben's. Her skin cooled as the breeze brushed the tears from her cheeks like tender fingers.

"Never is a long time," he murmured. "It doesn't have to be that way with us."

Sitting here, with God's canopy spread above her, Ben's hand holding hers, she could almost believe that. But there was another world out there, wide as the mighty Missouri. And she wasn't certain she was willing to cross it, even knowing Ben was waiting on the other side.

Ben blinked as the sky began to pale in the east. He'd spent the night sitting up, letting Dot and Meg sleep. He'd dozed off once or twice but kept waking to make sure Meg was all right. Seven people and more than two dozen mules and horses relied on him, and she remained at the top of his mind.

She'd fallen asleep next to him, curled on one side. He watched as the rosy light inched past her chin, less determined-looking in sleep, to her soft lips and the golden fringe of her lashes. They fluttered, opened, to reveal eyes like jade glowing up at him.

Ben looked away.

"We made it through the night," she marveled, sitting up.

On the other side of her, Dot stirred, then sat, frowning as she glanced from where Meg should have been sleeping to where she was lying now.

"Let's confirm everyone's fine," Ben said. Raising his voice, he called out. "Pike, Adams, Meadows, Larson, Newcomb, report!"

"Here," came Pike's voice, sounding more annoyed than usual.

"Here," Larson shouted with a less forceful echo from Meadows.

"Here, sir," the corporal offered.

"Here," Hank called.

Ben climbed to his feet. "Soldiers, see to our mounts and the mules. Pike, let's discover where our feline friend went. Hank, Meg, help Dot start breakfast."

"Sir," his men chorused.

Meg yawned before she waved her hand in agreement.

The hand he'd cradled until she fell asleep.

Had she heard his whisper in the dark? Was her silence his answer?

Pike approached around the corner of the picket line. Though he'd likely slept as little as Ben, he looked no scruffier than usual, black hair and beard unkempt. With a last glance at Meg, Ben hoisted his rifle, and he and the guide set out.

The dry golden soil made it difficult to track the cat, but they found a few prints too close to the camp for comfort.

Standing from examining the clearest impression, Pike looked away from the rising sun. "Headed west along the canyon by the look of it. We'll be following it if we continue the way you wanted. We must have strayed into its territory. Best we move inland for a while, circle back a few miles on."

Ben shook his head. "Our task is to search

along the rim for ways to cross. We already detoured once for water. Take Hank with you this morning and scout ahead for the next camp, as close to the rim as possible."

"I can move faster alone," Pike offered.

"Hank can keep up, and two make a less likely target."

Ben turned and started back, and Pike fell in beside him.

They broke camp that morning. Adams, Larson, Meadows, Dot, and Meg all pitched in to return the photography boxes to the van, righting the metal canister that had fallen in their wild ride yesterday. They struck the tents and loaded the supplies and equipment on the mules and into the wagon and van. Hank and Pike had already set out. Ben intended to meet them returning with the news of the next site.

He left his gear to the last. Meg and Dot had already packed his tent. The saddlebag with his personal belongings stood waiting. Crouching, he opened it to reach for his gauntlets.

A wildflower lay on top, the red of the paintbrush bright against the blue of his spare uniform.

Ben glanced up. Meadows and Larson were busy with the mules. Adams was checking the harness on his. Dot was sprinkling water over the last of the coals to cool them before leaving. Meg was down by the spring, filling the canteens. Was that pink in her cheeks, or the shadow from her hat?

Had she noticed his attempt to bring her flowers the other day after all? He'd thought it lost in the greater urgency to replace her shot. Was this flower her response?

Never had a single bloom held such hope. He picked it up, snapped off the short stem, and tucked the plume into the band on his hat. If she was bent on encouraging him, he'd return the favor.

## 19

The ride to the next camp seemed endless. Meg tried not to think about the cougar, but any movement among the trees caused her muscles to stiffen. At least the mules had calmed. They walked with no more than an occasional twitch of their long ears or swish of their long tails. The horses remained skittish, shying away from bushes close to their path, the sudden appearance of a chipmunk scurrying away. Meg patted and cooed to Stripe, who was carrying her plate. At least the mare proved sensible when the rain started once more.

This shower was less powerful than the storm that had rolled through earlier. The two young cavalrymen had time to don their rubberized canvas ponchos. They looked like crows with slick black feathers riding among the mules. Ben cantered back and offered his poncho to Meg.

"Mighty gallant, Captain," Dot said where

she sheltered under the canvas vault of the wagon.

"Thank you," Meg said, accepting the oblong material. She pulled it over her head, ducked through the central opening, and put her hat back on. His smile made her feel as if she were wearing the most fashionable gown at the ball.

The squall was over a few minutes later, leaving the sky looking newly washed. Once more steam rose from foliage and rocks, until she and the others moved through a silver mist.

Perhaps the greatest source of calm was Ben himself. He rode along, head high, one gauntleted hand resting on his thigh, as if he was on his way to a dress parade instead of another wilderness camp. Somewhere he'd picked up a red flower, long and tufty, which he wore like a crimson feather in his hat. Every time Meg looked at it, bedraggled now from the rain, she found herself smiling.

Or maybe it was the man wearing the flower that made her smile. She tried not to think of that too often.

They followed the canyon where they could, each turn bringing new perspectives, vaster prospects. In places, the steep and rugged terrain forced them inland, among stands of pine and spruce dotted with aspen, the leaves fluttering in the breeze. As the day warmed, the tang of pine resin filled the air. Meg took off Ben's poncho and draped it over her saddle.

Deeper fissures caused more detours. Ben dismounted and studied each, but none seemed suitable for a wagon road up from the river. She was glad when they reached an open plain between stands of trees.

"Such a purposeful fellow, that Captain Coleridge," Dot said from where she drove the wagon beside Meg and Stripe. "Always working."

"He is that," Meg said, tipping her chin to see the latest view. So many of them would have made fine shots, but she could not delay Ben, not today.

"Nice that he picked you flowers," Dot said.

Meg turned to her with a frown. "When did he pick me flowers?"

Dot blinked as if the sun had reached under her wide-brimmed straw hat. "Two days ago. Saw him myself as he was coming back toward camp, fist full of posies. I doubt he gave them to Larson."

So did she. And she couldn't help remembering the stems she'd crushed after finding her plate destroyed. Had Ben intended to present her with a bouquet?

"He never gave them to me either," she told Dot.

Dot eyed her. "Funny. Wouldn't have been like him to turn tail. He strikes me as a fellow who knows what he's about when he's courting."

Meg focused her gaze forward. "He was probably just being thoughtful."

"Thoughtful?" Dot slapped her hand down on her skirts with a crack that set the mules to stepping higher. "A lad bringing daisies for his mother is thoughtful. A man bringing flowers to his sweetheart is much more."

Inside her, something reached for the hope in Dot's words. She shoved it down.

"Captain Coleridge and I are not sweethearts," Meg informed her, meeting her gaze.

"You could be," Dot said with a wiggle of her brows. "Likely he's thinking that direction, especially after finding that pretty red flower."

Meg gasped. "Did you leave it for him?"

Dot glanced skyward. "Well, I'm not saying I did, and I'm not saying I didn't. If I had to guess, I'd say he thinks it came from someone who dotes on him."

Very likely he did. Meg drew in a breath

to slow her temper. "But it didn't. Stop trying to play matchmaker."

Dot's eyes widened. "Me? I don't have a romantic bone in my whole body. Hank, now . . ." She glanced ahead to where her husband rode with Ben and sighed happily. "Hank knows how to touch a lady's heart."

It was impossible to stay mad at her friend. Dot just looked so happy. "I'm glad you two made up," Meg said.

Dot sighed again. "That grin, a few charming words, and I melt."

"I suspect the mint didn't hurt," Meg said.

Dot laughed. "No, ma'am, it did not. He knows what touches my heart. And he knows how to calm my odd humors. That's the sort of man you want in your life — someone who challenges you to be the best you can be."

Ben certainly believed in her abilities with a camera. But she knew her ability and willingness to fit into good society.

"That lets Captain Coleridge out," Meg said.

Dot urged her team to keep moving. "Why would you say that? He encourages everyone."

"He does," Meg agreed. "His family is different."

Dot nodded. "When Hank and I were

with the Colonel in California, he didn't take Hank's refusal to sign another contract well. Hank wanted to pan for gold. Too many of the Colonel's men ran off and did the same. Much good it did me and Hank. He ended up surveying for the territorial government while I cooked in a mining camp, just to make ends meet. Still, the Colonel recommended Hank for survey work after all the fighting was over, so the man didn't hold a grudge. A shame he's gone."

A great shame. Yet Ben held on to hope. Meg had a feeling he wasn't just looking at the terrain down those side canyons. He wanted to catch any sign his father had traveled the same path.

"Colonel Coleridge was a strict disciplinarian," Meg acknowledged. "He had high expectations too. But he's nothing to his wife."

Dot glanced her way. "You met her? She was at the Presidio in San Francisco, but she wasn't likely to say good day to folks like me and Hank."

Perhaps it was time Dot knew more about Meg's past. If she understood the gulf between Meg and Ben, she might stop trying to match them up.

"She didn't like saying good day to me

either," she told her friend. "My father ran the photography studio at West Point when Captain Coleridge was a cadet there. I met him socially a number of times."

"Met him socially," Dot repeated. "What does that mean?"

"Oh, you know," Meg said with a wave of her hand. "Dances, church services, picnics."

Dot smiled. "He was courting you."

"It started out a courtship," Meg said. "But I realized I wasn't looking to marry."

Dot's smile faded. "Why not?"

This was harder than she would have thought. She glanced ahead, made sure Ben and Hank were far enough away that they might not overhear. "I like taking pictures, Dot. A husband might not approve."

Dot shook her head. "Not the captain. He admires what you do."

"He might. His mother didn't."

"Well," Dot said, squaring her shoulders, "it's a good thing you're marrying the captain and not his mother, then."

Despite herself, Meg laughed. "I am not marrying Captain Coleridge. He's like his father, determined to make the Army his career. I would never fit in his circle."

"I don't see why not," Dot insisted. "I've been attached to the Army my whole life.

I'm nothing special."

"You and I are never going to agree on that," Meg told her. "I find you quite special indeed. But don't you feel the least uncomfortable next to some of the officers' wives?"

" 'Course I do," Dot said with a hitch of her shoulders, as if she could feel the proud beauties staring at her all the way out here. "But I love Hank too much to let him go."

"Then perhaps," Meg said, "I don't care for Captain Coleridge enough, because it wasn't all that hard to let him go."

Dot frowned as if she couldn't believe that. Even Meg heard the false note to the statement. But words had to be true. She wasn't made for marriage to an Army officer. Ben's mother had understood that all too well. Meg could still see the uplift of her nose, the gaze that went past Meg as if seeking someone of greater worth. Meg had to fight for her right to ply her trade everywhere else. She wasn't about to fight with a husband and his family over it.

Dot, however, clearly hadn't given up.

"You could still win him," she said thoughtfully, gaze on Ben's back. "At the moment, you have his attention. Seize the skillet while it's hot."

"No," Meg told her again. "Ben and I had a falling-out at West Point. We've since settled our differences, and we can be cordial. I won't push for more."

"Then you settle for less," Dot said, voice laced with frustration.

"It's my decision," Meg reminded her. "Not yours, not Hank's."

"Sounds like it was Mrs. Colonel Coleridge's decision," Dot muttered, then she flinched when Meg glanced her way.

"Just think on the matter," Dot urged. "That's all I'm asking."

Meg nodded. Thinking was all she could do. For if she opened her mouth, she very much feared she might hear herself give in to Dot's persuasion.

Hank rode back to meet them later in the day.

"No sign of the cougar," he reported. "We may have moved beyond its hunting ground."

They'd moved all right. Too far, in Ben's opinion. He'd done no more than peer into the many side canyons that led like cracks to the larger draw. None had seemed ideal for the Army's road across the canyon, but at least one had held promise.

"How far to where Pike wants us to camp?" he asked the cartographer.

"Another few miles, and a bit inland."

Ben felt his temper rising and knew it wasn't just from lack of sleep. "I told him I wanted to camp close to the rim. We can't tell if there's a way across the canyon if we never venture close to the canyon."

Hank pressed his lips together a moment. "Nothing says we can't follow the rim for a while now."

Ben cocked a grin. "You're a man after my own heart, Mr. Newcomb."

"I feel the same way, Captain Coleridge."

That decided, they continued along the rim, just far enough away to be certain the weight of the horses, mules, van, and wagon wouldn't set the ground to falling. Hank looked back to where Ben had already noticed Dot and Meg deep in conversation. Meg's horse had been close to the wagon, and each woman's face had been serious.

"What have those two been discussing?" Hank asked.

"I have no idea," Ben told him.

"You have no idea, huh?" Hank teased him. "For all you know, they're talking about you."

Ben couldn't help another glance back, enough to catch a glimpse of Meg smiling about something Dot had said. That one look was enough to set him smiling. He schooled his face and turned to the front once more. "Nonsense."

Hank laughed.

The trees were thinning here, brush as well. They rode down into a sheltered draw, white rocks poking up through the soil and grass plentiful. The mules were balking, ready to partake. Ben could hear Meadows and Larson calling to the beasts to keep them moving.

Hank tipped his head toward a thicker clump of trees. "Spring that way. I can hear it."

So could Ben. A stream meandered away from the water, heading for the deeper canyon beyond. He raised his hand and reined in. Meg and Dot caught up to him and stopped as well. Adams drove the van up beside them.

Ben looked to Hank. "How close are we to Pike now?"

Hank pointed up over the farther side of the draw. "That way another mile."

"Good water?" Ben pressed.

Hank scratched his ear. "Some water, not as much as this. And not as much forage either."

Ben shook his head. "Then I say we stop here instead. Do you see any reason to continue, Mr. Newcomb?"

Hank grinned. "None in the slightest,

Captain. I'll ride on and fetch Pike for you."

Ben agreed, and the others began setting up camp. Ben was drawn to Meg's side. She had dismounted and had yet to fetch her camera from the van, while Adams was unharnessing the mules. She was gazing down the draw, one hand stroking the stripe on her horse's nose.

"I like it here," she said when he stopped beside her. "It's pretty."

Cool shadows danced across her face in the breeze. "Yes," Ben said. "It is."

Her cheeks darkened in a blush as rosy as the sunset. "I should help Dot." Tugging on the bridle, she led her horse away.

If she had left him the flower to encourage him, she was certainly rethinking her actions now. Aware of a distinct lowering of his spirits, he went to unload his own belongings.

Hank and their guide returned quickly, horses in a bit of a lather. Ben looked up from where he'd been helping Dot build her fire ring, then stood up as they reined in. Meadows came to take charge of their horses.

Pike strode up to Ben, eyes narrowed and face dark. "Did you hire me as guide or not?"

"You know very well why you were hired,

Mr. Pike," Ben said, refusing to show so much as a hesitation in the face of his anger.

"I thought I knew. But I spend all day finding you a campsite, and you stop anywhere you please. Let me guess. Little miss thought it was pretty enough for a picture."

Near her tent, Meg raised her head, cheeks once more turning rosy. She might think the place pretty, but that wasn't why he'd chosen it.

"I didn't consult Miss Pero," Ben said. "I don't need to consult you, for that matter. There's water, forage, and shelter. If I've missed some danger to the place, speak now, and I'll reconsider."

Pike's beard wiggled with his jaw. "Danger? Flash flood good enough for you?"

Hank was watching the guide. "That spring is unlikely to swell enough for a flash flood, even with a driving rain."

Pike rounded on him. "You sure about that?"

Hank met his gaze. "Positive."

Pike threw up his hands. "I give up. Camp on the moon if it suits you. Just remember. I warned you." He stalked off to see to his horse.

Hank shook his head. "Prickly fellow. But he'll come around."

Ben wasn't so sure. The air felt tense, as if

a storm was brewing, and he wasn't sure the thunder would be entirely above them.

As if he knew Ben needed a distraction, Hank nudged his arm. "Found something. You need to see this."

Intrigued, Ben followed him through the trees to where the draw dropped off into a side canyon running southwest toward its bigger sister. Even after eight days, the sight of the canyon stretching away in the distance never failed to leave him humbled.

"Look there," Hank said, pointing.

It had once been a sizeable outcropping. Now the sides had crumbled away, leaving bright stone at the top. The rocks below glowed red in the setting sun.

Ben grinned at Hank. "That's a picture."

Hank grinned back. "I know someone else who'd agree."

Ben cuffed him on the shoulder as they started back to the others. "You didn't need my permission to tell her. That's too good to miss."

"Well," Hank said, ducking under a low-hanging branch, "I thought it might raise your status in her eyes if you told her."

Ben glanced at him. The cartographer loped along, gaze on the ground before them, mouth relaxed. "You're not playing matchmaker, are you, Hank?"

Hank shot him a look, eyes wide. "Who, me?"

Ben shook his head. "Save yourself the trouble. Meg Pero isn't interested in having me court her."

"You sure about that?" Hank pressed, sounding a little like Pike.

"More sure than I'd like," Ben admitted. "We knew each other at West Point. I proposed marriage. She refused. Told me we could never be more than friends. I thought she might have reconsidered, but I don't seem to be making any headway."

Hank shrugged. "Times change. People change. You could keep trying."

"And give my pride another beating?"

"Huh." Hank scratched his grizzled chin. "Never thought you'd be one to run scared."

Ben jerked to a stop. "I've never run from a fight, never withdrew from danger. I wasn't raised that way."

"So how come you're willing to give up on love without a fight?" Hank didn't wait for his answer but continued on to where Dot and Meg were helping Larson and Meadows set up the tents.

Ben remained still, feeling as if his cartographer had planted a fist in his gut. He'd been so sure once that Meg was the one for him. Even now he felt the tug toward her, like a moon caught in her orbit.

So, if she was the perfect woman for him, why had he given up years ago? Had it been only pride, as he'd told Hank? He'd been young, altogether too full of himself. Her refusal had hurt. Instead of trying to overcome her reservations, he'd let her go.

They were dancing the same pattern now — him pursuing, her retreating. But winning her wasn't about his pride this time. She was more than an intriguing beauty across the ballroom floor. She was clever, talented, caring.

Could he find a way to break the pattern and reach a happier end, for them both?

# 20

Meg had the routine memorized. Unload and carry the lashed tents to the sites. Pound in stakes six feet apart in a square using Adams's mallet or a handy rock. Unlash and erect the poles, setting them deep and tying them to the stakes to keep them upright. String the rope between them. Hang the canvas and stretch it out. Go back for the folding cots and bedding as well as her personal items.

She had the tent up and her gear stowed in short order. She was walking along the edge of the draw, helping Meadows gather wood for the fire, when Hank and Ben returned.

"We have an appointment at dawn, Miss Pero," Ben announced.

Meadows raised his head. Meg glanced at Hank for a clue, but the cartographer excused himself to go help Dot prepare dinner.

"An appointment?" she asked Ben.

"Bring both your cameras," he said. "And plates."

A tingle ran through her. "Yes, sir." She snapped a salute.

"You do that real well," Meadows said as he passed her with a load of wood bundled in his arms.

She tried to pry the truth out of Ben over a dinner of salt pork and hardtack soaked in water and fried with dried apples.

"Did you find another window?" she asked.

Mouth full of Dot's cinnamon apple concoction but eyes twinkling, he shook his head.

"A field of wildflowers, all the colors under the sky?" Dot guessed.

Ben shook his head again.

"A Roman temple," Hank offered.

"There's a heathen church in the canyon?" Larson asked with a frown.

Ben swallowed and spoke at last. "No. It's more like a courthouse, and I would have said Greek. I was thinking the Acropolis."

Larson's frown deepened, but Adams perked up. "The Acropolis?"

"What's a cra-po-lis?" Dot asked.

"An ancient palace," the corporal answered. "But I hardly think you'll find such out here."

"You'll all see tomorrow," Hank promised. And Meg could get nothing more out of him or Ben.

"Teases," she complained to Dot as she helped clean up after dinner, the men standing near Ben's tent debating the need for sentries. "Courthouses, temples, and palaces. What am I to make of that?"

"Hank has the right of it," Dot said, scrubbing dried apples out of her biggest skillet. "This place is a temple of sorts. If all this beauty doesn't make you think of your Creator, I don't know what would."

"I know what you mean," Meg said. "I understand enough about geology to know this canyon formed over many years. Captain Coleridge said God put it here for us to find. Why does it make me feel as if every vista was carved with me in mind, meant to take my breath away?"

"You're an artist of a sort," Dot said. "Aren't artists supposed to be a little mad?"

She laughed. "So the story goes. I never believed it, until now."

The others must have felt a similar awe, for she found Larson, Meadows, Adams, and Hank near her tent at the edge of the campsite, gazing out over the shadowy draw.

"Something about it calls to one," Adams

315

murmured.

Larson elbowed Meadows. "Maybe we should call to it in return. Halloo!"

The word careened down the canyon, growing fainter and deeper.

"Twelve," Meadows said.

"Twelve?" Meg asked.

Larson glanced over his shoulder at her. "The number of times it bounces. You try."

They all looked to her.

"I'm not sure what to say," Meg admitted.

"Say your name," Ben suggested, striding up to them. "Like this." He raised his voice. "Ben!"

*Ben-Ben-Ben,* the canyon replied.

"Meg!" she shouted.

*Meg-Meg-Meg,* started the echo, but the words collided on their way down the draw, until all she heard was *Ben-Meg-Ben-Meg.*

Ben and Meg.

Did the canyon know something she didn't? Hank and the two privates thought so, for they were all grinning at her. She excused herself, cheeks warm, and escaped to her tent.

She was awakened by the sound of the canvas snapping as someone shook it the next morning.

316

"Rise and shine, Madam Photographer," Ben called. "The light will be here before you know it."

Meg had laid out the bottles holding her chemicals the night before, so it was easy enough to prepare the collodion, soak the plates, and load them into the cameras before extinguishing her lantern and exiting the van. The sky was still pearly gray. Ben carried the tripod and one camera, and she carried the other, and they headed out just as Dot went to start breakfast.

He led Meg through the trees, careful to point out roots jutting up through the soil and offering a hand over fallen limbs. In places he used the tripod to prop up branches, so she could walk more easily. In the smoky light, she could see the canyon, an empty space beyond the last tree, but she wasn't prepared for the sight when he drew her out onto a vantage point.

The canyon was broader here, impossibly craggy, with outcroppings and ridges at odd angles, debris fallen around their bases. Directly ahead, row after row of red rock was crowned by nearly white stone in sheer square blocks that thrust up into the sky, like monuments in a proud city.

"Acropolis indeed," she murmured.

"Sun's coming up," Ben said.

"Hurry." She took the tripod from him and settled it into place, then reached for the big camera and positioned it, judging the angle before she screwed it into place. She glanced back over her shoulder. Light sprang into the world, washing the stones pink. She would never have enough time to take two pictures before the light changed again.

"Man this lens," she ordered Ben, straightening away from the camera to reach for her stereographic one.

He started. "But . . ."

"Do it, or we'll miss the shot."

She didn't wait for his reply. She had to trust he would follow her lead.

She stretched out on the ground, propped the stereographic camera on a rock, as level as she could make it.

"Focus on the closest block," she instructed him. "Try to get as much as you can of the second in the background." She ducked inside the hood and fiddled with the lens until Ben's mythical courthouse came into view, centered on her perspective. "There!"

"Got it," he said a moment later.

"On my mark," she said. "Take the shot in three, two, one, go!" She set the exposure in time to hear the click and whirl of the

318

second camera.

She emerged from the hood the same moment Ben did. His hat was askew, and sweat gleamed on his brow for all it was still cool.

"I think I got it," he said.

"We'll find out when we look at the negatives later," Meg replied. "That was quick action, Captain. You've earned your breakfast."

Ben saluted her. "Ma'am."

He did not seem in a hurry to return to camp, moving slowly over the rough terrain. He might have been protecting the camera in his grip, but she too felt the need to pause, to breathe in the world around her. Light filtered through the trees, making lacy patterns on the golden soil. Birds sang before darting away from her steps. Such beauty, such peace.

Ben tucked the tripod under his arm and reached for her free hand. She took his, allowing his strength to help her, encourage her. For a moment, his company was all she needed.

He hesitated in the trees at the edge of camp. She could hear Dot calling for more wood, the whinny of a horse welcoming Larson or Meadows. She could not take her eyes off Ben, who was gazing down at their joined fingers, eyes as misty as the morning light.

"I'm not the boy who let you go, Meg," he murmured. "I find myself wondering whether we might be more to each other than the friends you claimed."

He stopped, and her heart started beating faster.

"I wonder too," she whispered.

He squeezed her hand. "Then let's follow the path and see where it leads."

Her lips trembled. "Spoken like an Army engineer."

He raised his head, the blue of his eyes drawing her closer. "Then let me state it in your terms. Take the shot, Meg. Let's see what develops."

What develops. Most times, her preparations and eye for the angle brought forth a picture worth sharing. But sometimes, no matter how well she prepared the plate, calculated the light, and focused the lens, the picture was flawed.

Useless. No good to anyone.

She swallowed the lump in her throat. "I always take the shot."

His smile widened even as he bent his head toward hers. Her eyes drifted shut, chin tilted up, every part of her waiting for that touch of his lips to hers, that moment when, for a fleeting moment, they shared one heart, one kiss.

"You coming for breakfast?" Pike asked.

Meg's eyes snapped open in time to see Ben jerk upright. He released her to adjust his hat and fix his scowl on the guide. "On our way."

Pike stepped aside to let them pass, but not before Meg caught his smirk.

She'd just agreed to a courtship with the one man she wasn't sure she should have, in a camp where no one had any expectation of privacy. Perhaps she really was a little mad.

Ben walked into camp with Meg beside him. He wouldn't have been surprised if his step held a swagger. The smartest, prettiest, most talented woman he'd ever met had agreed to a courtship. And this time, he wouldn't give up so quickly.

Adams had something else on his mind. He approached Ben after they all finished a breakfast of cornmeal mush and Dot's cinnamon rolls.

"Would you be willing to say a few words to the troops, sir?" he asked.

He made it sound as if Ben had a regiment at his command. "Something wrong, Corporal?" Ben asked.

"Just attempting to maintain morale, sir," Adams said, chin inching up.

One of the corporal's duties was to see to the well-being of the men. If he thought they needed encouragement, Ben should offer it.

He assembled everyone at the rear of the camp, his back to the canyon, their faces toward it. He wasn't sure what Adams wanted him to address, but the corporal seemed to have an idea, for he handed Ben the Bible, already open, and pointed to a set of verses.

"I thought these would be fitting under the circumstances, sir." He stepped back next to the privates with a stern look to them. Larson and Meadows stiffened their spines.

Ben glanced at the verses. Interesting choice. What was the corporal trying to achieve? Looking up, he found all gazes on his, ranging from expectant to wary. Ben straightened.

"Thank you for joining me," he told them all. "I have before me Philippians two, verses fourteen through sixteen: 'Do all things without murmurings and disputings: That ye may be blameless and harmless, the sons of God, without rebuke, in the midst of a crooked and perverse nation, among whom ye shine as lights in the world.' "

He paused to glance around. Meadows and Larson appeared to be listening intently, their gazes latched onto Ben. Hank was nodding along. But Adams, Dot, and Meg were all looking at Pike with narrowed eyes. Had they heard the altercation yesterday over the campsite? Or had Pike been sowing more dissent?

" 'Holding forth the word of life,' " Ben continued, " 'that I may rejoice in the day of Christ, that I have not run in vain, neither laboured in vain.' "

"Amen," Meadows said, then blushed as Adams frowned in his direction.

Ben closed the Bible, more sure of the purpose of this meeting. "We've all been working hard. I can see that, and I appreciate your efforts. I know it feels futile sometimes. It's easy to get disappointed and irritable."

His mind brought up a picture of the Colonel, as if taunting Ben with his own failure. He pushed the vision aside.

"We haven't found anything of import yet, but that in itself is telling. We've ruled out whole sections of the canyon. And I have high hopes that, in the end, we won't have labored in vain. Hold on to your faith, hold on to hope. In the end, like the apostle Paul,

323

we can rejoice in having done our all. Dismissed."

Adams came to take the Bible from him.

"Will that settle things, Corporal?" Ben said.

The skin around the corporal's brown eyes tightened. "Only time will tell, sir," he said with a sidelong glance at Pike, who stalked off as if glad to distance himself from them all.

Ben thanked him and intercepted Meg before she could go prepare more plates.

"Has Mr. Pike been troubling you?" he asked.

She looked to where the big man was saddling his horse, while Meadows hovered helpfully nearby. "You know I didn't much like the way he carried tales to you. Dot mentioned he'd said something to cause a rift between her and Hank as well."

"Corporal Adams isn't much pleased with him either," Ben told her. "I'll speak to Pike when he gets back from hunting. The last thing we need is internal strife."

"Agreed." She tucked back a strand of hair before he could reach out and do it, and disappointment tugged at him anew.

"Dine with me tonight?" he asked.

She fluttered her lashes. "At such a fine establishment? Why, Captain Coleridge, you honor me."

"Only the best for my sweetheart," he said.

Her smile faltered only the slightest. "Let's take that path slowly."

He felt shackled, but he didn't want to push her. "Consider dinner no more than mixing the collodion. Nothing commits you to taking the shot." With a tip of his hat, he moved away when everything told him to stay.

He couldn't stay. He had work to do.

He set Larson and Meadows to measuring off the grid and asked Meg to assist Hank and Adams with the surveying. With no sign of predators, four-footed or two-footed, he felt comfortable enough letting each work as they willed. As the others went about their tasks, he crouched beside Dot near the fire.

"Pack me hardtack and water," he told her. "And if there are any cinnamon rolls left from breakfast, I wouldn't mind one of them either."

Dot's smile widened. "Coming right up. You heading out on your own?"

"I just want to make sure we didn't miss anything important on the way here," he explained. "I'll be following the rim back a little way. Send Pike after me if I'm not here by midday break."

Dot nodded, then went to gather what he'd requested.

Food and water in the saddlebag, rifle in its saddle sheath at his thigh, Ben set out, guiding the horse carefully through the trees. The rim was rough and jagged. He had to detour inland a few times for more stable ground. Pike had been wise to counsel them to avoid the area. At least that was to the guide's credit. If the ground couldn't support a man on horseback, it would never support a loaded wagon.

He stopped from time to time, trained his field glass down a draw. He caught no sign of human occupation. If his father had passed this way, he'd left nothing behind. Ben still loathed having to report his lack of progress to Diana and their mother. That the Colonel's disappearance might have to remain a mystery was a bitter pill.

Once more he forced himself to focus on his work. That's what his father would have wanted. He dismounted here and there, always keeping firm hold on the reins in one hand as he bent to examine a plant or rock. Nothing seemed any different from what they'd recorded so far. At least that meant he hadn't overlooked anything obvious.

Good thing the canyon was more predictable than Meg.

He smiled as he remounted. Truth be told, her unpredictability was part of her charm. Like lightning, she flashed through his life, thrilling in her brilliance. Could he truly hold lightning in his arms?

It was midmorning. He ought to start back. Ahead, the rim bent inward, as if determined to keep its secrets. He had time for one more draw. He clucked to his horse and turned the beast along the edge of the curve.

This draw was deeper, he saw immediately, cupping a creek that looked strong enough to run all year. It tumbled down the draw, through a field of wildflowers Meg would surely love, past fallen trees, over rocks. The clear water flashed in the sunlight.

Once more, he dismounted, ground-tying his horse. Crouching, he cupped a handful of the water, which sparkled in his fingers. He took a long drink, feeling as if energy flowed with the water's clean, bright, cool taste.

Rising, he stared down the draw. It ran steeply toward the canyon to disappear at another rim below. But it wasn't as rough as most of the draws they'd passed, and it was certainly wide enough to accommodate a wagon. If that drop could be negotiated . . .

Frowning, he glanced around. If he could have found this spot, so could Pike. Once again, good grass waved in the breeze all around. The ground was relatively flat; plenty of room to pitch tents. With clear water and a promising approach to the Colorado, why pass it up?

He wiped the last of the water off his hands and glanced down the creek again. On Powell's trip two years ago, the explorer had named several features of the canyon. He'd been particularly impressed with the clarity of the water from a stream entering the canyon about midpoint, calling it Bright Angel Creek. Could this be close to its headwaters?

He returned to the horse, gathered the reins, and swung up into the saddle. This location was too good to pass up. He'd break camp, relocate here, and spend the next few days following that creek as far as he could. He might just have found the answer to the Army's quest. They could finish the survey early and return to the fort triumphant.

And then he'd be free to court Meg and win her heart.

# 21

Meg was the only one who didn't grumble when Ben returned at the midday rest to announce they were breaking camp. Meadows and Larson, who had spent the morning on the grid, exchanged dismayed glances. Hank fondled the theodolite with a frown, Adams clutched his notes close, and Dot hunkered over the split pea soup she'd already set cooking.

"You found some place better than this?" Pike scoffed. The guide had recently returned with a brace of quail. "You folks just want to amble all over this land like schoolboys on a holiday. I thought you hired me as a guide, not a nanny."

Adams, Larson, and Meadows bristled at that, but Ben merely smiled. "I'm not sure how we missed this spot in passing, but it deserves to be considered. Be ready to mount up in an hour."

That made them scramble. Meg had

already set up her camera and taken the southern exposure. She pulled out the exposed plate and hurried to prepare it for travel. Three verses of "Amazing Grace" would have to do this time. The shellac was barely dry when she slipped the plate into a frame and cushioned it with the others. Now for the camera itself.

"Need any help?" Dot asked, bustling past with arms full of dishes.

"I'm fine," Meg assured her. She dismounted the camera from the tripod and secured both in the van. She finally packed the stereographic camera and went to strike the tent and gather her and Dot's belongings.

The cook met her heading for the mules, arms around another load. "Thank you. It was hard enough figuring how to carry the soup. It would never have survived the jostling in the wagon." She nodded to where Meadows was rigging a travois with the pot slung between wooden poles, which he appeared to have newly cut and stripped. He'd lashed the lid to the handles with twine to keep it from bouncing off.

"Good thing that boy likes my cooking," Dot said with a shake of her head that only made her hair fly more wildly.

The private glanced up as if he knew they

had been talking about him. He looked to Larson, who came to Meg's side.

"I hope you don't mind, Miss Meg," the more talkative private said, "but we need to use your horse. Stripe is the most reliable, and Corporal Adams says we shouldn't rebalance the load among the mules so as to spare one for you."

Dot nudged Meg with a grin. "You can ride up with me."

"It seems I'm well accommodated, Private," she told Larson, who offered her a grateful smile. "Just be careful with that saddlebag. It has my best plate in it."

"We'll guard it like a babe, ma'am," he promised. He took it straight to Meadows, who clasped it close, eyes wide, as if he was honored by the trust she'd placed in him.

It took a full hour, but when Ben called "Mount up!" they were ready.

Meg would have liked to ride beside him and question him about this sudden change, but that was impossible with her on the bench next to Dot. Even if she'd been riding Stripe, she might not have been able to close the distance. The way was crowded with trees, making it difficult to ride two abreast. And their guide stayed as close to Ben's side as possible. Every time she caught a glimpse of Pike's face, his jaw was moving, beard catching the light. And Ben's face only grew more determined and set.

Dot must have noticed too, for she glanced at Meg. "I'd give my last cinnamon stick to hear what those two are arguing about."

"So would I," Meg said.

Whatever the problem, Ben never wavered from his course. It was late afternoon when they came out of the trees to a grassy clearing dotted with wildflowers and creased by a bubbling creek.

"Why, it's kind of pretty," Dot said with a smile.

It certainly was. As if they thought so too, the mules and horses raised their heads, nostrils twitching. Aspens on one side chattered a welcome in the warm breeze.

"I approve," Hank declared, swinging down from the saddle. "Two tents, either side of the stream, fire circle about there." He pointed to a slight rise to one side of the creek.

"On it," Dot said, jumping down from the bench and heading for her pot as Larson came to take charge of her mules.

Pike shook his head. "Perfect place for predators to meet prey. And you were worried about a brush with a cougar."

Meg chilled, but Ben showed no concern. He was on the ground, loosening the cinch on the saddle. "We'll deal with that problem when we come to it, Mr. Pike. Settle your gear. We should be here a few days at the least."

Pike planted his fists on his hips. "I've been this way before. There's a steep drop below — no access to the river. Your settlers' wagons would never make it up."

The others exchanged glances, and Ben turned slowly from his horse. "You're positive?"

Pike dropped his hands. "Positive. This site is a waste of time. I could have told you that if you'd taken me with you."

She could almost feel the disappointment fall over Ben like a winter coat. "My apologies, Mr. Pike," he said. "I'll confirm your findings in the morning. If you're right, we'll move on."

"No ifs about it," Pike insisted. "And I'm getting tired of you doubting me." He stomped off.

Meg left the tent poles on the mule and went to join Ben. "It's a promising spot. I can see why you were drawn to it."

He glanced down the slope, hands working at the saddle. "Apparently I didn't plan ahead."

Meg shrugged. "My father never planned ahead, and he had a fairly successful life."

"He wasn't an Army engineer," Ben pointed out, pulling the saddle from his horse.

No, Papa would never have been happy with rules and regulations. Could she be happy as the wife of an engineer?

She tried to ignore the thought as she went to set up her tent. The wildflowers whispered to her, promising a vista with the creek and surrounding pines, but she kept glancing at Ben. He worked swiftly and surely to prepare the camp before twilight fell. How would he feel in the morning if Pike proved to be right?

He looked up from rigging his own tent and met Meg's eyes. Warmth seeped through her.

"How much time until dinner, Dot?" he called.

"Half an hour, give or take," Dot answered.

He moved across the camp to Meg's side. "Care for a stroll before dinner, Miss Pero?" He offered her his arm.

So formal, but she could see the hope in his eyes. They both needed a little break.

She put her nose in the air like the brightest West Point belle and draped her hand over his. "Delighted, Captain Coleridge. But don't make me late for that dinner you

334

promised. I understand the establishment only serves the best people."

With Dot grinning at them, they set out.

The grass brushed her skirts as they moved south along the meadow, following the stream. Ben bent and plucked a tufted red wildflower from the grass and offered it to her. Meg accepted it with a smile.

"Thank you," she said. "But this isn't the first wildflower you brought me, is it? I'm sorry I didn't notice."

"You had other things on your mind," he allowed. "And wildflowers, no matter how pretty, do seem rather small against this backdrop."

They had reached the rim, where the land made its first drop into a draw carved by the creek as it tumbled toward the Colorado. Trees clung precariously to the sides, white as bone in places where the root systems must have failed. Farther down, the ground disappeared in another drop.

Ben stood regarding it a moment, then he raised his head. "We might have to use switchbacks in places, but I think we could put in a wagon road just there." He pointed to the gentler slope on the east side of the draw.

"What about that next drop?" Meg asked, trying to imagine the route.

His jaw hardened. "I'm going down to-morrow to find out."

Her fingers were itching again as she considered the prospect. "Ought to be quite a view from there, halfway down the canyon."

Ben shot her a look. "Are you asking to come with me?"

"Are you willing to take me?"

He laughed. "Yes. But think carefully, Meg. It's possible to fall. Even a little slide could damage your camera."

Sometimes that was the price for the pictures she took.

"I've seen it happen," she told Ben. "All my father thought about was getting the shot. He sprained his ankle multiple times, broke his leg once, landed on his head and knocked himself senseless another. The big camera I'm using is his fourth. I won't tell you what happened to the first three."

He turned to face her, one hand coming up. His fingers brushed her cheek, tender, sweet. "I hope you'll be more careful."

With him looking at her like that, it was hard to disagree.

"I know," she said, making herself smile. "I can't afford to replace that camera right now. But a few good pictures, Ben, and my fortune's made, at least for a while."

Still he continued to regard her, as if she were impossibly precious. Her cheeks were growing warmer in the glow of his regard.

"If you married," he ventured, "you wouldn't have to worry about making your fortune."

He said it nonchalantly, but he stood still, as if waiting for her to argue. She should argue. She'd certainly disputed the matter with her aunt and cousin and the well-meaning minister who'd presided over her father's funeral. Not all husbands were successes. Not all wives lived in the lap of luxury. Look at Dot and Hank. Women had been cooking and sewing and tending the wounded for centuries to make ends meet. But she couldn't seem to muster her arguments.

"I thought we were going to follow the path, see where it led," she said, breaking his hold to bend over the stream. The water was so clear, every pebble magnified — gold and gray and white. The last rays of the setting sun pierced the surface to set them gleaming.

"Like with this canyon, I'm beginning to hope I see the end," Ben said.

She couldn't offer him more, not yet. She dipped her fingers in the cool water, let the stream wash against her. "This water is lovely. I wonder if I could capture the beauty with the right light."

He sighed as if giving up on the deeper conversation for the moment. "Always thinking about the next shot, aren't you? Even your camera would be hard-pressed to catch that sparkle."

Meg cocked her head. Something in the silt between the pebbles was winking at her, brightening and darkening with every movement of the water. "I don't think it's just the clarity of the water making it sparkle. Is that gold?"

Ben started. He released her hand to crouch beside the stream and study the spot she'd indicated. He easily identified the pearly white of quartz, the golden brown of feldspar. Could she have spotted pyrite? She wouldn't have been the first to mistake the shiny gold rock for the real thing.

"Lots of minerals sparkle," he told her, but he scooped up a handful of the rocks and silt and sifted it through his fingers.

A tiny flake, gold and flashing, stuck to his forefinger. He pressed his thumb into the speck, watched it bend to the pressure. He drew in a breath.

"It is, isn't it?" Meg murmured as if awed. "There's gold in this creek."

"There's gold somewhere," Ben corrected her, dipping his hand in the water to free the flake. "The vein could be miles upstream or embedded in a cliff the stream or one of its tributaries passed. A little color doesn't mean a lot in this part of the world."

She shook her head, her look eager. "I know many people who'd disagree. A few flakes, a nugget or two, and you'll have a gold rush on your hands."

Something tightened inside him. He'd been a boy of eleven when his father had been sent to serve at the Presidio in San Francisco shortly after gold had been found in the hills. At nine, Diana had considered the trek across country an adventure. Even his mother had begun to appreciate the beauty of the area, though she, like his father, had deplored the actions of those rushing into the hills beyond.

"It's as if they've turned their backs on all civility," she'd said when their third cook had resigned in as many days.

"Some men will do anything to answer the call of wealth," his father had said. "You remember that, Ben. Duty may be a harsh lady, but serving her will give you a satisfaction you cannot gain with gold."

Thanks to the Colonel's loyalty to duty, his family had never suffered privation.

Indeed, his father's influence had opened, and closed, doors for Ben. How could he stand in judgment over men with fewer privileges?

Gold held a powerful pull. He'd seen it himself. The proud once-Spanish city had emptied. Civilians attached to the fort had quit, soldiers had disappeared in the night. More than a hundred ships had been abandoned in the harbor. Sailors had to be confined to their quarters to prevent them from jumping overboard. All had been lured away by the promise of riches. Even now, Meg crouched beside him, running her hands through the pebbles as if sure she'd find something.

Was that why his father had left the fort with only a guide for company? Had he feared how his men would react if gold was found in the canyon? What did it mean that only a piece of his spur remained?

He rose, pulling Meg up with him. "There's not enough gold for a rush," he told her. "There may be a few flakes, but nothing more."

"How can you be sure?" She glanced up and down the stream as if expecting to find a pile of golden nuggets waiting. "Oh, Ben, this could be our making."

He caught her hand, held it close. "I'll

take samples tomorrow to be certain. But a gold rush is no place for a lady."

"If the lady wants to get rich, it is," she countered.

"If the lady wants to stay safe," he said, "she'll have no part in it. It's a fool's quest, Meg. Your stereographs have far greater potential for giving you a solid future."

She stilled, took a deep breath, and met his gaze. "You're right. I don't know what came over me."

"What comes over most who stumble across gold in a creek," Ben assured her. "It's natural to dream, Meg, particularly when you're facing a future you're unsure of. But you don't have to worry. You can count on me."

"Thank you." She offered him a smile. "But I tend to count on myself." She glanced around the draw again, then stiffened to clutch his arm.

"When you prove there's no gold, you better publish your findings widely. Because we might not have been the first to discover this spot." She nodded toward the tree across the creek.

A symbol had been carved into the bark.

Ben released her hand to jump the creek for a closer look. A moment later, and she was beside him, skirts barely wet.

341

"Do you recognize it?" she asked.

Ben traced the shape with his finger. The bark had healed around the cut, so it hadn't been carved in the last few weeks.

"It's not an Army code," he mused. "And I haven't seen any territorial marks like it."

She was studying it with eyes narrowed. "It looks like two mountains with a creek cutting in between. And that shape at the top could be a half moon."

"Reference to when the discovery was made, perhaps?" Ben mused.

She glanced around. "My father set up shop at Boise City once. We didn't stay long. The miners were more interested in panning than having their portraits taken, and they didn't much like someone wandering their claims looking for pretty vistas to capture. Still, I seem to recall that there should be more than one of these, like your survey photographs, north, south, east, and west."

Ben dropped his hand. "This could be west, north, or south."

She pointed farther down the creek. "Is that another one?"

Ben grinned at her. "Only one way to find out."

They scrambled through the brush on that side of the creek, over fallen trees, around boulders tumbled from the cliff. Sure enough, another of the strange symbols had been carved in the trunk of a spruce, at about eye level.

"There should be two more on the other side of the creek," Ben said. "I'll draw that symbol for Hank. Maybe he's seen something like it before. But you're right. Someone started a claim."

"Maybe our night visitor," Meg suggested. "It would explain why we were followed."

"And why he wanted to see that picture you'd taken," Ben realized. "Maybe you caught something on your plate, Meg, besides his shadow." He released the snap on his holster, so he could draw his pistol quickly if needed. "Come on. We're heading back to camp. I want Pike and Hank's thoughts on this."

Meg nodded and accepted his hand to start back up the draw. The sunset must have been spectacular, for the sky danced with red.

Once more she clutched his arm, drawing him to a halt. "Something's wrong."

As if to prove it, the trees at the top of the draw went up in flame.

## 22

Ugly, jagged orange rimmed the hilltop. Dusky smoke billowed up through it, reaching greedy fingers into the draw. Ben could hear the sizzle and pop of the resin reacting to the heat, the crackle of limb and brush.

He whirled toward a white-faced Meg. Everything in him demanded that he protect her, but he had a duty to the rest of the team.

"Follow the creek as far down the canyon as you can," he told her. "Walk in the water if you have to." He pressed a quick kiss to her mouth, then turned for the top.

She seized him, fingers trembling against his arm. "Where are you going?"

"To make sure the others are safe." He squeezed her hand. "You can take care of yourself, Meg. You've more than proven that. I'll come back for you. I promise." He made himself break away and scrambled up the draw.

The air grew hotter, the blaze greater, the higher he climbed. An invisible rope tugged at him, urging him back to Meg's side. He couldn't obey the pull.

*Please, Lord, keep her safe.*

The prayer fueled his legs, lent strength to his heart. He raced up the last slope and crested the edge to where the camp should be.

He entered chaos.

Flames danced across the ground, embraced the trees as if intent on waltzing. Already one of the tents was ablaze. Smoke billowed toward him, reaching into the sky. Flashes of red inside the gray told him the pines on the edge of camp were on fire.

"Hank! Adams!" he yelled over the roar of the flames.

No one answered.

He started forward, arm up and bent to protect his nose and mouth. Now another tent was burning, the poles cracking in the heat. He couldn't see farther through the smoke. Where were they? He darted past the closest tent, and the flames licked within inches of his arm.

Ben jerked to a stop, then backed away as the blaze climbed higher on all sides. What had happened to his team? How could he help?

345

The wind parted the smoke for only a moment, but it was enough for him to glimpse Hank and Larson mounted on mules and leading the others north, into the wind. Relief pushed him back more surely than the fire. They were doing all they could to stay safe. Now he needed to find Meg and do the same.

As Ben disappeared up the creek, Meg drew in a breath and instantly regretted it. Though most of the smoke was rising into the darkening sky, the air around her had turned hot and acidic. She moved along the edge of the stream, through brush and trees, following the curves and pools deeper into the canyon.

She wasn't the only one. She heard the crash behind her a moment before a deer ran past, tawny rump flashing as it leaped away from the fire. A chittering in the trees told her squirrels and chipmunks were fleeing as well. Glancing up, she saw birds plunging through the smoke for safety near the river.

Another thud warned her something bigger was coming. She turned to meet it head-on.

A cougar raced toward her, bounding from rock to rock, muscles bunching.

346

*Please, Lord, protect me!*

The prayer hung in the air like the smoke and far less tangible. If there truly was a God who cared, she could only hope that now was the time he'd show it. She squared her shoulders, threw out her arms.

"Here I am!" she shouted.

The cougar passed without even glancing her way.

Meg sagged into the mud beside the stream and trembled.

*Thank you.*

How long she sat there, she wasn't sure. A thousand thoughts flitted through her mind, passing as quickly as the cougar. Her father's last days, lying on the hospital bed, breath ragged. The first time she'd taken a picture, the anxious waiting to see whether something good would come from it, whether Papa would approve. The glorious moment when he produced the print and looked at her with a smile and a "Not bad."

"Not bad?" she'd said. "It's good."

The moment she'd felt as if God was standing beside her, guarding her. That was better still.

As the sun set, it was easy to see the spiral of the fire, running through the grass along the edge of the rim, gobbling up the wild-flowers, edging ever closer. The pines stood silent in the glow, as if prepared to endure. The aspens roared with the heat, flaming up to leave a blackened shell behind. She made herself rise and follow the stream lower.

*Please, Lord, protect Ben.*

Fear for herself faded as fear for him rose. He was commanding and clever, but what could he do against such a conflagration?

The draw closed in around the stream. She had clearly wandered away from Ben's wagon road. Not even a horse could have passed easily this way. She stepped into the stream, felt her way along. A boulder seemed to offer safety, at least for the moment. She climbed up onto it and drew in a breath of the smoky air. The sky was a dusky pink above her.

Something else was moving through the smoke. She could hear the plunk as feet broke the surface of the stream. She couldn't seem to move to escape. All she could do was hunch against the rock and close her eyes against what was coming, as if by blocking the view she kept it at bay.

"Meg!"

"Ben!" She forced open her eyes, straightening away from the boulder. A darker shadow splashed through the creek to her side and reached up his arms.

She slipped from the boulder, sobbing in fear, in thanksgiving. He gathered her close a moment, his presence the surest place in the twilight. Then he leaned back and wiped the tears from her cheeks. "It's all right. You're safe."

"Are you?" Meg asked, hiccoughing back a sob.

In the last of the light, she could see him nod. "I'm fine. The others were already moving when I got there. Hank and Larson drove the mules north before they were cut off by the flames. As soon as this burns out, we'll climb up and rejoin them."

As if to disagree with him, a wrenching creak came from above. Over tumbled one of the trees, still smoking. It plunged straight down to crash through the undergrowth.

Ben pushed her against the boulder and sheltered her with his body.

Light flared, then dimmed, and the tree lay, crackling, upper branches piercing the creek with a mortal wound. Flames began to lick up around it.

Ben leaned back. "We have to get deeper, away from the blaze. Come on."

He took her hand. She swallowed, wanting only to stay on the safety of the rock, in the shelter of his arms. But he was right. They were still in danger here.

They had to pick their way down in the gathering gloom. The light from the burning tree slowly faded. So did the light from high above as the fire retreated from the edge. Quiet fell, until the only sound was the bubbling of the stream.

Ben inched along, placing each foot carefully before bringing her forward. Once he stumbled, and she cried out, reaching for him to find only air. A moment more, and he was back at her side.

"Just a slight miscalculation," he assured her. "No harm done."

Yet it could have been. He had to know that. He was being brave for her sake. She could do the same.

"I believe your definition of a stroll differs from mine, sir," she said as her feet splashed in the creek. Her toes were turning numb inside her boots. Her hem must be sodden; she could feel it dragging.

"Ah, but I thought you preferred adventure," Ben said, helping her over a fallen log. He held her in his arms a moment, and she wished she could see his face. Was he searching the dark with his gaze, trying to see her too? Was the look in his eyes as tender as when he'd kissed her?

"Perhaps not this much adventure," Meg said.

He stopped suddenly. "Wait here."

"You're leaving again?" Oh, but she'd never wanted to sound so desperate.

"Only for a moment, I promise." His shadow faded into the dark.

Meg stood, stream tugging at her legs, chill climbing through her. Now that the sun had set, the temperature was dropping. It might be warm on the rim after the fire's passing, but here in the depth of the canyon, the night came forward with icy hands.

"See, only a moment," Ben said, and she had to swallow her squeal of surprise. "There's an overhang along the cliff here, not deep enough for a cave, but it should provide some protection. Shall we?"

He was offering her his arm again. She felt it brush against her, and the courtly gesture nearly made the fears start falling.

"Why, certainly sir," she said, and he led her deeper into the dark.

How game she was. His mother would have sat near the rim and refused to move, sure someone would be along to rescue the Colonel's wife. She had relied on his father's reputation and consequence for so long, she sometimes seemed to have none of her own. His sister Diana might have screamed and cried and clung to him. Meg willingly put

351

her life in his hands. She trusted him and her own skills, and he would never let her down.

He felt past the brambles that tumbled over the edge of the outcropping, pulling her into the recess until his other hand scraped against the rock of the wall. He bent, feeling the ground before sitting, then urged her down next to him as he put his back to the wall.

"Not the most comfortable place to sleep," he acknowledged. "Not the worst, either."

"Pretty close," she disagreed, settling next to him. She shifted, shoulder bumping his, then he heard a rock skitter away. She must have thrown it.

"Ah, but you've never slept on an Army-issued bed," he said, trying to keep his tone light when weariness fell harder than the night. "Even worse than the cots we were issued for the survey. Stiff where it should give, giving where it should support. And with lots of tiny company eager to make your acquaintance."

"Can't be any worse than the campsites my father chose," she said. "He had a knack for selecting rocky ground. I'll have to thank Mr. Pike for doing better." She sucked in a breath. "That is, if we see Mr. Pike again."

"We'll see Pike," Ben promised, willing

his body to relax. "It just might take a day or two."

She pulled away from him. "A day or two?"

He urged her closer again. She needed the warmth, and so did he. As much as he'd maligned the Army's accommodations, he would have willingly shared a bed with vermin right now. He'd never been so thankful for the Army's wool uniform either.

"You saw that tree come down," he said. "There'll be more before the night is over. We can't climb back that way."

"Then do we head to the Colorado?"

For the first time, he heard fear in her voice. He put his arm about her waist.

"Only if we must. You should know what we're up against, Meg. There is no way to float out without a large, well-built boat. Powell will be farther downstream by now. It could take months before anyone mounts another expedition to come after us."

Her voice caught. "I understand."

He gave her a squeeze. "Did you notice the shape of this draw?"

Her hair tickled his cheek as she must have nodded. "Rough and craggy. Is that important?"

"It is. That means there are branches on both sides of the stream. At least one should lead back up to the plateau, where we can regroup with the others."

Her breath caressed his ear. "Oh, good. And searching for a way out is an efficient way to confirm your wagon road."

Ben shook his head. "Why am I continually amazed by you?"

Once more her hair brushed him. This time he was fairly sure she'd tossed her head. "Because I am a thoroughly amazing woman, Captain Coleridge."

He laughed.

She shivered.

Ben frowned in the dark. "Cold?"

"This skirt's soaked." She shifted away from him as if examining it with her fingers. "Give me a moment to find my knife."

He'd never considered her armed, just dangerous. "Your knife?"

Her voice was prim. "My knife, sir. My father gave it to me. Surely all good Army officers carry one as well."

He touched the leather sheath at his side. The knife and the few cartridges in his revolver might be all that protected them at the moment. He'd left his cartridge box and ammunition belt at the campsite.

"May I ask what you intend to do with yours?" he ventured.

His answer was the ripping of fabric.

"There," she proclaimed. "Much better." The faint light from the front of the overhang disappeared a moment as she straightened away from him and flapped the fabric up and out. "I can only hope it will dry by morning, and we can make use of it."

Had she cut off her skirt? His mind boggled. "Meg, you'll freeze."

"Not at all," she replied, settling back against him. "Hadn't you noticed? I wear breeches under the skirt. The boots protected them from the worst of the wetting."

It seemed the breeches he'd glimpsed earlier were everyday wear for her. His mother would be scandalized. Diana would probably want some. All he could think was that Meg was the most practical, intelligent woman he'd ever met.

"So how shall we make use of this windfall?" he teased. "Bullfight, perhaps? Though I seem to recall bullfighters using red cloth, not navy."

"You won't laugh when it's keeping us warm tomorrow night," she predicted. "Though I do wonder how we're to keep warm tonight." Another shudder went through her.

"Stay close to me," Ben said. "The overhang will cut some of the breeze. Our body heat should do the rest."

355

She snuggled against him, and suddenly he was quite warm indeed.

"Do people really fight against bulls using red fabric?" she asked.

"Major Daunton mentioned it at West Point," Ben replied. "He was trying to impress on us that strategy rather than brute force could win a battle."

"Using red fabric against a bull doesn't sound like much of a strategy to me."

He chuckled. "Ah, but the fabric was only a diversion. The fighter had a sword as well."

"And we have your revolver and our knives. I'm not sure they're any more use than a sword against a bull, though. I saw the cougar, Ben. It ran from the fire the same direction we did."

He kept his body still so as not to worry her further. "Probably all the way to the river by now. And it has the luxury of being able to scale those downed trees when it's ready to climb out."

"Does nothing worry you?"

She sounded incredulous. He could not tell her that, of the many things that concerned him — finding the truth about his father's disappearance, reuniting with the rest of the team — his biggest fear was for her safety.

"Try to get some sleep, Meg," he murmured, arm slipping about her waist once more, as if it belonged there.

She laid her head against his chest.

Again he marveled. He could only imagine what some of the young ladies who had visited West Point would have said. How dare he take liberties? They would have preferred to freeze rather than damage their reputations. Meg did what had to be done to survive.

Even if her reputation could be damaged by this night alone with him. He'd have to note details in the expedition journal or at least inform Colonel Yearling. Ben knew how quickly word could spread from there. But, time enough to contend with that when they returned to the fort.

And they would return. He refused to lose her now that he'd found her again.

He had intended to stay awake, on guard, but he must have fallen asleep, for the change in light woke him. Meg slumped against him, one arm about his waist, pretty mouth soft in sleep. Aspen leaves, yellowed away from the tree, stuck like feathers in her hair, and dirt smudged one pearly cheek.

Sunlight strayed into the canyon from the east. They had made it through the night. Now they had to find a way back out.

# 23

"Meg, sweetheart, wake up."

Meg smiled, eyes still closed. It had been a long time since she'd dreamed of Ben calling her sweetheart. She could imagine the warmth in his eyes, the gentle smile that softened his firm cheeks. And if she raised her chin, her lips would meet his. His kisses always made her feel treasured, beautiful. Loved.

"Meg, honey, I need you."

Oh, how she'd longed to hear him say that, until she'd realized his mother would never accept an unconventional daughter-in-law like her.

"Margaret Pero, attention!"

Meg jerked upright to meet Ben's surprised look.

"I would never have thought that would work," he said.

"Well," Meg said, gathering her dignity, "don't make a habit of it."

He grinned, then sobered. "No, ma'am. An officer of lower rank should never presume."

"Humph." She climbed to her feet, and he joined her. "It looks like we survived."

"And so did the canyon."

Meg glanced out. The stream rolled along, muddy now with ash and clogged with debris. Higher along the cliff opposite them, uprooted soil and rock gave testament to fallen trees. At the top, blackened skeletons reached leafless fingers toward the sky, as if begging for mercy. The air still hinted of smoke.

"I see why it might be difficult to climb out the way we came," she said.

"Ah, but look there." Ben pointed across the stream to where another draw opened. "That might be our escape. I was going to explore, but I didn't want you to wake alone."

The thought was terrifying, and she had to stop herself from reaching for his hand. "I'm glad you waited. I'll come with you." She bent and picked up the skirt of her riding habit, stiff now with dried mud.

"Still think it will be useful?" he teased.

Meg shook it hard, the snap releasing dust that sparkled in the rising sun. "Yes, quite useful," she said, draping it about her shoulders like a cape. "Come along, Captain Coleridge, and do try to keep up."

With a laugh, he followed her out into the canyon.

The rest of nature seemed unconcerned about the havoc of the night. Birds welcomed the morning in the trees along the stream. Meg and Ben surprised a herd of deer in a small meadow. They raised their heads from the grass, long ears swiveling this way and that, as if trying to decide whether they faced friend or foe. Oh, for her camera.

Meg stopped with a gasp that sent the deer bounding down the stream for safer ground. Ben turned to her, body tensed as if ready to defend her from whatever she'd sighted.

"My cameras," she said, tremor in her voice. "Do you think Dot or Hank had time to take them?"

His face confirmed her fears. Tears burned her eyes.

Ben gathered her close. "I don't know for certain, Meg. It's possible they salvaged something before lighting out. But if they didn't, I'll see that the Army replaces whatever was lost."

She leaned against him, let him carry her load for a moment. Her cameras were replaceable. The pictures she'd taken far less so. When would she ever get another shot like her heavenly window?

*I thought you cared, God.*

No. Enough of that. She didn't want to be ungrateful. She and Ben were alive, miracle enough. Besides, there was something right, something satisfying, in believing Someone was watching over her. And she needed him most of all now. She refused to give up that comfort for petty thoughts and blame. She'd been the one to bring her cameras into the wilderness, to leave her best plate behind when she and Ben went strolling. She had to believe this would all work out in the end somehow.

She pulled back. "Thank you. I'm sorry I lost my head. The important thing is that Dot and Hank and the others are safe."

"Let's see what we can do to find them," he said. He offered her his hand, and they set off once more.

The way remained open only a short distance. The creek fell in three- and four-foot drops between rusty-looking soil that crumbled under their boots. Ben had to detour wider, help her clamber down boulders. The air was warming, until the skirt heated her shoulders.

It felt odd moving without it flapping

about her legs. She'd grown used to the breeches she wore underneath, but her limbs felt more vulnerable without a skirt over them. It didn't help that her stomach reminded her that she hadn't eaten dinner. A rumble from Ben's direction told her his stomach was protesting too.

She stopped, then glanced around. There, by the stream, the nearly round emerald leaves bobbed in the breeze. Oh, and that lighter green plant with the jagged-edged leaves. And the fanciful one with the purple stem. She bent and gathered up handfuls.

"Here," she said, mixing them together and offering him a batch.

He frowned at it without accepting it. "You want me to graze like a mule?"

"I do believe we have discussed the traits you share with a mule before," she said. "But at the moment, I'll settle for you eating this. That's miner's lettuce, wild mint, and cabbage. Think of it as a salad."

He stuck out his lower lip as if impressed and accepted her offering.

"Where'd you learn about miner's lettuce and wild mint?" he asked as they crossed the stream on boulders jutting up from the rushing water.

Meg took another bite of the crisp leaves before answering. "One of the private

362

expeditions Papa and I joined hired a native guide. He was happy to show me."

He helped her down on the other side of the stream. "Just like Hank showed you how to use the theodolite."

"Everyone is good at something," Meg allowed, letting herself enjoy being in his arms. "Everyone has a story to tell. You just have to listen."

Ahead, the mouth of the draw opened, yet Ben seemed no more eager to reach it.

"What's your story, Meg?" he murmured, head cocked as if he would see inside her.

"Oh, you know it," she said. "Raised by a father fanatical about his profession. Finding myself drawn into it as well. There's not a lot to tell."

He released her at last and turned toward their goal. "So you just plan on taking pictures for the rest of your life."

Why did that sound less than a lofty purpose? "More or less," she admitted. "Papa never thought beyond that."

"You could."

Heretical idea. She stopped in the middle of the path he had broken through the brush. "Stop taking pictures?"

"Or maybe add something more." He paused as well, one foot higher than the other, gaze going into the draw. "This one's no good. Look at that overhang."

She could see it now that they were aligned with the fissure. The cliff above jutted out, its underlip cutting back into a mass of tumbled stone. They'd never be able to scale it.

"Not to worry," he said, turning and starting back past her. "There are plenty more."

With a sigh, she followed.

He stopped when he reached the stream. The lettuce had had a certain amount of moisture in it, but the bubbling brook called to her. A shame it was so dirty now.

"Thirsty?" he asked as if he'd seen the direction of her gaze.

Meg wrinkled her nose. "Not enough to try drinking that."

"We can drink it," he said. "If you'll sacrifice a corner of your new cloak."

Meg glanced at the skirt, then unfurled it from around her shoulders. "Certainly. What did you have in mind?"

In answer, he took it and snapped it tight between his hands. Bending, he scooped up water so that it pooled in the middle. Silver drops fell from the underside.

"Catch it," he said.

She cupped her hands to collect the precious water, then brought it to her mouth to drink. The wool filtered out most

364

of the ash and mud. Oh, but she'd needed this. The cool trickle down her throat brought life and vigor with it. After several rounds, she insisted on holding the material for him.

"What now?" she asked as he finished and she began wringing the last of the water from the wool.

He wiped his lips with the back of his hand, gaze scanning the wall of rock beyond her. Already stubble lined his jaw, shining gold in the sunlight. He pointed. "We try that one."

But that one didn't prove worthwhile either, and neither did the next. Always the draw ended in an ascent too steep to climb.

"I don't think much of the chances of making this your wagon road," Meg informed him when they stopped to drink again later in the morning.

"If the Army wanted to build a road, we could clear this brush and go straight down Bright Angel Canyon," he said.

She glanced around at the walls growing taller with each step toward the Colorado. "Bright Angel Canyon?"

"You wouldn't recognize it at the moment," Ben said, "but remember how clear that stream was when we first found it? Powell commented on a clear stream entering the canyon at about this spot on the river. He named it Bright Angel Creek."

She could see why. After so many of the muddy streams in the area, this was a rare find. "So you want the Army to roll right down it?"

"Right beside it," Ben assured her. "No doubt we'd need to find a way over the steepest part, and I don't know if there's a corresponding draw on the other side of the Colorado. Powell should be able to tell us when he finishes this time. For now, we have to find a footpath."

"For me," Meg realized. "You could probably climb out if you were alone, couldn't you?"

He made a show of studying the cliffs. "I'm not convinced. The rock's too weathered. Plenty of handholds, all of which could crumble when taking my full weight. I'd prefer to walk out rather than fall down."

So would she, but she could not help thinking that perhaps his mother had been right. Once again, her presence in Ben's life could hold him back, and this time it might mean his death.

Ben kept a cheery face as they climbed over another tumble of boulders on the way toward the west side of the canyon. In truth, the farther the sun moved in that direction, the lower their chances of escaping the canyon today. They were deeper now, the temperatures not as cold as they'd been higher. Trees, where they could root, were scraggly things, as were the bushes clustered between them. Deer had disappeared. Worse, the red limestone walls showed no sign of a cave, leaving less opportunity to find shelter. He didn't like the idea of sleeping in the open with Meg.

So, he kept moving, though his legs and back protested, and his stomach demanded more of the greens Meg had found earlier.

Shadows were lengthening when he spotted a good-sized gap in the cliff. He led Meg to it, then paused, gazing up. The walls were wide enough apart, the way steep but steady. In the distance, he could see the rim. Hope surged through him. "This could be it."

Meg clutched his hand. "Oh, Ben, you did it."

"Let's hold the celebration until we're on top," he cautioned. "We have a lot of climbing to do."

They drank their fill of the creek before starting. A stream trickled down the side draw, but Ben wasn't sure how easy it would be to reach from the path they would follow. At least the water was relatively clear, proof that they'd outdistanced the extent of the fire. There appeared to be a game trail of sorts, just a flattening of the undergrowth, but he followed it gratefully.

*Only a little farther, Lord. Help me save her.*

Up and up they went, past massive gray stones with rain-smoothed sides, tufts of grass and shrub clinging to the red soil. His legs were leaden, each step a chore. The warm air didn't seem to fill his lungs. She never complained, though he heard her gasp in a breath from time to time.

Partway up, they reached a small plateau, where the cliff had slumped. The stream pooled in a rocky basin before falling a few feet and continuing down to meet Bright Angel Creek. Ben called a halt, and they both collapsed beside the stream and quenched their thirst.

He glanced ahead, noting the rugged golden stone. "Looks like it gets a little steeper above here. But I think we can make it."

She glanced up as well. "I can see the top. I'm not turning back."

He smiled at her. "So catch your breath. We're almost there."

She shifted as if trying to find a comfortable position on the sandstone. "What happens when we find the others?"

When, not if. He appreciated her confidence. "We assess the damage. If they saved enough equipment and supplies, we continue at a faster pace, making sure we didn't miss a better approach than the one down Bright Angel Canyon. But if we lost equipment, we'll have to return to the fort."

She drew in a breath. "I must be mad to hope we can continue."

Ben shook his head. "Even after all this?"

Her cheeks were turning pink. "Well, it has been nice to have the bulk of your attentions, Captain Coleridge."

Ben laughed. "I should have known it would require an act of nature to get you to take me seriously."

She fussed with the fraying end of her skirt. "I always took you seriously, Ben. It was your courtship I refused."

He rocked back on his heels where he crouched by the pool. "Why? We've always done well together."

"Well, you thought so." She straightened her legs and flexed the toes of her boots up and down. "West Point society made me feel like an oddity."

He could not understand her. "You seemed perfectly poised to me."

"All an act," she insisted. "I wasn't raised

for fancy dress balls and teas in pretty parlors. I'm sure more than one lady noticed."

"I never noticed," he protested.

She shook her head. "I'm better suited to this life. I know where to plant my tripod, how to take the shot." She gestured toward the trees at the edge of the plateau. "How to find food. I'm a disastrous cook, you know."

He could not see that as such a fault. "Dot doesn't think so. You taught her a trick with the bacon."

"And salt pork, Ben. No one outside the Army or pioneers eats salt pork."

He wasn't so sure about that, but she continued before he could comment.

"Admit it, Ben. I'm better out here than I am in society, even a society as limited as an Army outpost."

"You'll never get me to agree," he told her. "The girl I met at West Point was admired, respected. Every cadet envied me."

She shook her head. "I can play the part for a while, but sooner or later I say something, do something, and everyone knows the truth."

"What truth? That you are talented and clever as well as beautiful?"

Her gaze was militant. "That I am outspoken and headstrong and determined to pursue my work. Most men don't like that."

"I do."

When she looked at him askance, he rose and offered her his hand. "I do," he repeated. "You wouldn't be the woman you are if you didn't believe in what you do. I've seen the power of your photographs, Meg. I would never ask you to give that up."

She eyed his hand as if accepting might commit her to something. "What about your career? An Army officer goes where he's told. He's not free to follow his wife on expeditions."

Wife. The fact she'd even used the word lifted his heart. "But wives accompany their husbands on expeditions. Look at Dot. Look at General Custer's wife, for that matter. And most engineering expeditions require a photographer."

She blinked as if she hadn't considered that.

"And if, for some reason, the Army refused to hire you," he said, "you could still shoot your stereographs. And you wouldn't have to ask permission."

A smile curved her lips. Slowly, she reached for his hand, and he pulled her up and into his arms.

Sunlight brushed her cheeks as she tilted

her chin, inviting his kiss. His heart started beating faster as he lowered his head and obliged.

Warmth, light, and joy broke over him in waves. What was it about Meg, sweet Meg, that thrilled him more than discovering an ore deposit, finding a way to cross the Colorado? She touched his heart in a way no one and nothing else ever had. He had to force himself to break the kiss. Her eyes opened slowly, the green as deep and inviting as a cool pool. She seemed to want to linger as much as he did.

"You can be very persuasive," she murmured, stepping back from him. "I'll consider the matter. I think that might be a raspberry bush near those trees, or at least some miner's lettuce. Let me gather some before we climb."

He grimaced but nodded. "If I have to eat much more of that lettuce, I'll turn into a horse."

"Maybe we'd get out faster if you did," she teased, moving closer to the cliff face, where more of the broad emerald leaves clustered among prickly looking bushes. She ducked under a tree limb and stumbled. As she righted herself, she gasped, stiffening.

"Ben!"

The terror in her voice galvanized him,

and he was at her side in an instant. Her gaze was latched onto something on the ground, the thing that had caused her to trip.

The body lay face down in the brush. The hat had tipped off and rolled to one side, the insignia clearly visible: the crossed sabers of a cavalry officer.

# 24

Meg couldn't breathe, couldn't think, couldn't move.

"Is he . . ." she started.

"Dead," Ben confirmed in a flat voice. "Probably for a long time. Go back to the pool, Meg. I'll take care of him."

Relief almost made her comply, but confusion kept her immobile. "But who is he? How did he get all the way out here?"

He stood as still as a statue. "I believe it's my father."

Of course. Why hadn't she realized it? She could see where the rowel from one of his spurs had broken off. Pain lanced through her, and she turned and took Ben in her arms, held him close. "Oh, Ben, I'm so sorry."

He was stiff against her, unwilling to accept even this little kindness. "Go back to the pool, Meg. I'll be with you shortly."

She released him. His face was as set as

his voice, eyes gazing at nothing.

"What are you going to do?" she asked.

"I'd carry him out if I could," he said. "But I can't make the climb with so much extra weight. I'm going to bury him."

Meg frowned. "How? We don't even have a shovel."

He wiped his nose with the back of his hand. "We have plenty of rock."

Meg nodded. She went to fetch two, one in each hand, from the tumbled stone around the pool.

When she returned, he was kneeling beside the body, calmly removing the insignia. "Mother will want them," he said in that same lifeless voice.

Every part of her hurt for him. When she'd finally realized the extent of her father's illness, little time had been left, but she'd been seated beside him, holding his hand when the moment came. She'd heard the last rattling breath leave his body, felt his grip grow slack in hers. When she'd risen to kiss his forehead in farewell, his skin had already been cold. He had gone, and she was alone.

Ben had held out hope his father was still alive. He'd searched every draw, every crack in the wall of the canyon, expecting any day to find him injured but alive, awaiting rescue. How awful to face the Colonel's death so suddenly, knowing he could never say goodbye or ease his father's passing.

She laid a hand on his shoulder, felt it shaking. This strong, sure man had every right to weep. She wept with him, for all the words that couldn't be said, the moments that would never come again. When he straightened his shoulders, she released him to fetch more rocks.

They worked in silence, passing each other as they ferried stones to cover the body. Every moment only seemed to deepen the burden on her heart. If only she had a bucket or a pail so she could carry more rocks at a time.

As she made another trip to the pool, she spotted her skirt where she'd left it to dry. It rippled in the breeze as if just as ready to escape the canyon and its deadly secrets.

Meg smoothed it out. Who needed a bucket when a sling would do? She began piling rocks in the center of the material. She had just tied the corners over the top and was testing the hold when Ben paused beside her.

"Let me," he said.

She stepped back, and he took the bundle and tossed it over one shoulder.

She went in search of more rocks.

The sun had disappeared over the rim,

leaving the clearing in shadow by the time they finished. Ben had found a fallen limb with branches set nearly perpendicular. He shoved it into the rocks near where his father's head had been. Meg stared at the crude cross, tears stinging her eyes again.

"Do you want to say something?" she asked.

"No." He turned for the pool.

She lingered a moment, remembering the tall, proud man who had figured so largely in his family's life and many a cavalry legend.

"Thank you," she whispered. "Thank you for accepting me, and thank you for raising a man any father would be proud of."

She closed her eyes.

*Thank you, Father, for allowing Ben and his family to understand that the Colonel is gone. I don't know the choices Colonel Coleridge made when he was on this Earth, but I think he had faith in you, likely more than I've had lately. I hope he's safe in your arms now. I hope Papa is too. I'm sorry I never thought to pray about that until now. I'm sorry I haven't prayed much at all. Help me.*

Peace flowed through her, allowing her to draw her first deep breath in hours. She turned her back on the grave and went to join Ben.

The Colonel was gone. Even after checking the body for signs of what had caused his father's death, removing the silver eagle on the shoulder strap, and burying the man, Ben had to repeat the fact to himself. The whole world seemed to have dimmed, as if the light had left with the Colonel.

He stared down into the pool, his reflection wavering back at him. He looked dusty, worn. Every bone and muscle ached, and he knew it wasn't just from the exertion. He'd started this expedition with two goals: find the Army its road and learn what had happened to his father. Only Meg understood the latter goal.

What would she think if she knew what he'd discovered about his father's body? The way the Colonel had been lying, it had appeared he'd died trying to crawl out of the canyon. Nothing could be further from the truth. Ben could still feel the brittle bones under his hands, broken in places, likely from a fall from a height. And there had been no mistaking the gaping hole in his chest.

Right now, Meg didn't need to know any of that. She had enough to worry about without looking for murderers around every bend. It was one more secret to keep, one more burden to carry. At the moment, he felt bowed by them.

He stiffened as she touched his arm.

"The sun's nearly down," she murmured. "Should we keep climbing?"

He'd wanted to be out of the canyon before dark. That didn't seem possible now. He'd have to pick his way carefully up that craggy cliff. But he couldn't stay here with the body. Scavengers had been at it. They could return, and he didn't want Meg to be waiting. They had to keep moving.

"We'll climb," he said. "We may not make the rim, but we'll look for better shelter along the way."

She nodded, then bent over the stream. "Drink up."

Food or drink held no interest, but he knew she was right. He bent and cupped water into his hands. That's when he noticed hers.

Swallowing the water, he reached for the long fingers, took them in his own. The nails were chipped and filthy, the skin roughened and torn. The climb was partially to blame, but these wounds were from what she'd done for his father, for him.

"Thank you," he murmured, pressing a

kiss into her damp palm.

A tremor went through her. Looking up, he found that her smile had softened, become something more. How easy to let himself float in it, forget he had more to do. He made himself release her and started out of the clearing.

It was harder going now, and he was glad for something else on which to focus his mind. He had to think like Hank and the theodolite, calculating angles in his head, determining the most stable path that would lead them upward. He barely noticed that the plants were changing again, growing fatter, greener. The air cooled with the coming night, but another scent sparkled in the air.

"Pine," she said behind him with a sniff. "We must be close."

So it seemed when he glanced up, but the path kept running into sheer drops or towering walls, requiring him to backtrack. They kept climbing, but they never reached the top.

Twilight wrapped the draw when he stopped again. Trees draped over the canyon here, their roots partially exposed against the golden rock, fallen needles softening the ground and branches creating a canopy against the elements.

"We'll stay here," Ben said. "We'll be safer

380

starting out once it's light."

She sank and stretched her legs in front of her. "You'll get no argument from me. I'm not sure I could take another step."

Ben sat heavily beside her, feeling as if he'd marched twenty miles with a loaded pack. "Good, because I don't think I could fight you." He leaned against the cliff and stretched his legs as well. They throbbed, and so did his feet.

She unslung the skirt from where she'd once more wrapped it around her shoulders and opened it to reveal the shiny black clusters of elderberry, which she must have picked as they climbed. "Dinnertime. Look what I baked over a hot stove all day."

Ben chuckled. "Gingerbread couldn't taste sweeter right now." He selected a cluster and began pulling off the little round berries.

"Now, that I will argue." She leaned back against the wall as well, munching a moment before speaking again. "I was always fond of gingerbread. Gingersnaps too."

"Mmm." He smiled, remembering the tart taste. "Frosted sugar cookies were my downfall. Mother always claimed I had an endless appetite for them. Then there's Dot's cinnamon rolls."

She twisted her legs from side to side as if

381

trying to work out the kinks. He still couldn't get used to her in breeches, not that he could see much in the growing dark.

"I hope Dot's all right," she said.

"Dot will be fine," he assured her. "She's tough, experienced, and savvy."

"Bad things still happen to people like that."

As they had happened to the Colonel.

The berries were like straw in his mouth, but he made himself swallow another bite.

"I'm sorry," she murmured. "I didn't mean to remind you. If there's anything I can do . . ."

"Nothing," Ben said.

"It might help to talk," she encouraged.

She made it all too easy. Though she was a fading shadow, he could imagine that engaging smile, the tilt of her head, the way she leaned forward as if eager to hear what he had to say.

"Did it help, when your father died?" he asked.

She shifted on the hard stone. "It might have. I didn't really have anyone to talk to. Aunt Abigail never understood. She seemed to think Papa brought his illness on himself. Something about living outside society's expectations, I suppose." She humphed. "She certainly wouldn't think much of our current circumstances."

"Neither would my mother," Ben assured her.

"I can hear Aunt Abigail now." Her voice took on a higher, nasal pitch. "Young ladies eat sparingly, Margaret, if they eat in public at all. And they do not masticate their food like a milk cow."

As if in defiance, she pulled off more berries, shoved them into her mouth, and smacked her lips. Even in the dim light he could see the purple juice dribbling from one corner of her lips.

He reached out and wiped it away with the pad of his thumb.

She stilled, and he could feel her gaze on him. "I'm sorry, Ben. I asked you to talk, and here I am prosing on."

"I like it when you prose," he said. "I always learn something."

She snorted. "Oh yes. Like the fact my aunt finds me detestable."

"Like the fact that she held you to a ridiculous standard," he countered. "I know something about that. My father was in the Army most of his life, starting as a volunteer in the local militia and continuing with the standing Army after the War Between the States. There was one and only one acceptable occupation for the Colonel's son."

"The cavalry," she said.

He nodded, then settled himself more comfortably against the soil at his back as his tense muscles began to relax. "Every spare minute he had, he taught me to ride, to shoot, to use a saber. Geology studies were only useful if they helped me take advantage of terrain. History was best suited to teaching lessons on how previous military men waged war."

Could she hear the bitterness that had crept into his voice? He forced it back.

"Make no mistake. The Colonel wanted the best for me. We just disagreed on what that was."

"But he must have come around in the end," she protested. "You entered West Point. You graduated. You're serving as an engineer now."

"Because of him." The words nearly choked him, but he made himself continue. "He convinced the admissions committee at West Point to let me in. I didn't know it at the time, or I would have refused the appointment. I took a spot meant for someone else, someone who *had* earned it." Admitting it aloud brought back all the shame he'd felt when he'd first discovered the truth.

"He must have believed in you to take that

chance," she insisted.

He drew a breath. "He didn't. He thought I'd fail and then I'd have no choice but to attempt the cavalry instead. He told me so when I received my first promotion."

"Oh, Ben." Her voice echoed his sorrow.

"He didn't stop there," he said. "I was surveying with Wheeler, exactly the sort of work I'd hoped to be doing. But that wasn't good enough for the Colonel's son. He wanted to see me make major, and he couldn't believe I might achieve that as a surveyor. He arranged for me to be appointed to a monument committee in our nation's capital. Lots of prestige. Men who would gladly promote his son. Not much earthly good."

She edged closer. "No wonder you jumped at the chance to lead this survey team."

"That and to learn what had happened to him. Now I know, but I'll have to ask for leave to go home and tell Mother and Diana. They deserve to hear it from me instead of a telegram. So, you see, even from the grave, the Colonel manages to dictate my life."

The bitterness was back. He couldn't swallow it so easily this time. What was wrong with him? He wanted to help his mother and sister. He wanted to respect the legacy his father had left. He may not have wanted the opportunities the Colonel had given him, but he wouldn't be the man he was today without them.

Something bumped his arm. Looking down, he made out a white palm filled with round black berries.

"Have some," Meg said as if the tart fruit would solve all his problems.

For her and for no other reason, he took a few and ate them. "Thank you for dinner, Meg, and for listening. Try to get some sleep."

She disappeared for a moment, as if squirreling away the berries for the morning. He saw her skirt flip up to drape like a blanket. She hesitated a moment, then leaned against him. Ben put his arm around her.

"It will be all right," she promised.

He nodded, but he couldn't tell her he very much doubted that. Even when he returned to the fort, he would have to tell the commander what he'd learned about his father. There would be inquiries, accusations. His work was just beginning.

Around him, night sounds rose with the moon: the furtive movement of something small and likely vulnerable in the branches above them, the howl of a coyote on the rim. A bat glided silently past the opening to their shelter as moonlight brightened the canyon. Meg's breath was soft beside him. His body demanded that he sleep, but his brain refused to obey orders for once.

He was the head of the family now. He'd have to provide for his mother, his sister. He wasn't sure what that meant. Would they be content with him sending money, or would they expect him to end his career and join them? His mother had stayed behind while his father campaigned before. Surely she'd want to remain somewhere with a society, and something finer than that of a wilderness fort. Neither she nor Diana would ever be able to handle a survey expedition the way Meg had, even if the Army would consent to allow him to bring them along.

He shifted on the rock, cushioned Meg's head against his chest. Beyond his feet, the world dropped away to the blackness of an abyss. The loss of his father felt as wide and deep.

*Why, Lord? Mother needed him. Diana needed him.*

*I needed him.*

He would never have admitted it to the Colonel. Pride again. They both had had it, to excess. He'd wanted to make his own way, blaze his own trail. Knowing his father was behind him.

Once more the coyote howled, a wavering, forlorn sound that reached inside his chest. Meg was there beside him, but he had never felt so alone. Though at times he'd resented his father's unasked-for intervention, the Colonel had always been there, a solid presence at his back. How would he go on without him?

*My grace is sufficient for thee.*

The remembered verse whispered like a breeze through the trees, chasing away the sound of the coyote, humbling him.

Why had he forgotten? He wasn't alone, and he never would be. He might have lost his earthly father, but his heavenly Father was always listening, always ready to help. He never went off on campaign, never disappeared into the wilderness, never slept. His intervention would always be to Ben's good. He was the One to be counted upon.

Ben bowed his head, drawing in a breath with his prayer.

*Thank you, Lord, for the life he lived, for the inspiration he provided me and countless other soldiers. Help me to rely on your inspiration from here on.*

Sleep stole over him. The last thing he remembered was resting his head against Meg's and relaxing at last.

# 25

Meg woke first this time. Birds darted past the branches of their shelter, and others sang above. One landed on the rock by her outstretched feet, head cocked as if eyeing the pitiful pile of elderberries she'd tucked into a corner. She moved, and the bird flew off. She grabbed a handful of the tart berries, cold from the night, and swallowed them down before turning to look at Ben.

He was tipped back against the rock. Two days in the canyon had left the beginnings of a beard that showed signs of red in the rising sun. Brown lashes swept his cheeks, and his lips were parted, as if he craved more of the sweet, cool air.

Her heart turned over.

She couldn't wake him. Yesterday had been grueling, emotionally and physically. All this time, she'd thought Mrs. Colonel Coleridge the one with impossibly high expectations, when the Colonel had been

389

far worse. Her father had been tough on her at times as he taught her to take pictures. And he had tended to make decisions that benefited his needs, not hers. But he'd never manipulated her, tried to force her to be something she wasn't. Small wonder Ben had mixed feelings about his father's death and his own future. He deserved his sleep.

She crawled carefully out onto the cliff.

The golden stone glowed in the light, shadows clearly outlining every crease, every indentation. She could almost plot the path up with her eyes. Another hour, maybe two, and they would reach the top. Relief nearly flattened her.

The breeze brushed her cheeks, and a lock of hair danced past her eyes.

Her hand flew to her head. Leaves and pine needles seemed as numerous as the tangles. The skin of her cheeks felt hot, dry. She wouldn't have been surprised if her nose was peeling. Certainly her lips were chapped. Her breeches were filthy, boots scuffed and crusted with red earth. And she was a little afraid that faint sour musty smell was her.

No way around it. She was a mess. At least Ben would have no illusions about her. The thought was lowering.

She forced herself to focus on the situation instead. She knew it couldn't be much farther up. And down . . .

The depth of the canyon was nearly dizzying. She was glad when Ben came out to join her.

"Ready to greet the day?" he asked.

He certainly was. A few leaves stuck in his thick hair, his skin had turned a golden brown, and his uniform still looked serviceable. It wasn't fair.

"Certainly," she said. "Eat the rest of the berries, and let's get started. I'll look for better breakfast along the way."

He did as she bid, and they started up the path.

Her body protested. Her legs were stiff; her neck ached from the angle she'd slept. The wool of her riding skirt slung about her shoulders chafed her sunburned neck. But if he could keep going, so could she.

Once again, the cliff fought them, leading them in promising directions that stopped at a sheer wall or dwindled to a drop-off. But every setback took them a little higher, until the rim was within reach.

They stepped out of the draw midmorning. The pines and spruce, tall and proud against a cloudy sky, felt like old friends, welcoming them back. Meg sank onto the ground. "We made it."

"Not yet," Ben said as if determined to dampen her hopes. "We have the afternoon to find water, shelter, and food, in that order. And we need to attract attention."

He pulled the pistol from his belt and fired it into the air. "Halloo!" he shouted after the echo faded. "Captain Ben Coleridge of the U.S. Army Corps of Engineers. Can anyone hear me?"

His voice rolled down the canyon, but no one answered.

Meg sagged. It couldn't be easy. With a sigh, she climbed to her feet. "Which way?"

"East," he said. "We stay close to the rim and keep calling."

Meg nodded, and they set out.

It was more comfortable going here, the land mostly flat with the occasional gentle slope up or down. Through the trees on her right, she caught glimpses of the canyon. A squirrel with tufted ears darted out of sight. As the temperatures climbed, pine scented the air.

"Are we beyond the burned area, then?" she asked, glancing around. "I don't see any blackened ground or trunks."

"It must have started between here and the last camp," Ben said, detouring around a fallen branch.

"But how?" Meg squinted into the distance but saw only more pines. "Please don't tell me Dot was careless."

"Dot knows her way around a fire," Ben assured her. "And even if an ember strayed beyond her circle of stones, the ground near the camp was fairly green because of Bright Angel Creek. The fire must have started in the undergrowth outside the draw. It wouldn't have taken much when the land there was dry. Perhaps a lightning strike or sunlight through a water drop. They can act like a magnifying glass to concentrate the heat." He paused to raise his voice. "Halloo! Anyone near?"

Birds darted out of the trees ahead, but even they didn't answer.

And Ben didn't stop. Every few minutes, he hollered, until his voice grew rough. Meg took up the call then. She also gathered what she could, finding red raspberries and more wild cabbage among the brush.

Ben ate them readily enough. He had to be as hungry as she was.

"Oh, what I wouldn't give for a nice roasted chicken about now," she said.

He winked at her. "At least this is better than salt pork."

"Or hardtack," she agreed.

He ripped off more of the cabbage with his teeth, chewed, and swallowed, Adam's apple bobbing. "The Wheeler survey had a cook who favored pork rind."

Meg frowned. "What part of the pig is that?"

"The skin. He used to deep fry it before setting out on the trail and keep it in a vat of vinegar."

Meg shuddered. "That sounds horrible."

Ben wiggled his brows and toasted her with the last of the cabbage. "Makes miner's lettuce and cabbage seem like a treat, though."

Meg laughed, then winced as her throat protested. All that calling was taking a toll.

So was the lack of water.

She tried not to think about that. The raspberries helped a little. But the scratch in her throat grew worse, and her head began throbbing. Ben's stories dried up as well, and she couldn't find it in her to tell any herself. Every step, every breath, seemed harder.

He bent and plucked some rocks from the ground.

"What are you doing?" she asked, voice croaky.

"Picking up chert," he said. "It's hard enough to act like flint. I didn't have wood or spark for a fire the last two nights, but I might here."

The idea of another night on their own was never less appealing. Neither was starting a fire. Still, he was right. With no cave or overhang for protection, and them higher now in elevation, it would be cold tonight. Her battered skirt wouldn't be enough to keep them warm.

She glanced up at the clouds, which were only growing more numerous, dimming the day. "Do you think it will rain?"

He smiled, and she noticed his lips were cracking too. "We can only hope. If we don't come across a stream, we'll need to look for a stand of aspen and wildflowers. They're often the first to colonize when a pond fills in. We might still find water near the surface if we dig for it."

Meg craned her neck to see around the trees ahead of them. "What about that?"

He followed her pointing finger. Aspens clustered around a rainbow of wildflowers as if to protect them from the encroaching pine and spruce. He started in that direction, with her right behind.

The ground felt softer under her dirty boots. It looked darker too. Ben hurried forward, dropped to his knees, and began scrabbling at the soil. Meg crouched beside him.

"There's something here," he said, hope

lacing his voice. He dug harder. Water seeped into the hole, muddy, clotted. It had never looked more appetizing.

She wanted to hug him from sheer relief, but she wanted a drink more. "Use this," Meg said, offering him her skirt, and once more, he filtered water through the wool.

The seep rose slowly. It took a while for both to drink their fill. Finally, he rocked back on his heels and glanced up at her. "We can't stay here. It's too open."

Meg sat back and began rubbing life into her leaden legs. "Isn't it better to stay close to water?"

He glanced around. The aspens waved their leaves like friendly hands as if encouraging them to remain. Ben didn't look appreciative, frown gathering. "Meg, there's something else we should discuss. This adventure will have repercussions. Your reputation, for one. You've spent two nights in my company, unchaperoned, and you may have to spend more before this is over."

"I spent the time surviving, same as you," Meg said. "Surely Dot would understand."

His blue-gray gaze crossed back to her. "Dot would. The rest of the world might not."

Meg waved a hand, then regretted it. Even her fingers felt heavy. "The only part of the world that matters is the part that pays me for my work. Most people buying stereographs won't know I had the misfortune of getting trapped in the Grand Canyon. If they do, they might see that as part of the glamour of my profession."

He chuckled. "Yes, this has been quite glamorous."

That only made her think about her hair again. She raised her head instead. "No one who matters will care about my reputation."

"I'm not so sure about that," he said. "Our disappearance will have to be noted in the expedition record. I'll have to brief Colonel Yearling. Word will get out. You'll have to negotiate the next contract, likely with officers who have only heard about your reputation. I don't like the idea of how they might treat you if they thought you less than a lady." He went down on one knee before her, mud-streaked face earnest.

"I won't let you bear the censure, Meg. We'll get married."

She stared at him. She must know it was the perfect solution to the problem. She didn't deserve the whispers, the sly looks. Some men thought a lady, once ruined, should be glad for any attention. If she married him, he could protect her. He could imagine working side by side, exploring the country, opening new lands. They could settle in a cottage somewhere, raise a family together — she'd make a wonderful mother the way she listened and advised. Perhaps he'd be invited to teach at the Point. They could grow old together, unlike his parents.

"No," she said.

Ben blinked. "No?"

"No," she repeated. "I'm not marrying you to save my reputation or your conscience. We haven't done anything wrong."

Ben rubbed the back of his neck, which felt unaccountably hot. "Of course we haven't. That's not the point."

She cocked her head to look up at him as he rose. "Then what is the point?"

Ben shook his head. "At the moment, I have no idea. My mother and sister always insist that a lady's greatest treasure is her reputation. Being alone in the wilderness with me damaged yours. I just wanted to make things right."

"Nothing you can do," she said, climbing to her feet as well. "But if the matter doesn't bother me or my clients, I don't see why it should bother you."

Frustration pushed at him, like a hot wind from the canyon. He knew it was the weariness, the struggle of the last two days, but he couldn't stop the words that came out. "I thought we had an understanding."

"We do." She bundled up the wet wool, still maddeningly calm. "We agreed to see whether our friendship might lead to something more. I certainly never agreed to be pushed into marriage."

Pushed? He'd felt as if he was walking on eggshells most of the time, picking his way along. He blew out a breath. "I'm not pushing you, Meg. I want this to be a joint decision. Why don't you wait here while I see if I can find us some shelter for the night?"

"You're not leaving me behind," she declared. She reached toward her legs as if preparing to twitch her skirts aside, then paused as if remembering she no longer wore them. "Where you go, I follow."

"Apparently only if it doesn't involve a wedding ceremony," he said, but he turned and headed back toward the rim.

The rain she'd predicted came, a gentle shower this time, pattering down around them. Ben ducked under a tree, but Meg stood out, head tilted back and hat off, letting the water run down her face. With her pale hair coming loose from its pins, her smile warm, she looked as bright as sunshine. His heart tugged at him.

Why had she refused him again? He was

an officer now instead of a cadet, someone with a sure future ahead of him. An Army engineer was an excellent prospect, or so his sister claimed. He could almost hear Diana.

*A lady with little means of support, concerned for her reputation, ought to jump at the chance to marry someone like you, Ben.*

He winced. He wasn't a finer catch than any of the other officers at the fort. If Meg was interested in marriage, she could have had her pick. Or not. She had a chance to make her own future with her photography. He ducked out from under the trees, stood beside her in the rain, let the water wash him clean.

The rain slowed to a shower, then moved on. She smiled at him. He couldn't let her go, let his feelings go.

"Am I so abhorrent?" he murmured.

Her smile was sad. "You're not abhorrent at all. I care about you, Ben."

Once more hope leaped up, brighter than the sun coming out from behind the lingering clouds. "Then help me. What am I doing wrong?"

"Nothing," she assured him, pulling away. "Shouldn't we be calling?"

Ben shook his head. "You're avoiding the issue."

She ignored him. "Halloo!" she shouted, voice tight and shrill. She tilted her head to look around him as if expecting to see someone riding to their rescue.

He caught her hands. "Meg, please. I care about you too. I want to get this right."

She clamped her lips shut, eyes as stormy as the clouds heading for the rim.

"Halloo!"

Ben stared at her. Her eyes widened, and her body stiffened.

But her lips — her soft, sweet lips — hadn't moved.

He released her and whirled even as she crowded closer to him.

"Halloo!" he shouted, cupping his hands around his mouth. "Captain Ben Coleridge. Is anyone there?"

For a moment, he heard nothing. Had it only been an echo? Or was his mind that desperate for an answer? Meg clutched his arm, gaze on the distance, as if she could will help closer.

"Halloo!" came the call at last. "Corporal Christopher Adams of Fort Wilverton! Stay where you are. We'll come to you."

Meg turned in his arms, buried her head in his shoulder. Ben held her close a moment, thanksgiving pulsing through him.

The sight of his team coming through the

trees had never been more welcome. It looked as if they'd saved most of the mules, for each was riding one bareback, and Larson and Adams were each leading a string. The beasts looked odd, and it was a moment before he realized why. Only a few carried a pack, and none pulled a wagon or van. His stomach sank.

Dot, who was riding in the lead, skirts hiked up to accommodate the lack of a sidesaddle, urged her mule forward, and Hank let out a cry. Ben started running, and Meg joined him.

Dot struggled to get off her mule, then ran to meet them and hugged Meg close.

"Oh, I thought we'd lost you," she said, rocking back and forth.

Hank clapped Ben on the back even as Adams and Larson saluted.

"Sight for sore eyes, Captain," the cartographer said.

"You too," Ben assured him, hand on his shoulder.

Meg pulled back. "Where's Private Meadows?"

"Here, ma'am." The private moved out from among his charges. One side of his face was an angry red, blisters showing white, and one hand was wrapped in cloth. Ben stiffened.

Meg reacted more strongly. "What happened?" she cried.

Adams raised his head. "Private Meadows ran into the flames to cut the horses free."

Meg's face crumbled. "Oh, poor Stripe! She won't know what to do."

Meadows hung his head. "Sorry."

"No apology necessary, Private," Ben said. "You did what you had to do to save their lives. If they don't find their way back to the fort, natives may come across them and take them in or a trader might capture them."

"I'd like to request an official commendation for bravery, Captain," Adams put in.

"Wasn't bravery," Meadows muttered, averting his gaze. "Just couldn't see a critter burned."

Meg shifted on her feet, as if she wanted to rush up to the fellow and wrap her arms around him. Ben was glad she didn't. The youth was embarrassed enough as it was.

"That *is* bravery, Private," she told him. "You faced something that had robbed you before, and you refused to give it another opportunity."

"Corporal Adams is a hero too," Larson put in as if hoping to draw attention away from his friend. "He spotted the fire coming and warned us all in time."

"He took charge and kept us together," Hank confirmed, though the tone in his voice said he was still surprised by the turn of events.

Adams's chin inched up. "I was simply doing my job to the best of my abilities." He glanced at Meg for some reason, then started as his gaze dropped to her breeches. Pink gathered in his cheeks.

Time to turn attentions back where they belonged. "Well done, both of you," Ben said. "I'll speak to Colonel Yearling at the fort about your efforts."

Meadows ducked his head. Adams nodded with evident satisfaction.

Ben couldn't help looking over the team again. Each bore some testament to their harrowing escape. Dot's skirts had blackened circles, like polka dots on the blue denim, where embers must have landed and been beaten out. Hank had lost part of a sleeve, his arm showing scarlet through the tattered remains of his flannel undershirt. Adams's eyes were red-rimmed, as if he had looked too long into the flames as he helped the others out. Larson moved with a limp. And Pike . . .

Meg must have noticed the missing member of the expedition, for she spoke even as Ben was opening his mouth to ask the ques-

404

tion. "Where's Mr. Pike?"

Dot's face fell.

"Lost," Hank spit out. "And that's all I'll say on the matter in present company."

# 26

Meg had never been so happy to see anyone in her life. She wanted to hug them all close, tend all their wounds. And the thought of Mr. Pike's loss was heartrending. She'd never liked the taciturn guide, but she wouldn't have wished this fate on him.

She'd seen the same dismay cross Ben's face, but he straightened, and the air of command slipped over him like a well-worn cloak. "The sun will be going down soon. I need a situation report. Anyone else injured?"

The others rallied as well, the cavalrymen straightening until they stood at attention, Dot raising her chin, and Hank meeting Ben's gaze.

"Not seriously," the cartographer said. "Private Larson was hit by a falling limb."

The private kept his gaze straight ahead. "Nothing that will prevent me from doing my duty, sir."

"The good Lord spared us," Dot agreed.

*Thank you, Lord.* The prayer speared skyward with Meg's relief.

Ben remained focused as he glanced over the mules. "How'd we fare as far as supplies and equipment?"

"The tents and most personal gear are gone," Hank said. "Corporal Adams helped me save the theodolite and one set of the expedition journals."

The corporal nodded, narrow face redder than usual. "We also managed to load a few saddlebags with gear: a compass, blankets, canteens, and part of the picket line among other minor articles."

Ben looked to Dot. "What about food and cooking equipment?"

"One pot and the cinnamon," Dot said. "The fire just swung in so fast!"

"Never saw anything like it," Hank agreed. "It ran along the bushes, jumped from tree to tree."

"Like it was alive," Meadows murmured.

Meg shivered, remembering. "It looked terrifying from the canyon."

Dot nodded. "Couldn't tell the sky from the ground with all the smoke. But Hank pointed us north, and we kept going until it petered out."

"We have our knives, pistols, and a rifle,"

407

Hank added, "but only the ammunition that was in them or on our ammunition belts. We hunted and gathered what plants we could the last two nights."

"There's a stream down there," Dot said, pointing back the way she and the others had come. "We've been following the rim, figuring you'd come up somewhere along here, if you could." She gave Meg another squeeze. "Don't you go running off on me again!"

"I won't," Meg promised, hugging her back.

"We'll camp at your stream tonight," Ben said. "It's clear with this setback we can't continue the survey. The only way forward I can see is to return to the fort."

Adams and Meadows brightened, but Larson eyed the golden soil with a sigh. "Might as well admit our defeat."

Ben's smile was grim. "We aren't defeated, Private. We didn't fail in our duty. When Miss Meg and I were down in what I believe was Bright Angel Canyon, we found the Army a possible wagon road. We just need to live long enough to tell them."

Hank clapped him on the back again, and his men offered their congratulations.

Dot was watching Meg. "You don't seem so happy about this," she murmured.

Meg made herself smile. "I'm glad Ben found a promising route, but I'll be sorry to see the survey end. I had higher hopes for what we might accomplish."

Dot started. "Your cameras! Of course. I'm sorry. There just wasn't time to save them before Hank dragged me off and set me on a mule."

She would not think of her loss, not when she'd just gained so much back. "The important thing is that most of us survived," she told Dot, but she couldn't help glancing at Ben. Weariness must be riding his shoulders, yet he had taken charge of the group, was even now charting a course home.

He had to be hurting. It was one thing to lose their guide, another to have lost all hope of finding his father alive. He hadn't confided in the others that he had a secondary mission. Would he tell them what else he'd discovered in the canyon?

Ben had never liked riding a mule. The sturdy animals had their own opinions as to pace and direction. But he was grateful for the ride as the mule carried his weary body back toward the spring. Their path to return to the fort wouldn't be easy, especially with Pike gone, but with what they had, they should be able to reach safety.

He glanced back along the short column. Hank rode at his side, with Dot and Meg right behind. Adams came next, and Larson and Meadows led the rest of the mules, stretching out behind like the tail of a kite. They were all blessed to have survived.

He caught Meg's eye, and she smiled. He felt lighter. Her knowledge of plants and quick thinking about her skirt had quite probably saved his life. She had never complained, always contributed to decisions. He could not imagine a better person to have at his side, in that canyon, or through life.

*Thank you, Lord.*

As if he knew the direction of Ben's thoughts, Hank spoke up. "Miss Meg asked about Pike."

Ben faced front to give the cartographer his attention. "What happened?"

Hank's gaze went into the distance as if seeing something other than the tall pines. "I'm not sure. He left camp before the fire started. You saw how mad he was we didn't take his advice."

Ben remembered. "I should never have gone down along the creek."

Hank shrugged. "You couldn't know a fire was coming."

"You navigated in the smoke by the sound

of it," Ben said.

"I figured if we could head north, we might outrun the fire. Thanks to the right wind, we did. It burned itself out when it hit the canyon on the other side of that dried-up pond Pike had been hoping we could camp at. Saw it on our way back south."

Once again, all Ben could feel was thanksgiving. If the wind had turned, if the mules had balked, someone might have died. Then again, it seemed someone had.

"How do you know Pike didn't make it?" Ben asked.

Hank's face lengthened. "The next morning, we went back over the burnt area, hoping to find you all alive. We knew you and Meg had gone down that side canyon, so we stood at the top and hollered."

"The creek must have drowned the noise," Ben said. "We didn't hear you. Either that, or we were too far down the canyon by then. Too many fallen trees to climb back the way we'd come."

"We thought the way looked blocked. I figured you'd search for another way up."

"Which is exactly what I did," Ben told him. "But it took a while. Sometimes it seemed every direction was blocked there as well. I don't like thinking about what

411

would have happened if you hadn't found us."

"Glad to help," Hank said with a nod. "I only wish we'd been able to save Pike. We found a body yesterday, right about where the fire started, from the look of the scorched dirt. It was burned beyond recognition, but about the right size. Adams, Meadows, and Larson helped me use sticks to carve out a shallow grave."

Ben glanced at him. "You're sure it was Pike?"

Hank shared his frown. "It had to be. Who else would be out here?"

Their nocturnal visitor, perhaps? But if so, then where was Pike?

"You forget," Ben said. "More than one person disappeared out this way recently."

"That guide McCoy and the Colonel," Hank agreed. "But what would either be doing here alone, and where was the other?"

His throat felt tight as the memory washed over him. "Meg and I found the other body down in the canyon. It was my father."

Hank's face tightened. "I'm sorry to hear that. The Colonel was a good man."

Ben turned his face forward. "He was. I didn't always appreciate that. I would have brought his body back if I could. We buried him in rocks."

412

"But how'd he get down in the canyon?" Hank asked. "Did he and the guide go exploring and get trapped on the way out by a storm or rockslide? Did you find the guide too?"

"No," Ben said darkly. "That's why I questioned you about the body you found."

Hank eyed him. "You think it was McCoy? Why?"

"Because the Colonel had one more story to tell."

Hank frowned. "What?"

In his mind's eye, Ben saw the crooked body, felt the fragile bones under his hands as he'd searched the corpse while Meg was gathering stones. "You and Meg both assume he died trying to escape the canyon. His body was feet away from a pond, lying in a thicket of berries and miner's lettuce. Lack of food and water didn't kill him."

"Then what did?" Hank asked.

The matter left a bitter taste in his mouth. "He had several broken bones and a gunshot to the chest. The Colonel was murdered, his corpse left for nature to destroy. And I think I know why."

Hank was staring at him so fixedly he didn't appear to notice his mule was veering for the trees. Ben tipped his head, and the cartographer urged the mule closer again.

"I found indications of gold in Bright Angel Creek," Ben explained. "Not enough to make a profit from what I can see, but all it takes is a rumor and men will clog its banks. I think the Colonel heard such a rumor. Meg and I found claim markers in the canyon. After what he'd seen in San Francisco, my father wouldn't have risked taking his men to investigate. He commandeered someone he trusted and went out himself. I don't know if McCoy turned on him, or someone else caught them both. But he wasn't supposed to make it back and inform the Army."

He reached into his pocket and drew out the rowel. The steel winked in his palm as he held it for Hank to see.

"I discovered this on the slope our second day at the canyon, in an area where someone had overturned a number of rocks. It's my father's. Maybe he lost it in a fight for his life, and his murderer only went back to look for it when he knew we were in the same area."

"Our midnight visitor," Hank guessed. "Makes sense. And he likely had help to move that body to a different location."

Ben started, and his mule shied. Pocket-

414

ing the rowel and urging his mount closer to the cartographer again, Ben lowered his voice. "That's it, Hank. McCoy must have had a partner. They were working together all this time. That's how he slipped into camp unseen. That's why he destroyed Meg's plate, so no one would know she'd caught something that might implicate them — a camp we missed, a second claim?"

"The only person who could have been his partner is Pike," Hank said, the name a growl.

"You're right." In his mind, he saw the symbol carved into the trees again. What they'd seen as two mountains could well have been the letter *M,* the half moon, part of the letter *P.*

"Well, he won't be around to enjoy his gold," Hank said. "Looks like McCoy double-crossed him too."

The thought brought no comfort.

Next to him, Hank cocked his head. "You sure there wasn't enough to pan?"

Ben chuckled. "Don't you go getting gold fever on me."

Hank held up his hands, then hastily clutched the mule again. "Not me. Dot would kill me if I ran off. And I don't like the idea of her living in a mining camp again. But you can be sure that if the

415

Colonel heard the rumor, others will too, and they will come looking."

"Then we'll hold them off with the truth," Ben said, gaze going forward once more. "There's not enough gold to fund two prospectors, much less hundreds. We can look for samples before we return to the fort and prove it."

They reached the campsite and settled in around the spring. Meg took a long drink of the cool, crisp water. Someone had shot a rabbit. It was a small meal for seven people, but they augmented it with the berries and greens Dot had gathered along the way.

As night fell, the air chilled, and coyotes howled in the distance. Everyone huddled near the fire, men along one side and Dot and Meg close together. Ben might have been sitting on the ground leaning back on one elbow, but his gaze was sharp.

"We have a long trek ahead of us," he said. "The mules are hardy, but we can't push them. We'll start at dawn, stop midday to rest them, then move on and ride until twilight. We have a compass and the theodolite. Even without Pike, we should be able to retrace our steps."

Someone sighed with obvious relief.

Ben glanced around, gaze lingering a moment on Meg. "As before, I need each of you to use your skills. We have limited ammunition — every shot must count. Private Meadows."

The youth perked up. "Sir?"

"You were raised in Tennessee. Did you ever trap?"

He nodded, eyes bright in the firelight. "Some, as a boy."

"See what you can do to set up traps each night when we camp. Use the remains of dinner, your bootlaces, and Dot's pot if need be. The more animals we catch, the fewer bullets we'll have to expend."

"Yes, sir. I'll set up a snare in a tree tonight."

"And I'll trust you and Private Larson to take care of the mules," Ben continued. "If I overtax them, if they need a longer rest or more time to graze, speak up. They are our ticket home."

Both Meadows and Larson saluted.

"Corporal Adams, you are our best marksman," Ben continued. "If you see meat you're confident you can bring down with one bullet, do it."

"Yes, sir." Adams pulled his rifle closer.

"Hank," Ben said with a look to the cartographer, "man the compass and use the theodolite morning, during afternoon break, and evening to chart our way forward."

"Yes, sir," Hank said, with a salute to match that of the cavalrymen.

Ben smiled before turning to Meg. "Miss Pero."

Meg met his gaze. "Whatever you need."

Something flashed behind his eyes, as if he intended to take her up on that promise. "You've proven wise when it comes to finding food. Point out plants to us. We'll gather as we go."

"Count on me," Meg said.

He turned to the cook. "And Dot?"

She nodded eagerly. "Yes, Captain?"

"You stretch that cinnamon as far as you can."

Dot snapped a salute too.

Ben nodded as if satisfied. "If everything goes well, we should reach the fort in a week to ten days. Any questions?"

To Meg's surprise, Meadows spoke up. "Should we mount a guard, sir?"

Ben's face tightened. "I believe we've seen the last of our midnight visitor, but it would be wise to watch for tricks of nature."

Ben took the first watch, and the others settled themselves to sleep as best they could around the fire. Meadows huddled back to back with one of the mules. Larson bundled himself in a saddle blanket and leaned against a tree. Dot and Hank shared a blanket. Meg draped her skirt about her shoulders and tried to find a comfortable spot on the ground.

Ben moved past on quiet feet.

She watched as he patrolled around the edge of the firelight, his own gaze sweeping the darkness beyond as if he could keep it at bay. Once more confidence cloaked him.

She forced herself to close her eyes, take even breaths. Still sleep refused to come. It felt odd lying here alone after spending the last two nights against Ben, his arm about her, and the steady beat of his heart lulling her to sleep.

*You could have that every night if you'd just say yes.*

The voice in her head sounded suspiciously like Ben's.

*You don't understand,* she argued. *Take a good long look at me — my drive to be the best at my profession, my outspoken nature. Is that really what you want in a wife?*

The Ben in her imagination looked forlorn, and she knew what his answer would be.

*No.*

That was why she'd refused his proposal

at West Point. That was why she'd refused his proposal today. He was still the eager young man looking across a crowded room and seeing a pretty girl. He'd been taken in by the glamour of her, not understanding the life that came with it. He couldn't understand why she wouldn't fit in his world. He'd see the truth once they reached the fort.

Ben moved around the group, too restless to sleep. Once more the responsibility for their lives sat on his shoulders, heavier than before because the stakes were higher. Their lives were in danger. The life of the woman he loved was in danger.

He glanced to where Meg had curled up on one side, hugging the wretched remains of that riding skirt about her. Firelight turned her pale hair to gold. Now, there was a treasure worth dying for.

He'd asked her twice and been refused twice. Some would have cautioned him to give up. She was firm in her convictions, determined to yield in no way. She reminded him a little of his father.

But he wasn't his mother. He wasn't content to watch Meg's star blaze across the sky. He wanted to be beside her, urging her higher. He wanted her beside him, encouraging, supporting. There had to be something he could say, something he could do, to prove to her that they were better together.

She might still refuse. That was her right. But as long as he had any hope of success, he would keep trying.

## 27

Eight days later, they reached the fort. The mules knew it before Ben did. Their heads came up, their nostrils twitched, and they broke into a trot as if ready for their pens. The cluster of square adobe buildings on the plateau looked more like home than ever.

The ride had been long and hard, but he'd never been more impressed with those under his command. Each member of the team had served with distinction. Meadows had snared two squirrels and trapped several rabbits using Meg's miner's lettuce as bait. Adams had brought down a pronghorn with a single shot. Larson had kept the mules watered and fed. Hank had helped Ben collect samples at Bright Angel Creek to confirm that only isolated flakes populated the stream and plotted the course with unerring accuracy. Dot had figured out how to turn the most plentiful plant in the area

— pine — into nourishing and refreshing tea.

Then there was Meg. She'd pointed out plants as he'd asked and gathered more than her share, until her fingers were stained with raspberries. But, more than that, she listened in her forthright, encouraging manner. Her optimism and practicality buoyed them all. And when her warm alto raised the first verse of "Amazing Grace" on the Sunday of their journey, he thought his heart might swell right out of his dusty uniform.

Their forced proximity, however, did not allow for private conversation, and Dot seemed to be taking her chaperone duties even more seriously since their separation after the fire. She stayed within sight of Meg, giving Ben no opportunity to talk further to her about their future. He could only pray things would be different once they reached the fort.

The sentries stared at them as the mules trotted into the parade now, and Ben could understand why. Everyone on his team was riding the mules bareback, after all. He and the other men sported beards of various lengths, from Hank's grizzled locks to Meadows's scraggly chin-hugger. Dot and Meg were sunburned, and Meg still wore her breeches, battered skirt draped about her shoulders. They were all thinner and dirtier than when they'd left, but they carried their heads high as they rode into the fort and reined in before post headquarters late in the afternoon.

The commanding officer strode out as they dismounted.

"Captain Coleridge," he proclaimed, and Ben and his men stood at attention and saluted.

"At ease," he ordered them as other members of the fort gathered around. A tall, lean fellow with a shock of iron gray hair and sideburns that bristled as much as his mustache, Colonel Yearling looked them over, taking in their disheveled state. "I'm surprised to see you back."

In the short time Ben had been at Fort Wilverton before setting out on the survey, he'd come to realize that Yearling did everything according to regulations. He wouldn't take surprises well.

"I'm prepared to give a full report, sir," Ben said. "But, in short, we fell afoul of a wildfire and barely escaped with our lives."

"That's exactly why I'm surprised," Yearling said, hands braced on his hips. "We were told you all perished."

Meg gasped. Hank and the others stared

at the commanding officer as if he'd gone mad.

Ben took a step forward. "Who told you that?"

"Rudy Pike," Yearling answered, "right before he collected his pay and headed south for the pleasures of civilization in Prescott."

Anger surged through him. So, it hadn't been Pike's body Hank and the others had buried. It must have been McCoy's. Had he or Pike started the fire, or just made use of it to cover their dark deeds?

"As you can see," Ben said, struggling to keep his voice civil, "we survived. Pike's story is one more reason for me to suspect he is a liar, a cheat, and a would-be murderer."

Murmurs ran through the assembled crowd.

"Is that so?" Colonel Yearling looked more thoughtful than shocked. "I'd like to hear your full report before I make any decisions. At the moment, however, I know two others who will want to welcome you back."

Still fuming about Pike's betrayal, Ben frowned. Before he could ask, an unmistakable squeal sounded behind him. Whirling, he saw Diana running toward him from the officers' quarters.

"Ben! Oh, Ben, you're alive!"

She hugged him so tightly he couldn't catch his breath. Over her shoulder, another woman came out of the adobe building. Slow and calm as ever, she made her way to his side, amber-colored silk skirts brushing the dust of the parade aside.

"My prayers have been answered," she said, laying a hand on his and his sister's shoulders.

"Mother," he managed. "Diana. What are you doing here?"

Watching the reunion made Meg warm and cold at the same time. Mrs. Colonel Coleridge's mouth trembled, and her daughter's face was stained with tears. It must seem miraculous to them — to have thought Ben lost and here he was found.

They had changed in the last five years. With her honey-colored curls and warm smile, Diana Coleridge had blossomed into a lovely young lady, and more than one officer was watching her now as if wondering how he could make her notice him. Mrs. Colonel Coleridge looked grayer, thinner, as if worrying about her husband had worn her away.

"We came here to see you," Ben's sister was explaining. "Mother was certain you

426

would find a way to locate Father and bring him home."

The ground beneath Meg dipped. How Ben would hurt to tell them the truth. He'd located his father, but the Colonel would never be coming home.

"I'm glad you're here," Ben told them, looking from one to the other. "And I'll explain everything soon. Right now, I need to report to Colonel Yearling and clean up." He pulled away from them.

The commanding officer nodded. "Mrs. Coleridge and Miss Coleridge are staying in my quarters for the moment. I'd be delighted to host the three of you for dinner tonight." He looked to Meg, gray eyes keen. "And you too, Miss Pero. You didn't receive a proper welcome, I understand, when you were here last."

Ben's mother turned as if to see who the colonel had invited to share a table with her. Her eyes widened as her gaze moved from the worn boots to Meg's torn and filthy breeches to her dry face. If Meg had had any thought of convincing Ben's mother to accept her, it would have evaporated now.

Meg turned to the colonel, feeling as if her sunburn had suddenly intensified. "Thank you, but after our ordeal, I should rest."

Only Ben looked disappointed. She tried to console herself with the idea that his disappointment would soon be tempered by relief that she hadn't agreed to his proposal.

The commanding officer accepted her refusal more graciously, inclining his head. "Of course. Mrs. Newcomb, can you make room for Miss Pero in your quarters?"

Either the officers' quarters had no more room or Colonel Yearling had decided she didn't really belong in them. Meg couldn't mind. She'd have far rather stayed with her friend.

Dot must have felt the same way, for she took a step closer to Meg. "Miss Pero is a hero. We wouldn't have made it back without her. Anyone would be honored to host her."

The dear woman overstated, but the men crowding around wouldn't know that. They offered her admiring glances. Ben's mother turned away as if dismissing them both.

"That's settled, then," Colonel Yearling said. "Corporal, see to your men and take your mounts to the corral, then turn in. The three of you are off duty for the next two days."

Adams saluted, and Meadows grinned.

"Captain," the colonel continued, "join me."

"You too, Hank," Ben put in as the commanding officer turned for the door.

"In a moment," Hank promised.

Ben gave Meg one last look before joining his family and the colonel. The world felt smaller.

As Hank accepted the theodolite from Adams, Dot put an arm around Meg's waist. "Come on. I could use a hot bath, and so could you."

All at once, the weariness hit her, and she nearly collapsed where she stood. She made herself go with Dot and Hank to the small house at one side of the parade ground.

Dot's home was neat as a pin, with plank floors and a colorful weaving separating the bedchamber from the main room. Darker patches on the sand-colored walls over the hearth spoke of good meals cooked with love.

"It isn't much," Dot said, "but it's a lot better than a cot or a bedroll on the ground."

"Yes, it is," Hank said, following them inside and setting the theodolite on the table that graced the center of the room. "If you're all right, I need to report."

Dot swatted him on the shoulder. "Get along, ya big galoot."

"I'll be back as soon as I can." He pecked

his wife on the cheek, smiled at Meg, and left.

Dot went to pull out a massive pot from a cupboard near the hearth. "Water's right out the door. Fill this, and I'll come help you carry it back in."

Thank goodness for Dot's pushy nature. Meg couldn't seem to muster thought. Now she just did as she was told — taking the pot to the pump, cranking up and down on the iron handle until cool water splashed out to fill the vessel nearly to the brim, helping Dot carry it back inside. Dot scooped up a smaller kettle and set it on the fire she'd started in the hearth.

Meg didn't think about the past or the future, just the present, until she sat in the battered tin bathing tub Dot dragged onto the braided bedroom rug. Knees drawn up, she ducked her head and washed her hair with the lavender soap Dot had given her. The warm water relaxed overtaxed muscles. The steam removed the last scent of the fire from her body.

The water in the tub was muddy by the time she finished washing, and she stood and rinsed off with the smaller pail of water Dot had left, leaving her shivering in the warm air. The thought of putting on her soiled camisole and corset made her stom-

430

ach knot, but there was nothing for it. They were all she owned now.

Her shivering grew worse as the loss pressed down on her shoulders. She'd come with such high hopes, and she was leaving with nothing — her cameras destroyed, her plates lost, her bedroll and clothing gone.

*Oh, heavenly Father, what am I to do?*

Once more tears were falling. She brushed them away with her fingers. All she needed was a stuffy nose. She didn't even own a handkerchief!

She had filled the tub a second time for Dot and left the cook to her ablutions when someone tapped hesitantly at the door.

"It's safe to come in, Hank," she called, using her fingers to comb out her wet hair where she sat on a bench, back to the fire and face to the table.

The door cracked open, and Ben's sister peered inside. The proper manners couldn't mask the family twinkle in her blue-gray eyes. In the rustic cabin, the fine material of her dress was even more apparent. The blue and white creation boasted row after row of pleats down the front. Meg found herself wondering how she would ever manage to ride astride a mule, then had to stop herself from laughing when she remembered Miss Coleridge would never find herself in such a position.

Ben's sister offered a hopeful smile as she came into the house, material bundled in her arms. "Miss Pero? I don't know if you remember me. We met at West Point."

"Of course I remember you, Miss Coleridge," Meg said, pulling her fingers out of her tangled hair. "But I'm afraid I'm not in much shape to entertain visitors."

"I understand," she assured her. "Ben's still talking to Colonel Yearling, but Corporal Adams told us a little about what you all went through. I can't imagine."

No, she couldn't, and Meg was glad of that. "I'm just thankful to be back."

"The corporal said you lost everything." She took another step forward, fingers worrying at the material in her grip. "There are only a few women at the fort, and the sutlers don't carry ready-made. I checked. Then I realized I was the closest to you in size. I hope I won't offend you, but I thought you might find use for these." She held out the bundle.

Meg rose and closed the distance to take it from her. Wrapped carefully together were a dainty white chemise tied with satin ribbons, a ruffled petticoat edged with lace, an underskirt of blue flowers on white, with panels alternating between horizontal swags and vertical bouquets, an overskirt to match, and a blue-and-white striped bodice with lace trimming. So lovely, so fine. Another shiver went through her.

"You are very kind, Miss Coleridge," she said. "But I wouldn't want to put you out. You can't have brought too many clothes with you all this way."

That twinkle was back. "You might be surprised. But any minor inconvenience is nothing compared to what you endured. Why, we might not have Ben back without your help."

Meg thought it was the other way around. She might have died in the canyon but for Ben. She ought to refuse, but some part of her begged her to accept the gift. Clean clothes, pretty clothes. It seemed like forever since she'd had either. Meg nodded, pulling the bundle close.

"Thank you," she said. "You cannot know how much this is appreciated."

Diana Coleridge cocked her head, the thick coils of her honey-blonde hair swinging to one side. "You could do me a favor in return. Join us for dinner. I'd love to renew our acquaintance."

A shame Meg could not believe her mother would say the same. Even the most fashionable dress in Arizona, made from the finest fabric, wouldn't make her fit for the Coleridge family.

"I'm very tired," Meg demurred.

Ben's sister straightened. "Of course. How thoughtless of me. You will want to rest. Perhaps we could have tea in a day or so."

Tea. Society. Propriety. Normally she avoided such ordeals. But Ben's sister had been kind. For her sake, she'd try.

"That would be lovely," Meg said.

Diana Coleridge beamed.

As soon as she was out the door, Meg scrambled to shed herself of what remained of her battered clothing.

When Dot came out a short time later, also in clean clothes, a cotton skirt and striped bodice, she stopped and looked Meg up and down. "Where'd that come from?"

Meg spread the skirts of the blue and white dress. "Miss Coleridge brought it. It's a little short and a little tight in places, but I'm beyond grateful."

"And now you can go to dinner," Dot said.

Meg shook her head, but before she could explain, another knock sounded at the door.

"Come on in, Hank," Dot called. "We're decent."

But instead of her husband, Private Meadows stood on the stoop. He must have been to the infirmary, for salve was shining on

434

his burned face and his hand was wrapped in a proper bandage. Someone must have loaned him a spare uniform as well, for he looked newly scrubbed from head to toe.

He nodded respectfully to Dot before looking to Meg.

"This was in a saddlebag." He held out a framed plate with his unbandaged hand. "Thought you might want it."

Meg's feet moved her forward before conscious thought intruded. She took the negative from him, held it to the light streaming through the open door.

Her heavenly window glowed brightly, offering hope, a glimpse of the divine.

*Oh, Father, thank you!*

As tears streamed down her face, the private slumped. "Didn't mean to make you cry. Did I hurt it?"

"No," Meg managed. "It's perfect. Oh, Private, thank you. You gave me back my life."

# 28

"So that's why I believe Mr. Pike to be a criminal," Ben concluded.

Colonel Yearling had granted him and Hank the right to sit in his office. After days on the trail, the spindle-backed chair felt surprisingly confining. Or maybe it was his desire for justice that had him longing to get up and ride off after the treacherous guide.

Yearling shook his head as he leaned back in his chair behind the simple wood desk with its neatly stacked papers and precisely aligned pens. "Pike and his partner found gold, and they were willing to kill anyone to keep it a secret."

"Even the partner," Hank put in. "I thought the body we found burned was Pike's. Since he's obviously alive, it had to have been McCoy, the guide who went out with Colonel Coleridge."

"Bad business all around," the commanding officer said. "My condolences, Captain. Would you prefer I explain the matter to your family?"

"No, thank you, sir," Ben said. "I'll do it. And after that, with your permission, I'd like a cavalry detail to go after Pike."

Yearling spread his hands. "Much as I'd like to see the fellow punished, he could be anywhere."

Hank shook his head. "Not likely. He's either on his way east, then southwest to Prescott as he told you to make sure no one else has staked a claim in the area, or he's on his way back to the gold to protect his find. Since we didn't catch sight of him coming back, I'm leaning toward Prescott."

Yearling seemed to consider that, mustache wiggling as if he chewed on the matter.

"Very well," he finally said. "I'll have six men ready to accompany you in the morning, Captain. Dismissed."

Hank walked Ben out. "I hope you'll let me make the seventh. I'd like to see Pike brought to justice too."

"What about Dot?" Ben asked as they came out onto the parade ground.

"I'm sure she'd be delighted to make your eighth man."

Ben laughed. "She probably would. And

437

we'd eat better too. But I doubt the Army will requisition a cook."

"A shame," Hank said with a sigh. He cast Ben a look. "Nor a photographer, I gather."

Ben paused and rubbed his neck. "I don't know what to do about Meg. I can't take her with me on this assignment. She may not be willing to stay at the fort until I get back. I asked her to marry me, but she refused."

"You do have a way with the ladies," Hank joked.

"If only that were true. Besides, there's only one lady whose good opinion I crave."

Hank nodded toward the officers' quarters, where Diana had come out into the sunlight as if searching for Ben. "Only one?"

Ben sighed. "Tell Meg I'll come by this evening."

Hank nodded, and Ben went to join his sister.

She linked arms with him the moment he was close enough. "I'm so glad you're safe."

"Me too, though I think I brought a few visitors back with me." He scratched at his uniform, which seemed far more prickly than usual.

Diana hastily disengaged. "Forgive me. You wanted to clean up first."

"Perhaps it's better if we talk," Ben said.

Diana backed away. "No, no. Mother would have apoplexy if you came inside in all your travel dirt. Surely whatever you have to tell us can wait."

He nodded again, feeling craven for taking the excuse to escape his duty. Still, he couldn't help remembering another lady who had had no trouble being at his side, dirt or no dirt.

By the time dinner rolled around, Ben was exhausted. He'd washed and shaved and put on his dress uniform. The man who looked back at him from the mirror was hollow cheeked and weary eyed. But he was in no worse spirits than his mother and Diana after he went to break the news about the Colonel. His mother's reserve had cracked at last, and she had sobbed on Diana's shoulder while his sister sat, lips trembling and face pale, all her usual brightness extinguished.

"I'm sure Colonel Yearling would understand if you wanted privacy tonight," Ben had told them both.

His mother had raised her head. "We are Coleridges. We will do our duty."

He hadn't argued. She needed something to cling to, and there were worse things than duty.

The officers' mess was a small room off the main hallway of the quarters. A white cloth draped the table, and china plates replaced the tin used by the enlisted men. Colonel Yearling must have ordered his other officers to eat elsewhere, for though there were multiple chairs at the table, he was the only one in the room as they entered. He rose from the head of the table and came to meet Ben's mother.

"Mrs. Coleridge, may I extend my condolences? You are as gallant as the Colonel always said for joining us tonight."

His mother inclined her head and allowed him to lead her to the seat at his right. Ben led Diana to sit at his left. Before he could take the chair beside her, however, a sound came from the open door.

Turning, he found Meg standing there. Her hair was piled up behind her and confined with silver combs that must have belonged to Dot. The blue and white dress outlined her curves, made her eyes blaze green. She was every bit the beauty he remembered from West Point, and so much more.

"I was feeling up to it after all," she said. "I hope you'll allow me to join you."

Meg kept smiling politely as they all looked

her way. Dot had convinced her to come.

"You mean you refused a good meal out of pride?" she'd demanded when Meg had attempted to explain why even her borrowed finery would not make her an acceptable dinner companion.

"It's not pride," Meg had protested, a little stung by the accusation. "Ben and his family really don't want me there."

"Says you," Dot had retorted. "I know the Captain. He wants you at his side. He needs your support now."

And that idea, far-fetched as it had seemed, had been what had encouraged her to cross the parade ground, enter the officers' quarters, and knock at the door of the mess.

Mrs. Coleridge's frown almost had her turning heel, but Ben came to take her hand. She hadn't seen him in his dress uniform before, but the tailored navy wool frock coat with its brass buttons sat well on him.

"Meg, thank you."

The relief in his voice buoyed her, and she allowed him to escort her to her seat.

Next to his mother.

Meg tried not to look at her as she sat. The colonel and Ben sat as well, Ben directly across from Meg.

"What a pleasure having three lovely ladies at my table," Colonel Yearling said with a smile all around. He tapped his glass with his knife, making the crystal chime, and two of his men began bringing in the food. One hurried to set a place for Meg. She hardly noticed. Just the sight of the chicken and dumplings made her stomach rumble. As if she'd heard it, Mrs. Coleridge shifted away from her.

Colonel Yearling said the blessing and began serving them. Meg certainly wasn't going to pick at the meal, as her aunt insisted, not after starvation rations the last few days. It was all she could do not to gulp down the food and demand more.

Ben was eating nearly as quickly and taking long drinks from his glass of lemonade.

"I apologize, Colonel Yearling," his mother said with a frown at her son. "It seems the Captain has forgotten his manners since arriving at your fort."

Meg stiffened at the criticism, but Ben merely smiled at his mother. "Forgive me, Mother, but this is manna after the rabbit and miner's lettuce we ate the last two weeks."

His mother sniffed, but Diana glanced from him to Meg, eyes shining like silver in the candlelight. "I think you were both

442

tremendously brave. I don't know whether I could have lived that way."

"It's surprising what you can make do with when needs demand," Colonel Yearling said. "More chicken, Mrs. Coleridge?"

"No, thank you," she said, then dabbed at her stern lips with the linen napkin.

"What did you think of the canyon, Miss Pero?" Diana asked from across the table. "I understand it's quite something."

"Words cannot do it justice," Meg told her.

"But Meg's pictures can," Ben said. "I understand from Private Meadows that one survived."

Meg nodded, warm just remembering. "The window to heaven."

His smile brightened the room.

"Window to heaven?" Diana asked.

"A unique formation," Ben explained. "Picture a mighty outcropping of red stone, pierced by a hole. Meg caught it aflame with the setting sun. I can hardly wait to see what the public makes of it."

Colonel Yearling frowned. "The public? The picture was taken during an Army survey. That makes it government property."

Meg shook her head, but Ben jumped into the fray. "Sir, I must protest. That picture is all Miss Pero has to show from this venture.

443

Her cameras and equipment were all destroyed in the fire."

He was so determined to protect her. How could she not admire that?

As Colonel Yearling's frown deepened, Meg leaned forward. "Actually, sir, there should be a contract on file from when I was hired. I think you'll find that, while I will supply the Army with prints of any photographs taken during the expedition, all negatives remain my property. I supplied the plates, after all. You'll find Mr. O'Sullivan with the Wheeler survey has a similar agreement."

His face relaxed, and he nodded. "Very well, Miss Pero. I'll look forward to seeing a print of this heavenly window."

Ben beamed at her, as if he'd known she would win the argument.

The colonel turned to Ben's mother. "Forgive my intrusion at this difficult time, Mrs. Coleridge, but have you considered your plans?"

Very likely the fellow was hoping to move back into his own quarters soon. After all, Mrs. Coleridge had no more reason to stay. And, with her husband gone, her connection with the Army would grow tenuous. Despite her feelings toward the woman, Meg's heart ached for her loss.

Mrs. Coleridge kept her head high and her smile pleasant as she turned from the commanding officer to her son. "I imagine that will be up to the Captain. We always moved at the Colonel's pleasure. Now I expect we will move at his."

Had the Colonel failed to make arrangements for them in the event of his death? Had she no home to return to? What a burden to place on Ben!

"I'll be at Fort Wilverton until I receive my next orders," he told her. "We'll talk when I return from my current assignment."

Meg paused, fork halfway to mouth. "You're not going back to the canyon?"

"No, indeed," Colonel Yearling answered for him. "Captain Coleridge is leading a detail to apprehend Mr. Pike."

The food held no more interest. She lowered her fork and sat quietly. Conversation ebbed and flowed around her. Ben's mother and sister did not seem overly concerned about the colonel's announcement. All Meg could think about was that Ben was leaving. With a detail of cavalrymen at his side, the danger was possibly minimal. But Pike had proved crafty, and he would be desperate. If something happened to Ben . . .

"Meg?"

She blinked. He must have asked her a question, for his brows were up, his head cocked just the slightest. Everyone else was watching her, as if waiting for her answer. His mother looked the most displeased, likely because Ben had used Meg's first name.

"Yes?" Meg asked.

His smile inched up. "May I walk you back to the Newcombs'?"

Relief and pleasure crested in waves. "Yes, of course."

"You must get some rest, Captain," his mother put in. "You have a duty tomorrow."

One that did not include Meg.

"I'll be fine, Mother," Ben said. "But thank you for your concern."

They left a short time later. She felt his mother's gaze on her as they started across the parade ground. The moon was riding high on feathery clouds, turning the red soil to silver. Voices echoed here and there — the watch reporting, a sergeant calling for a private's aid.

"She hates me," Meg said.

Ben glanced at her with a frown. "Who?"

"Your mother."

He chuckled. "She doesn't hate you. She just has high expectations, of everyone."

Expectations Meg would never meet.

"How do you deal with it?"

"Mostly, I've managed to meet them," he said, moonlight reflecting in his hair. "But when I don't, I try to remind myself there's only one person I need to please."

"The Colonel," she said.

He stopped short of the door to Dot and Hank's home. The curtain twitched as if hastily being put back into place. Meg hid her smile.

"You know," Ben said, one foot up on the stoop, "for a long time, that's what I thought. Like Mother and Diana, I moved where my father moved, associated with those he pointed out, followed his least advice. As I grew older, I resented the way he loomed over my life. I realized in the canyon that I'd made him into a godlike figure. But he was just a man, and one who made mistakes. His last one cost him his life."

She had to touch him, going so far as to rest a hand on his arm. It was firm and strong beneath the navy wool.

"There's only one who matters, Meg," he murmured. "And he forgives our mistakes freely. All we have to do is do our best. It doesn't matter what anyone else thinks."

Do her best. That was something she'd done all her life. She felt as if he'd opened the shutter on her camera, widening her view. All this time, she'd focused on the differences between her and Mrs. Coleridge, the differences between the woman she thought Ben's mother wanted him to marry and the woman Meg knew herself to be. Perhaps she didn't have to measure up to Mrs. Coleridge's expectations any more than she measured up to society's. Perhaps the only expectations that mattered were God's.

Love him.

Love others.

Be her best self.

That she was capable of doing. Amazing grace indeed. Had Papa known that too? Perhaps that was why he had favored the song.

"Thank you," she told Ben. "I'll try to remember that."

His hand rose to touch her cheek, the movement slow, soft. "I don't know how long I'll be away, Meg. Would you stay on at the fort and wait for me? I know you refused my proposal, but I believe we can find a way back to each other. I'm not willing to give up. Are you?"

"No," she said, heart full. "But you'll have to be patient. I feel as if I've stretched myself wider than ever, and it scares me."

"What could possibly scare the intrepid Meg Pero?" he asked, but he gathered her close, sheltered her in his arms, as if prepared to protect her from whatever concerned her. She clung to him, breathing in the leather and wool scent that was an Army officer, imagined she heard his heart beating in time with hers. He had seen her at her worst — dirty, prideful, even fearful — and still wanted to court her. It was time she took a chance on what might be.

"I'll be here when you get back," she promised. If she had to fight the entire U.S. Army to do so.

# 29

Meg began her new life the very next morning. Head high, she stood next to Diana and her mother to wave the cavalry and Ben off. Private Larson made one of the detail.

"He wanted justice," Meadows told Meg as they turned from the parade ground, Corporal Adams behind her. Both the young private and the corporal seemed to think it their duty to help her while Ben was gone, and the commendation Meadows had earned for bravery seemed to have loosened his tongue at last. "I reckon after the way those Johnny Rebs burned his town, he doesn't take well to bullies."

Neither did Ben. He was determined to bring Pike back. Meg tried not to think of the many ways he might be injured, ways that were far too real to her now that she'd lived through them.

In the meantime, she kept busy. She helped Hank and Adams go through the notes from the survey, filling in pieces they had overlooked. The supply office had small amounts of the chemicals she needed, and Hank rigged her up a dark room, so she could develop the stereograph and make multiple prints of a single frame.

"Oh, how amazing!" Diana exclaimed when Meg gave Ben's sister a copy. "You're right. It is like peering into the sky. Look, Mother."

Mrs. Coleridge gazed down at the print, then up at Meg. "You took this?"

"She was the expedition photographer, Mother," Diana pointed out.

"Very nice," Mrs. Coleridge said, and Meg had never felt more pleased by praise.

In the limited society of the fort, it was all too easy to spend time with Ben's mother and sister. Diana also introduced her to the other women at the fort over tea. One was the fifteen-year-old daughter of a major. The other two were wives of cavalry officers. Meg was determined to be herself, so much so that she wore her navy riding habit, which Dot and she had repaired, replacing the wool skirt with one of denim.

Mrs. Wilkins, the oldest at about Dot's age, smoothed back her impeccably coiled gray hair as she picked up her teacup and held it precisely over her brown silk dress.

"I heard you lost everything on that expedition. Ladies, we must do something."

Miss Perkins nodded, flaxen curls bouncing. "I'll help. I have some nice emerald-colored wool put by."

"And I have some copper buttons left for a coat," the curvaceous Mrs. Bateman put in.

"Just the thing," Mrs. Wilkins agreed. She turned to Meg. "Would you mind terribly if we made you another dress, dear? Or would you prefer another riding habit?"

Mrs. Coleridge, who had said little until now, glanced up from her tea with a frown.

"A riding habit would be more practical," Diana mused with an envious look to Meg's skirts.

The rest of them were watching Meg, smiles eager and eyes bright. Even Ben's mother offered a nod.

Once more tears gathered. Meg blinked them back and returned the ladies' smiles. "I'd be delighted with either. Thank you so much for your kindness."

"Not at all," Mrs. Wilkins said. "We ladies of the frontier must stick together."

Ladies of the frontier. She'd never thought of herself that way. Perhaps she could fit in, just as she was. All she had to do was be herself.

She was even more thankful when, on the third day, Meadows brought an old friend to see her.

"Stripe!" she cried, going to stroke the mare's cheek where she stood beside Meadows outside Dot and Hank's cottage.

"Patrol found her and most of the others ambling our way," Meadows said with a fond smile. "I think she's glad to be home."

It was all too easy to begin thinking of the fort as home, partly because Diana went out of her way to befriend Meg. Ben's sister was bright and bubbly. She was a great favorite among the officers, many of whom appeared to be smitten. A pair always seemed to be out practicing saber drills, muscles flexing and swords clashing, whenever Meg and Diana crossed the parade ground. Others insisted on accompanying them whenever they strolled beyond the confines of the fort, even so near as Laundress Lane. Meg enlisted the aid of Corporal Adams, whose dour looks deterred all but the boldest. The clerk had come into his own after their adventures and was unafraid to state his opinion or hold his ground. Rumor had it he was about to be promoted to sergeant.

With all the attention being paid to Diana, the colonel was besieged by requests to dine with her and Meg at his table. The flowery compliments and longing looks would have melted many a heart.

Diana was kind but firm about refusing their attentions.

"I'm not marrying a cavalry officer," she told Meg. "I've had my fill of this life. I want a husband who stays put."

"I've never known a man who stayed put," Meg said with a laugh.

"Then *you* accept their offers," Diana said, linking arms with her.

Only one offer appealed to her. She could not stop thinking about it. She'd turned Ben away twice. God cared enough to offer her this new chance at life. If Ben asked a third time, she knew what her answer would be.

Given the way she and Diana appeared to be disturbing the activities of the fort, Meg wasn't surprised when Colonel Yearling called her into his office on the fifth day. The room was as regimented as the commanding officer, everything lined up in orderly fashion. She wouldn't have been surprised if the pens were required to salute him. He greeted her and waved her into one of the chairs across from his desk.

"I find myself in a difficult position, Miss Pero," he said, pacing back and forth across the planks while Adams stood on duty behind him. "You have done outstanding work, despite impossible circumstances. Yet I have an obligation to keep order."

"I can remain in my quarters if that would help," Meg offered. "It should only be a little longer. Dot and Hank won't mind."

"I fear keeping to quarters may not be enough to satisfy the legalities." He waved to the papers on his desk. "I've just received a warrant for your arrest."

Adams started. Meg pushed to her feet. "Arrest? For what?"

Colonel Yearling met her gaze. "Theft, Miss Pero. It seems you made off with your cousin's photographic equipment."

Cold and heat flushed up her in turn. "It wasn't his," Meg insisted. "My father left it to me."

The colonel's look was commiserating. "I'd like to believe you, but I must act on the information I've been given. There are regulations, you know. Be assured I will telegraph for more details."

Meg nodded, feeling numb. What details could he get? Only more of Cousin Harold's lies.

"In the meantime," Colonel Yearling continued, taking a seat behind his desk as if prepared to dismiss her, "I have no choice but to put you under arrest." Colonel

Yearling glanced over at Adams, who looked as shocked as she felt. "Corporal, escort Miss Pero to the guardhouse and make her as comfortable as you can."

Adams stepped forward. "Yes, sir. Should I then return and help you deal with Mrs. Newcomb and Mrs. Wilkins?"

Colonel Yearling frowned at him. "Do they have an appointment today?"

"No, sir," Adams replied, face neutral. "But I've no doubt they'll show up anyway. Miss Pero is something of a favorite. And you know how Mrs. Newcomb can be."

The darling! He was arguing far more effectively than she ever could. Meg kept her gaze down and her thoughts to herself. Perhaps that was why she noticed the colonel carefully rearranging his steel-point pens.

"Yes, well," he said, pausing to clear his throat. "Perhaps we can keep the matter quiet."

"Of course, sir," Adams said. "Perhaps Mrs. Newcomb won't notice when Miss Pero doesn't report for dinner."

Colonel Yearling stood, forcing her gaze up with him. He tugged down on his navy frock coat. "I'll have you know there are regulations, Corporal."

"I am well versed in Army regulations,

sir," Adams countered. "Would you like me to look up the one that says young ladies must be confined in the guardhouse while awaiting news? I don't recall seeing it, but it must be there somewhere if the colonel has retreated to it twice now."

"Retreated?" Colonel Yearling raised his head, mustache bristling. "An Army officer never retreats. I know there's a regulation."

"Very likely," Corporal Adams drawled, but his gaze went past the colonel as if seeing something else entirely.

Meg held her breath as the colonel frowned at her. His left eye twitched once, twice. Finally, he nodded. "Very well. Confine her to quarters. But I'll have no nonsense from Mrs. Newcomb or Mrs. Wilkins, or I'll lock up the whole lot of you."

# 30

Ben and his men caught up with Pike a few days later. The guide tried to outrun them across a craggy plateau dotted with orange and white knobs of sandstone, like pillars rising from the sage. But there was nothing quite like a cavalry charge, hooves pounding and sabers flashing, to make a man consider his likelihood of success. In the middle of it for the first time, Ben began to see why his father had refused promotion.

Pike clamped his mouth shut when Ben leveled the charges against him, eyes straight ahead and shoulders back. He never acknowledged his role or his avarice, even when Private Larson called him a polecat.

"You won't let him get away with it, will you, Captain?" the private asked as two of the other cavalrymen tied Pike's hands.

"Colonel Yearling may be able to learn the truth," Ben told him.

Ben was bone weary as he rode back to

Fort Wilverton. He'd survived wildfire, thirst, and hunger; captured the man most likely responsible for the murder of his father and the attempted murder of the men and women under his command. He and Larson ought to feel vindicated, jubilated.

All he could think about was Meg.

Had she kept her promise and stayed at the fort? Would she listen to his pleas? How could he convince her he loved her and wanted only the best for her?

Colonel Yearling ordered him to report as soon as he returned. Two of the cavalrymen brought Pike in, arms confined behind his back. The commanding officer shook his head in disgust.

"Have you nothing to say for yourself, man?" Yearling demanded. "You are accused of deserting your duty, attempting murder, and murdering an officer."

Pike's mouth curled in a sneer above his beard. "You can't prove anything."

Yearling stroked his mustache. "Perhaps not, but the case against you is credible. And what's this I hear about a gold claim?"

Ben held back a groan even as the two cavalrymen exchanged glances. This rumor was what his father had tried to quell. He'd died protecting Fort Wilverton and the Grand Canyon from becoming another Sutter's Mill.

"There is no gold," he said before Pike could answer. "I tested the samples myself."

"Liar!" Pike surged forward, and the two horse soldiers had to hold him back. "You want it for yourself, just like your father. I stopped him, and I stopped McCoy when he started to break. He couldn't handle not knowing what you were doing. He kept sneaking around, looking for a piece of spur your father had lost, breaking into camp, fussing with little miss's plates. He wouldn't leave well enough alone. Well, he's gone, and that gold is mine."

Colonel Yearling stepped back from Pike's panting. "Take him to the guardhouse."

The cavalrymen dragged Pike out of the room.

Colonel Yearling shook his head. "Mad. Utterly mad. You've handed me quite a problem, Captain."

Ben refused to back down. "There is no gold, sir. I'd stake my life on it."

"It appears you already have," Yearling said. "And I'll take your word on the matter of the gold. The fellow is clearly guilty as charged, as was McCoy. Pike will stay in the guardhouse until I can turn him over to the civil authorities. I suppose it's a good

460

thing I didn't have to put Miss Pero in with him."

He could not follow the man's logic. "Miss Pero? Why would you lodge her in the guardhouse?"

"I received a warrant for her arrest while you were gone."

Her arrest? His jaw felt so tight he could scarcely open his mouth. "Who," he gritted out, "would prefer charges against Miss Pero?"

"A Mr. Harold Finch," the colonel said with some distaste. "She tells me he's her cousin, interested in claiming her cameras as his own. I telegraphed for details and to tell the fellow the cameras were lost in a fire. Impudent cur demanded payment in lieu. Unfortunately, Miss Pero hasn't enough to pay the fee."

Ben leaned forward. "But if he's paid, he'll withdraw the charge?"

"So I understand."

Ben straightened. "Then I have a proposal to make."

Meg sat at the table in Dot's cottage, Mrs. Wilkins on one side, Diana on the other, and Dot busy getting a stew going on the hearth across from them. It had been like this for the last few days. One of her new

461

friends had been at her side, encouraging, from midmorning until past dinner. Dot was in her element cooking for them all.

Ben's sister visited every morning and afternoon. They played checkers, having borrowed the board with its red and green squares and round wooden pieces from Corporal Adams. They also traded stories about their childhoods. Meg loved hearing about how Ben had constructed elaborate sandcastles with interconnecting roads and bridges one summer when the Colonel had been stationed near the shore. It seemed he'd liked building things from an early age.

Diana had even raised the question about West Point.

"You're the one, aren't you?" she asked as they were playing checkers one day. "The woman who broke Ben's heart." Dot, who had been rolling out the crust for a dried apple pie on the other end of the table, had looked up in obvious surprise.

"I never intended to hurt him," she told them both, guilt tugging. "I thought breaking things off was the best for everyone. After all, it became clear to me that we never would have suited then."

Diana frowned. "Why not? You were both bright and eager. He thought the world of you. He wouldn't have brought you home

462

otherwise."

Meg shook her head. "I imagine he brought a number of girls home."

Diana jumped one of Meg's pieces and neatly removed it from the board. "No. Only you."

"You see?" Dot crowed, waving her rolling pin. "I told you he favored you."

Meg smiled. "So it seems. Even if I'll never be a society belle."

Diana wrinkled her nose. "No one needs a society belle out here. If there was a battle, we could be nurses. If there were children here, we could start a school. Where would this fort be with no laundresses, no lady sutler running the trading post? Why, how would Ben's expedition have gotten by without a cook or photographer?"

"That's right," Dot said, smacking her rolling pin against the table and setting the checkers to bouncing.

"I wish everyone thought like you two," Meg said, righting her pieces.

"I imagine more ladies think like we do these days," Diana said.

"Even your mother?" Meg couldn't help asking.

Diana glanced up from setting her pieces back into place. "So that's what's worrying you." She reached across the game and

463

touched Meg's hand, then winked at her. "You leave that to me."

Meg wasn't sure what to expect from that promise, but the very next day, Mrs. Coleridge had come to see her. Dressed in a burgundy silk gown with golden panels down the bodice and hem, she glanced around at the little cottage, and her upper lip curled. Dot stiffened.

"It is absolutely disgraceful that you must be locked up indoors," Ben's mother said, chin high. "It is very kind of you to play hostess, Mrs. Newcomb, but I cannot help but feel the imposition on you."

Dot thawed just the slightest, drying her hands on her apron. "I like company, normally."

Meg hid a smile. Mrs. Coleridge missed the hidden jab. "I told Colonel Yearling that you must be released at once, Miss Pero, but he refused."

Meg rallied. "He's only doing his duty."

Mrs. Coleridge fiddled with the cream-colored lace at her bell-shaped sleeves. "I understand about doing one's duty. A mother has a duty to ensure her son grows into a man who takes responsibility for his actions, who puts others before himself."

Dot nodded. "That's the Captain, all right."

She dropped her hand. "That is my son. I have always been proud of him. But I saw how the young ladies looked at him at West Point. They heard the Coleridge name and thought they could align themselves with it for no more than a pretty smile."

Meg raised her chin. "That's not me."

Mrs. Coleridge looked up at last, eyes soft. "No, dear, it isn't. I must offer you an apology. When Benjamin brought you home, I didn't see beyond your beauty. I thought you were just another one of those girls who wanted nothing but to marry well. You are so much more than that."

Why did these tears keep coming? "I try to be."

Mrs. Coleridge nodded to Dot, who was watching avidly. "I've had the pleasure of talking with Mrs. Newcomb, Corporal Adams, and that sweet Private Meadows. They can say nothing but good things about you. And your work speaks for itself. You are obviously a woman of character and talent. Please forgive me for thinking anything less of you."

"Of course." Meg had to look away to gain control of her emotions. "Thank you for telling me."

"It's plain the Captain still cares for you. I hope nothing I've done made you think less of him."

Meg drew in a breath. "Never. I admire Ben so much." She dared to look at Ben's mother again. Mrs. Coleridge was smiling at her.

"And I believe he admires you as well." As if suddenly aware of herself, she adjusted her sleeves. "I should go. I will continue speaking to Colonel Yearling on your behalf." She sniffed. "You would never have been confined to quarters if the Colonel was still alive."

The sniff became something more, and she'd had to excuse herself. Meg could scarcely believe it. She'd thought only a society girl would suit Mrs. Coleridge, when all the while Mrs. Coleridge had been hoping for more for Ben.

Someone who loved him, would encourage him. Someone who only wanted the best for him. That was a woman Meg could be.

Now Mrs. Wilkins set down the green wool she was sewing for Meg. "I don't remember a call to arms. Why do I hear running feet?"

Meg heard it too, footsteps pounding closer. Dot raised her wooden spoon as if prepared to defend them all.

Someone rapped on the door. "Meg Pero!

Come out."

She knew that voice. Meg rose, trembling. Diana was grinning at her. So was Dot.

Mrs. Wilkins folded up her work. "Well?" she challenged. "What are you waiting for?"

Meg hurried to the door and threw it open. Ben stood on the stoop, hat gone and hair wild. The rough navy wool of his day uniform made his shoulders appear broader, and the sky-blue trousers made his legs seem longer.

"Oh Ben," she cried, "I'm so glad you're back safe. Did you catch him?"

He grinned as broadly as his sister. "We did. And I've come to ask you to take a walk with me."

Her spirits soared even higher. "You convinced Colonel Yearling to let me leave my quarters for a little while?"

"Nope." He stepped aside as if to give her room to run. "You're free to go. All charges dropped."

Meg stared at him. "Cousin Harold agreed to let me off?"

"For a consideration."

"For a bribe, you mean." Indignation marched out of the house with her. "I'll pay you back, Ben. I promise."

"No need." He waved to his sister, Mrs. Wilkins, and Dot before shutting the door behind her. Meg paused to take a deep breath of the warm air, let the sun bathe her face.

*Thank you, Lord. Now, show me the path forward. I know I can trust in you.*

Ben put a hand on her arm, and she turned to face him. Tension sat on his shoulders, as if he had one more task to undertake before he could rest.

"You're a free woman," he said, "able to go anywhere, do anything you want. What can I do to convince you that you want to be with me most of all?"

Meg gazed into his dear face. Those blue-gray eyes, that long nose, the lips that could warm her with the merest touch, the capable hands that held her heart so gently. "It wouldn't take much."

His eyes lit. "So, what if I promise to carry your equipment, mix the collodion, polish the lenses?"

Those were the little jobs she'd done for her father. He was offering to perform the lowliest work, if that would please her. She swallowed. "That's very kind of you, but I can do all that."

He arched a brow. "What if I recommend you highly to the Army for future work?"

"Colonel Yearling would likely do the same, now that I'm cleared of all charges, of course."

He blew out a breath in obvious frustration. "Found you the perfect horse? Built you a house overlooking the sea?"

"Diana might appreciate the horse more, and your mother might like the house. You and I will be too busy exploring."

He searched her face. "What are you saying?"

What she should have said five years ago but hadn't had the courage. She'd changed. He'd changed. Together, they would only be stronger.

Meg went down on one knee, heedless of the soldiers moving around the parade, taking the cavalry horses to the stables, carrying messages between commands. Mrs. Coleridge must have heard the troop ride in. Was she watching even now? Dot, Diana, and Mrs. Wilkins were staring out the window. She ignored them all.

"Captain Ben Coleridge," she said, voice as firm as her convictions, "I love you. You are wise and brave and kind, and being with you I can be my very best. Nothing would make me happier than to be your wife. Will you marry me?"

"Yes!" As if he didn't trust she wouldn't change her mind, he seized her hands and pulled her up and into his embrace. In his kiss, she felt all the love and hope she'd ever needed, an acceptance so deep and full she could never fail it, and she knew she'd made the right decision at last.

Ben wanted to leap, to soar. His brave beauty had said yes. They had managed to bridge the distance between them. He was going to marry Meg Pero.

Visionary.

Artist.

Love.

He held her close, promised to encourage and protect her all the days of his life. For now, the vow was between him and God, but soon it would be before family and friends.

He leaned back, peered into her face. Tears sparkled on her lashes. "I love you, Meg. Since the day we met."

She smiled. "I won't argue with you this time. Just promise me you'll still love me when I'm old and gray and not as beautiful as you saw me then."

He cupped her face, pressed a kiss against her lips. "You will always be the most beautiful woman in the world to me."

She wiped at her cheeks. "Ugh! Even if I become a watering pot?"

"Even then," he promised her. He released

her to slip an arm about her waist. "We should tell Mother and Diana."

Meg glanced back at the house. Her friends hastily disappeared.

"Diana knows," Meg said. "So does Dot. She and Hank have been trying to bring us together for weeks. Oh, and we must tell Adams, Larson, and Meadows."

"I'm ready to tell the entire company, the fort, and the mules," Ben declared. He raised his voice. "You hear that, world? I'm in love with Meg Pero, and she's going to marry me!"

"Well done, Captain!" someone shouted back.

Meg laughed as he caught her close again. "I think the word is out."

"Then we better start planning. When?"

"As soon as you want."

He liked the sound of that. "Where?"

"At the fort? Everyone we care about is here."

"What about that aunt you mentioned?"

Meg shuddered. "The mother of the man who sent me to jail? No, thank you, although I may write afterward to tell her. She always said I should marry. It just took me a while to see that the perfect man for me was only a camera shot away."

Dear Reader,

Thank you for choosing Meg and Ben's story. Our national parks began in a time of exploration and wonder, much like Meg and Ben's love, and I hope I've captured that in this book.

The Grand Canyon was known to Native Americans and their forebears for centuries before the first white explorers ventured into the area. In 1858, Lieutenant Joseph Christmas Ives of the U.S. Army Corps of Topographical Engineers (as it was known at the time) attempted to take a steamboat up the Colorado. Though he reached partway into the Grand Canyon, he ultimately gave up the pursuit after losing his boat against the rocks. While he admired the scenery, he deemed the area "altogether valueless."

John Wesley Powell disagreed. His two trips through the Grand Canyon, one before my story is set and one concluding afterward, and his subsequent reports, books, and articles, opened the country's eyes to the undeniable beauty and majesty of the area. Meg's stereograph would only have helped. Still, the Grand Canyon wasn't made a national park until 1919, one hundred years before the publication of this book.

John Wesley Powell named many of the features in the area. He also discovered a little gold in Kanab Creek, west of Bright Angel Canyon, which sparked a short-lived gold rush. In the end, not enough gold was found to sustain more than a few weeks of work.

Ben's wagon road today forms part of Bright Angel Trail. However, there is still no way to cross the canyon itself except on foot. In late 1871, a ferry was set up to the east, outside the canyon itself, carrying riders and wagons across the mighty Colorado to new lands in the West.

The Army had a bigger role to play in the history of the national parks, however. Turn the page for a sneak peek of my next book for Revell, set in Yellowstone, the world's first national park, when the U.S. Cavalry was sent to take charge.

name of research, of course. Learn more about her at her website at www.reginascott.com.

# ABOUT THE AUTHOR

**Regina Scott** started writing novels in the third grade. Thankfully for literature as we know it, she didn't sell her first novel until she learned a bit more about writing. Since her first book was published, her stories have traveled the globe, with translations in many languages including Dutch, German, Italian, and Portuguese. She now has more than forty-five published works of warm, witty romance.

She credits her late father for instilling in her a love for the wilderness and our national parks. She has toured the Grand Canyon, Yellowstone, Crater Lake, Yosemite, the Olympics, and the Redwoods and currently lives forty-five minutes from the gates of Mt. Rainier with her husband of thirty years.

Regina Scott has dressed as a Regency dandy, driven four-in-hand, learned to fence, and sailed on a tall ship, all in the name of research, of course. Learn more about her at her website at www.reginascott .com.

The employees of Thorndike Press hope
you have enjoyed this Large Print book. All
our Thorndike, Wheeler, and Kennebec
Large Print titles are designed for easy reading, and all our books are made to last.
Other Thorndike Press Large Print books
are available at your library, through selected bookstores, or directly from us.

For information about titles, please call:
(800) 223-1244

or visit our website at:
gale.com/thorndike

To share your comments, please write:

Publisher
Thorndike Press
10 Water St., Suite 310
Waterville, ME 04901